350 TRADITI... HOME PLANS

TABLE OF CONTENTS

CRE∧TIVE HOMEOWNER®

Library of Congress
Catalogue Card No.: 99-068503   ISBN: 1-58011-034-7

Creative Homeowner A Division of Federal Marketing Corp.
24 Park Way, Upper Saddle River, NJ 07458

Manufactured in the United States of America

Current Printing (last digit) 10 9 8 7 6 5 4 3 2 1

Front cover photography by Donna and Ron Kolb Exposures Unlimited
Back cover photography supplied by the Meredith Corporation

COPYRIGHT © 2000
CREATIVE HOMEOWNER®
A Division of Federal Marketing Corp.
Upper Saddle River, NJ

Arched Windows

If open space suits your taste, here's a sturdy stucco classic that fits the bill with style. The vaulted-foyer is flanked by a soaring living room, with a huge palladiam window, and a formal dining room. Step up the stairs to the loft for a great view of the fireplaced family room, separated from the huge kitchen/dinette arrangement by a two-way fireplace. And while you're upstairs, be sure to notice the two bedrooms with walk-in closets and adjoining bath.

Design by The Garlinghouse Company

Deck

Family Rm
15-6 x 19-2
vaulted

MBr 1
15 x 13-2
pan vault

Dinette/Kitchen
22 x 13-8
bench

Balcony above

spa

UP DN

desk

ov

pantry

Living Rm
13 x 13-8
vaulted

Foyer
vaulted

Dining Rm
11 x 13-8

Garage
21-4 x 31-4

52'-0"

64'-0"

First Floor

Br 2
13-2 x 13-10
shelves

Loft
linen

DN

Br 3
12-6 x 10-8

Second Floor

Photography by John Ehrenclou

High ceilings and arched windows lend elegance and style to this outstanding family room.

A half circle window above the door and sidelights to either side naturally illuminate the foyer.

Plan info

First Floor	1,752 sq. ft.
Second Floor	620 sq. ft.
Garage	714 sq. ft.
Bedrooms	Three
Baths	2 1/2
Foundation	Basement, Slab or Crawl space

Warm and Charming

A stone and brick exterior is well coordinated to create a warm and charming showplace. The spacious foyer leads directly into the Great room which visually opens to the rear yard providing natural light and outdoor charm. A fully equipped kitchen is located to provide convenience in serving to the formal dining room with double soffit ceiling treatment or the breakfast area which is surrounded by windows. No materials list is available with this plan.

D esign by Studer Residential Design, Inc.

first floor

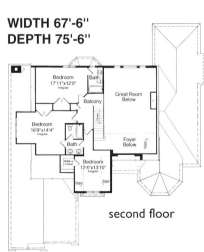

WIDTH 67'-6"
DEPTH 75'-6"

second floor

The Great room is truly grand with high ceilings and large rear facing window. The fireplace adds to the formal atmosphere.

The kitchen is open to the hearth room giving the illusion of more space with the added benefit of the fireplace, which enhances the atmosphere throughout the rooms.

Plan info

First Floor	2,479 sq. ft.
Second Floor	956 sq. ft.
Bedrooms	Four
Baths	3 1/2
Foundation	Basement

European Influenced

Twin arches add to the symmetry of this European influenced design. Inside, the floor plan provides all the elements demanded by every lifestyle including dual areas for entertaining in the living room and family room. The functional kitchen design with angled eating bar opens the area to the family room and the breakfast room. This plan is available with an optional basement, slab or crawl space foundation. Please specify when ordering. No materials list is available with this plan.

Design by Larry E. Belk

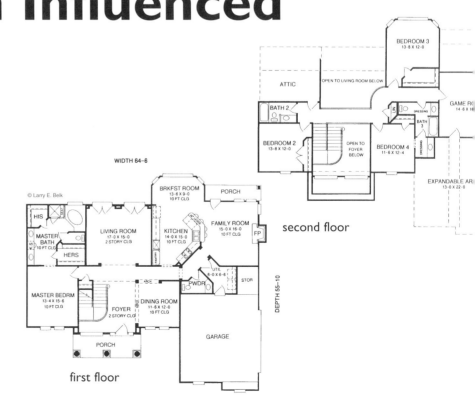

second floor

first floor

Grand two-story foyer is accented by a cascading staircase and gleaming wood floors.

Photography supplied by Larry E. Belk

The outstanding kitchen overlooks the family room giving this living space an open airy atmosphere.

Plan info

First Floor	1,919 sq. ft.
Second Floor	1,190 sq. ft.
Bonus	286 sq. ft.
Garage	561 sq. ft.
Bedrooms	Four
Baths	3 1/2
Foundation	Basement, Slab or Crawl space

Plan no. **99119**

Distinctive Master Suite

This two-level home invites guests into the living room with a vaulted ceiling and a see through fireplace. The large kitchen featuring an abundant pantry area, lots of work space, and a breakfast bar, will be a delight to the family cook. The sunny nook adjoins the screen porch. The family room provides a warm gathering place with built-in cabinetry and a see-through fireplace. Down the hall is a guest bath and a laundry center. No materials list is available with this plan.

Design by Ahmann Design, Inc.

first floor

second floor

8

The peninsula counter doubles as a snack bar and is all that separates the nook from the kitchen area.

The cathedral ceiling tops the living room giving more volume to the room.

Plan info

First Floor	2,157 sq. ft.
Second Floor	956 sq. ft.
Bedrooms	Four
Baths	2 1/2
Foundation	Basement

Plan no. 97714

Stone and Brick Styling

The stone and brick exterior with multiple gables and side entry garage creates a home that will enrich any community. The impressive foyer offers a dramatic view past the dining room and open stairs through the Great room and out to the rear yard. Exquisite columns, 13 ft. ceiling heights and detailed ceiling treatments decorate the dining room and Great room. No materials list is available for this plan.

Design by Studer Residential Design, Inc.

lower floor

WIDTH 84'-6"
DEPTH 69'-4"

main floor

Imposing columns grace the entrance and a dramatic arched window adds to the formal theme of the room.

This kitchen, breakfast room and hearth room combination creates an open living space that is both functional and efficient.

Plan info

Main Floor	**3,570 sq. ft.**
Lower Floor	**2,367 sq. ft.**
Bedrooms	**Three**
Baths	**3 1/2**
Foundation	**Basement**

Master Retreat

The master suite occupies the entire second floor and is accented by a window seat and a private balcony overlooking the backyard. The parlor may be used as a third bedroom, a guestroom, or an office.

Design by The Meredith Corporation

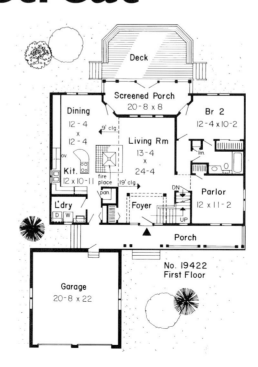

Deck

Screened Porch
20-8 x 8

Dining
12-4
x
12-4

9' clg.

Living Rm
13-4
x
24-4

Br 2
12-4 x 10-2

Kit.
12 x 10-11

fire
place

19' clg.

L'dry

Foyer

Parlor
12 x 11-2

DN

UP

Porch

Garage
20-8 x 22

No. 19422
First Floor

WIDTH 50'-8"
DEPTH 61'-8"

stor.   Balc.

seat

deco
box beams

MBr
15-8 x 11-9

beams @
foyer below

DN

make-
up

Second Floor   deco. beam

Photography supplied by The Meredith Corporation

An old-fashioned Country porch invokes memories of long ago while extending living space to the outdoors.

A four-sided fireplace offers cozy warmth to the living room of this home.

Plan info

First Floor	1,290 sq. ft.
Second Floor	405 sq. ft.
Garage	513 sq. ft.
Bedrooms	Two
Baths	2(full)
Foundation	Basement or Crawl space

13

Plan no.
34901

price code **B**

BL ✕ ZIP ЯR

total living area: 1,763 sq. ft.

Photography by Laurie Solomon

Farmhouse Favorite

Perfect for a family with young children all of the bedrooms are located upstairs close to each other. An optional deck in the rear provides outdoor living space. There is a convenient rear entry door to the garage.

Design by The Garlinghouse Company

Second Floor

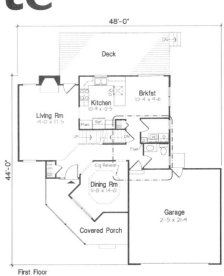

First Floor

Plan info

First Floor	909 sq. ft.
Second Floor	854 sq. ft.
Garage	491 sq. ft.
Bedrooms	Three
Baths	2 1/2
Foundation	Basement, Slab or Crawl space

Opt. Slab/ Crawl Space

total living area: 3,144 sq. ft.

BL

price code **E**

Plan no.
97734

Photography by Donna and Ron Kolb Exposures Unlimited

Hidden Attributes

FIRST FLOOR

- Master Bath
- Great Room 16'-5" x 17'-2"
- Breakfast 12'-0" x 12'-6"
- Hearth Room 19'-6" x 14'-10"
- Deck
- Kitchen 14'-6" x 15'-6"
- Laun.
- Master Bedroom 14'-0" x 18'-1"
- Bath
- Foyer
- Porch
- Sitting Area 11'-8" x 11'-8"
- Dining Room 13'-8" x 13'-0"
- Garage 21'-0" x 32'-10"

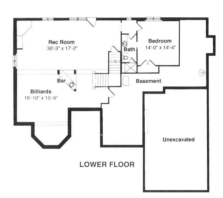

LOWER FLOOR

- Rec Room 30'-3" x 17'-2"
- Bath
- Bedroom 14'-0" x 14'-4"
- Bar
- Basement
- Billiards 16'-10" x 15'-6"
- Unexcavated

This home's beautiful exterior is inviting, yet hiding inside the floor plan is expansive. Family members are assured of their own space. Whatever your family's future needs may be there is plenty of bonus space for expansion. No materials list is available for this plan.

Design by Studer Residential Design, Inc.

WIDTH 70'-0"
DEPTH 56'-10"

SECOND FLOOR

- Computer Loft
- Walk-in Closet
- Bedroom 15'-8" x 11'-3"
- Great Room Below
- Bath
- Bedroom 15'-8" x 11'-10"
- Foyer Below
- Walk-in Closet
- Dining Room Below

Plan info

First Floor	2,237 sq. ft.
Second Floor	907 sq. ft.
Bonus	1,450 sq. ft.
Basement	787 sq. ft.
Garage	669 sq. ft.
Bedrooms	Three
Baths	2 1/2
Foundation	Basement

15

Photography by Donna and Ron Kolb Exposures Unlimited

Versatility and Charm

This one-level home is defined by its versatility and charm. At the foyer you will be immediately impressed by the view of the spacious Great Room with corner fireplace and tall transom windows. The location of the dining room allows for easy expansion of your entertaining area. The optional study or bedroom gives you the opportunity to utilize the living area to what best fits your family needs. No materials list is available for this plan.

Design by Studer Residential Design, Inc.

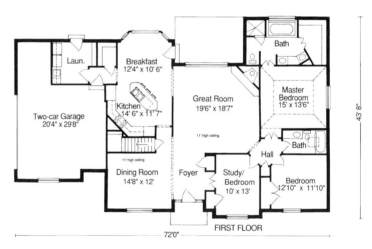

FIRST FLOOR

Plan info	
Main Floor	**1,998 sq. ft.**
Garage	**488 sq. ft.**
Bedrooms	**Three**
Baths	**2(full)**
Foundation	**Basement**

Photography supplied by Design Basics, Inc.

Victorian Accents

second floor

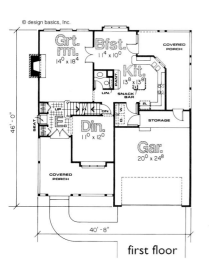

first floor

Plan info

First Floor	905 sq. ft.
Second Floor	863 sq. ft.
Garage	487 sq. ft.
Bedrooms	Three
Baths	2 1/2
Foundation	Basement

A covered porch and Victorian accents create this classical elevation. The double door entry opens to a spacious great room and elegant dining room. The gourmet kitchen features an island/snack bar and a large pantry. French doors lead to a breakfast area with access to a covered porch and kitchen. Cathedral ceilings in master bedroom and dressing area add an exquisite touch. His and her walk-in closets, a large dressing area with double vanity and whirlpool complement the master bedroom. A vaulted ceiling in bedroom number two accents the window seat and arched transom window.

Design by Design Basics, Inc.

17

Photography by Donna and Ron Kolb Exposures Unlimited

Family Favorite

The first floor laundry room and the attached garage add step saving convenience to this home. Stairs to a full basement, which can be used as a game room, are located near the kitchen. Small windows across the front of the home decorate the dormer and provide additional light to the second floor. No materials list is available for this plan.

Design by Studer Residential Design, Inc.

Plan info

First Floor	**788 sq. ft.**
Second Floor	**769 sq. ft.**
Bonus	**236 sq. ft.**
Garage	**452 sq. ft.**
Bedrooms	**Three**
Baths	**2 1/2**
Foundation	**Basement**

Photography by Donna and Ron Kolb Exposures Unlimited

Elegant Elevation

WIDTH 54' - 6"
DEPTH 41' - 10"

As you enter the foyer of this transitional two-story home, you will immediately be impressed with the high ceiling, the elegantly styled staircase and the arched opening to the formal living room. These features, combined with the open dining room, create a stunning effect. The kitchen is conveniently located in the center of the home and is visually open to the family room and the breakfast area, allowing light from the multiple rear windows to permeate through the combined areas. No materials list is available for this plan.

Design by Studer Residential Design, Inc.

Plan info

First Floor	**1,309 sq. ft.**
Second Floor	**1,119 sq. ft.**
Garage	**452 sq. ft.**
Bedrooms	**Four**
Baths	**2 1/2**
Foundation	**Basement**

Plan no.
32146
price code **F** BL ⚔ ZIP
total living area: **3,895** sq. ft.

Photography supplied by The Meredith Corporation

Luxurious Elements

Luxurious elements combine to create a custom looking exterior. Inside the home there is space for formal, casual and private moments, which is smartly arranged. Open areas provide many options for furniture arrangement.

Design by The Meredith Corporation

MAIN LEVEL

Plan info

First Floor	**2,727** sq. ft.
Second Floor	**1,168** sq. ft.
Bonus	**213** sq. ft.
Garage	**984** sq. ft.
Bedrooms	**Four**
Baths	**4 1/2**
Foundation	**Basement**

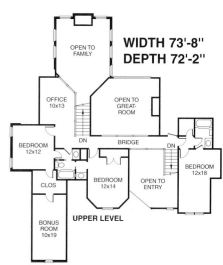

WIDTH 73'-8"
DEPTH 72'-2"

UPPER LEVEL

Cozy Three Bedroom

main floor

This small home is surprisingly spacious. There are three bedrooms, yet you may want to utilize the front bedroom as a study. It is adorned in a vaulted ceiling and has a private location. The great open area created by the Great room and dining room gives this home its initial feeling of spaciousness. This plan is available with a slab and a crawl space foundation. Please specify when ordering. No materials list is available for this plan.

Design by Nelson Design Group

Plan info

First Floor	1,601 sq. ft.
Garage	500 sq. ft.
Bedrooms	Three
Baths	2(full)
Foundation	Slab or Crawl space

Plan no.
82023

price code **C**   **BL**   total living area: **1,966** sq. ft.

Spacious Great Room

The Great room of this home includes a warm fireplace to gather the family around and a built-in media center. The kitchen /breakfast nook has a peninsula counter at an angle that views the Great room. This set up encourages family interaction throughout the rooms. This plan is available with a slab or crawl space foundation. Please specify when ordering. No materials list is available for this plan.

Design by Nelson Design Group

Plan info

Main Floor	1,966 sq. ft.
Garage	452 sq. ft.
Bedrooms	Three
Baths	2(full)
Foundation	Slab or Crawl space

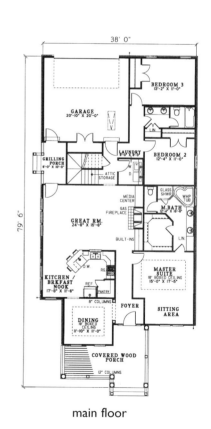

main floor

Room For Expansion

first floor

This home has been designed for now and later. There is a bonus area on the second floor standing ready for future expansion. This area could become a playroom, hobby room or an additional bedroom. This plan is available with a basement, slab or crawl space foundation. Please specify when ordering. No materials list is available for this plan.

Design by Nelson Design Group

second floor

Plan info

First Floor	1,155 sq. ft.
Second Floor	529 sq. ft.
Bonus	380 sq. ft.
Garage	400 sq. ft.
Bedrooms	Three
Baths	2 1/2
Foundation	Basement, Slab or Crawl space

Plan no.
82002
price code **B**
BL
total living area: 1,535 sq. ft.

Cozy Cottage

The cozy atmosphere of this home warmly embraces all who enter it. This three bedroom offers elegant details and built-in conveniences not usually found in homes of this size. Some of the sought after amenities featured are an island snack bar in the kitchen and boxed ceiling treatments in the master bedroom and the Great Room. There is even designated space to store your golf cart in the garage. This plan is available with a slab or crawl space foundation. Please specify when ordering. No materials list is available for this plan.

Design by Nelson Design Group

Plan info

Main Floor	**1,535 sq. ft.**
Garage	**550 sq. ft.**
Bedrooms	**Three**
Baths	**2(full)**
Foundation	**Slab or Crawl space**

main floor

total living area: 1,965 sq. ft. BL price code **B** **Plan no. 82024**

Eye-Catching Elevation

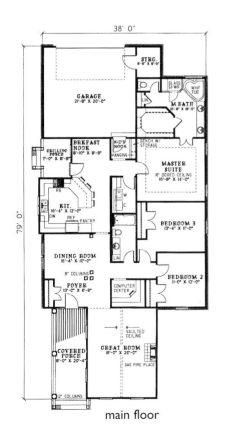

main floor

Bedrooms to one side of the floor plan, living areas to the other, this home is laid out for the way you live. The dining room and the foyer have an easy flow between them and the kitchen is close at hand. The Great room is a sight to behold with a gas fireplace and terrific windows. There is even a computer center located outside of the bedrooms. This plan is available with a basement, slab or crawl space foundation. Please specify when ordering. No materials list is available for this plan.

Design by Nelson Design Group

Plan info

Main Floor	1,965 sq. ft.
Garage	479 sq. ft.
Bedrooms	Three
Baths	2(full)
Foundation	Basement, Slab or Crawl space

Plan no.
92560
price code **C** BL ✕
total living area: 1,660 sq. ft.

Clever and Compact

This split bedroom design features walk-in closets in all of the bedrooms for increased storage space. A built-in cabinet in the dining room will give you a place to store your best china. Covered porches front and rear increase your living space to the outside. This plan is available with a crawl space or a slab foundation. Please specify when ordering.

Design by Rick Garner

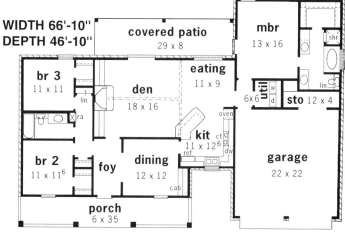

WIDTH 66'-10"
DEPTH 46'-10"

covered patio
29 x 8

mbr
13 x 16

br 3
11 x 11

den
18 x 16

eating
11 x 9

lin

sto 12 x 4

util 6x6

w
d
lin

shr

oven

kit
11 x 12⁶

ct

dw

ref

br 2
11 x 11⁶

foy

dining
12 x 12

cab

garage
22 x 22

porch
6 x 35

main floor

Plan info

Main Floor	**1,660 sq. ft.**
Garage	**544 sq. ft.**
Bedrooms	**Three**
Baths	**2(full)**
Foundation	**Slab or Crawl space**

Delightful Dining

Crawl Space/Slab Option

58'-0"

Deck

Dining
11-0 × 11-2

Br #2
10-10 × 11-10

Den/Br #3
10-0 × 11-10

Optional
Door
Location

Decor. Ceiling

Kit
10-0 × 11-2

Ldry

Sink

Range

DW

Ref.

Pan.

Solid Wall
w/ Opt. Door
Location

Plant
Ledge

DN

34'-4"

Decor. Ceiling

MBr #1
11-7 × 13-0

Living Rm
14-10 × 17-0
10' clg

Garage
20-4 × 21-8

Seat

main floor

A tray ceiling and a rear wall bay with sliders to the deck make for a delightful dining experience in the dining room. Choose a door location for the bedroom/den based upon how you utilize the room. The open rail staircase adds a beautiful touch to the living room.

Design by The Garlinghouse Company

Plan info

Main Floor	1,359 sq. ft.
Garage	501 sq. ft.
Bedrooms	Three
Baths	2(full)
Foundation	Basement, Slab or Crawl space

For Today's Family

Extra flexibility has been designed into this home with a study that could be converted into a guest bedroom when needed. The placement of the island in the kitchen allows you to prepare meals and be a part of activities in the Great room.

Design by Donald A. Gardner Architects, Inc.

FLOOR PLAN

© 1995 Donald A Gardner Architects, Inc.

Plan info

First Floor	2,192 sq. ft.
Bonus	390 sq. ft.
Garage	582 sq. ft.
Bedrooms	Four
Baths	2 1/2
Foundation	Crawl space

Private Master Suite

main floor

The secluded location of the master suite of this home provides a retreat from the day's stresses for the owner of the house. This home includes amenities not usually found in a home of this size. Decorative ceiling treatments and the openness of this floor plan add to its spacious feel. This plan is available with a slab or crawl space foundation. Please specify when ordering. No materials list is available for this plan.

Design by Nelson Design Group

Plan info

Main Floor	1,472 sq. ft.
Garage	510 sq. ft.
Bedrooms	Three
Baths	2(full)
Foundation	Slab or Crawl space

Plan no.	price code		total living area:	1,390 sq. ft.

Plan no. 92557 price code B BL X total living area: 1,390 sq. ft.

Elegant Brick Exterior

WIDTH 67'-4"
DEPTH 32'-10"

This home exudes elegance and style, using detailing and a covered front porch accented by gracious columns. The den is enhanced by a corner fireplace and adjoins with the dining room. The efficient kitchen is well-appointed and has easy access to the utility room/laundry. The master bedroom is topped by a vaulted ceiling and pampered by a private bath and a walk-in closet. The two secondary bedrooms are located at the opposite end of the home from the master suite and share a full bath located between the rooms. This plan is available with a slab or crawl space foundation. Please specify when ordering. No materials list is available for this plan.

Design by Rick Garner

main floor

Plan info

First Floor	1,390 sq. ft.
Garage	590 sq. ft.
Bedrooms	Three
Baths	2(full)
Foundation	Slab or Crawl space

30

Porches Aplenty

brz'way to detached garage

Deck   Deck

Covered Porch   Porch

Ma. Ba.   Sitting Rm.
10'-2" x 5'-9"

Util.

Brkfst.
13'-8" x 9'

Great Room
23'-6" x 17'-8"   Hall   10'clg
11'clg

Kit.
13'-8" x 13'-6"   1/2 Ba.   Ma. Bdrm.
13'-8" x 18'-10"

Porch
14' x 6'   Dining
12'-8" x 15'-6'   Living
13'-6" x 12'-8"   Porch
14' x 6'

Foyer

Porch
38' x 7'

first floor

Porches and decks provide plenty of outdoor enjoyment. Great for a family with older children the split bedroom design assure privacy for all members of the family. This plan is available with a slab and a crawl space foundation. Please specify when ordering. No materials list is available for this plan.

Design by Chatham Home Planning, Inc.

WIDTH 66'-0"
DEPTH 56'-0"

Bdrm. 2
13'-6" x 12'   attic storage

Dr.

Ba. 2   Balcony
ceiling   Ba. 3

attic storage   Dr.

Bdrm. 3
13'-6" x 15'

Bdrm. 4
12'-8" x 13'-6"   open to below

second floor

Plan info

First Floor	2,033 sq. ft.
Second Floor	1,116 sq. ft.
Bedrooms	Four
Baths	3 1/2
Foundation	Slab or Crawl space

total living area: 1,927   sq. ft.   **BL**   price code **C**

Plan no.
82022

This home has a "Kid's Nook" located inside of the garage entrance. This is the perfect place for all the paraphernalia the children like to leave about the home. This plan is available with a basement, slab or crawl space foundation. Please specify when ordering. No materials list is available for this plan.

Design by Nelson Design Group

main floor

Plan info

Main Floor	1,927 sq. ft.
Garage	448 sq. ft.
Bedrooms	Three
Baths	2(full)
Foundation	Basement, Slab or Crawl space

---

total living area: 2,301   sq. ft.   **BL ✕ ZIP ЯR**   price code **E**

Plan no.
96404

© 1993 Donald A. Gardner Architects, Inc.

Great for entertaining or just plain relaxing, there are covered porches on the front and the rear of this home. The best possible use of space is taken advantage of and is evident with the walk in pantry, wetbar, and bonus room.

Design by Donald A. Gardner Architects, Inc.

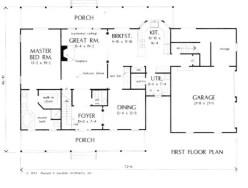

FIRST FLOOR PLAN

SECOND FLOOR PLAN

Plan info

First Floor	1,632 sq. ft.
Second Floor	669 sq. ft.
Bonus	528 sq. ft.
Garage	707 sq. ft.
Bedrooms	Three
Baths	2 1/2
Foundation	Crawl space

Design by Nelson Design Group

Brick and Siding

Total living area 985 sq. ft. ■ Price Code

No. 82029

This plan features:

- Two bedrooms
- One full bath
- The Great Room has the option for a gas fireplace
- The U-shaped Kitchen includes a peninsula counter/snack bar
- The Bedrooms have a full double vanity Bath between them
- A Patio Area extends the living area to the outdoors
- No materials list is available for this plan
- An optional slab or crawl space foundation — please specify when ordering

Main floor — 985 sq. ft.
Garage — 985 sq. ft.

MAIN FLOOR

33

Smaller Three Bedroom

Design by Nelson Design Group

Total living area 1,029 sq. ft. ■ Price Code A

No. 82064 BL

■ This plan features:

- Three bedrooms

- One full and one half baths

■ The covered Porch adds to the curb appeal

■ The Great Room and Kitchen are separated by a peninsula counter/Eating Bar

■ A walk-in closet provides storage in the Master Suite

■ No materials list is available for this plan

■ An optional slab or crawl space foundation — please specify when ordering

Main floor — 1,029 sq. ft.

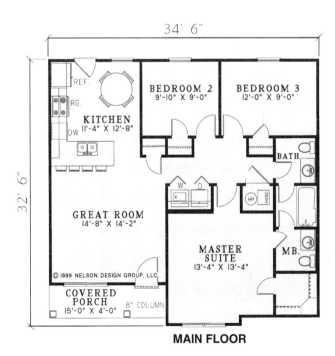

34' 6"

32' 6"

REF.

RG.

KITCHEN
11'-4" X 12'-8"

DW

BEDROOM 2
9'-10" X 9'-0"

BEDROOM 3
12'-0" X 9'-0"

BATH

W   D

WH   HVAC

GREAT ROOM
14'-8" X 14'-2"

© 1999 NELSON DESIGN GROUP, LLC

MASTER
SUITE
13'-4" X 13'-4"

MB.

COVERED
PORCH
15'-0" X 4'-0"

8" COLUMN

MAIN FLOOR

Decorative Ceilings Inside

■ *Total living area 1,104 sq. ft.* ■ *Price Code A* ■

No. 98468 **BL**

This plan features:

— Three bedrooms

— Two full baths

■ The Family Room has a vaulted ceiling and a corner fireplace

■ The galley Kitchen has a Pantry, and a serving bar opens to the Family Room

■ The Master Suite has a tray ceiling, a walk-in closet, and a private Bath

■ This home has a two-car Garage with storage space

■ No materials list is available for this plan

■ An optional basement, slab or crawl space foundation — please specify when ordering

Main floor — 1,104 sq. ft.
Basement — 1,104 sq. ft.
Garage — 400 sq. ft.

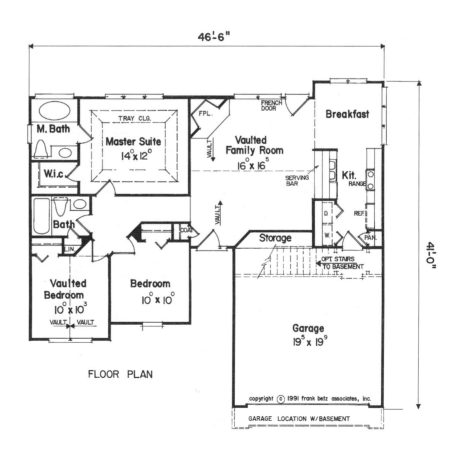

46'-6"

M. Bath

TRAY CLG.

FPL.

FRENCH DOOR

Breakfast

Master Suite
14⁰ x 12⁰

Vaulted
Family Room
16⁰ x 16⁵

W.i.c.

VAULT

SERVING BAR

Kit.

RANGE

Bath

VAULT

COAT

Storage

D.

REF.

W.

PAN.

LIN.

Vaulted
Bedroom
10⁰ x 10³

Bedroom
10⁰ x 10⁰

OPT. STAIRS
TO BASEMENT

VAULT VAULT

Garage
19⁵ x 19⁹

FLOOR PLAN

41'-0"

GARAGE LOCATION W/BASEMENT

Small Yet Stately

Design by Nelson Design Group

■ *Total living area 1,172 sq. ft.* ■ *Price Code A* ■

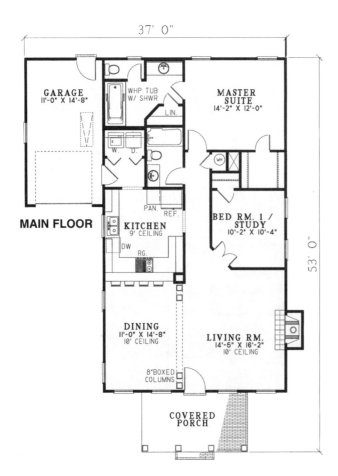

MAIN FLOOR

37' 0"

53' 0"

GARAGE
11'-0" X 14'-8"

WHP TUB
W/ SHWR

LIN.

W. D.

PAN. REF.

KITCHEN
9' CEILING

DW

RG.

DINING
11'-0" X 14'-8"
10' CEILING

8" BOXED
COLUMNS

MASTER
SUITE
14'-2" X 12'-0"

WH

BED RM. 1 /
STUDY
10'-2" X 10'-4"

LIVING RM.
14'-5" X 16'-2"
10' CEILING

COVERED
PORCH

No. 82040

■ **This plan features:**

— Two bedrooms

— Two full baths

■ The Living Room has a ten-foot ceiling and a fireplace

■ Decorative columns separate the Dining Room from the Living Room

■ The Kitchen includes a wrap-around counter and a breakfast bar and a Pantry

■ The Master Suite has a private Bath and a walk-in closet

■ An optional crawl space or slab foundation is available — please specify when ordering

■ No materials list is available for this plan

Main floor — 1,172 sq. ft.
Garage — 213 sq. ft.

Design by Nelson Design Group

■ *Total living area — 1,194 sq. ft.* ■ *Price Code — A* ■

No. 61004

This plan features:

— Two bedrooms

— Two full baths

■ The rear Deck and abundance of windows provide views of the backyard

■ A stone fireplace and a high vaulted ceiling with skylights accent the Great Room

■ The Master Suite has direct access to the Deck through French doors

■ The efficient Kitchen includes French doors to the Deck

■ The second floor Loft Bedroom has a full Bath with a skylight

■ No materials list is available for this plan

First floor — 862 sq. ft.
Second floor — 332 sq. ft.

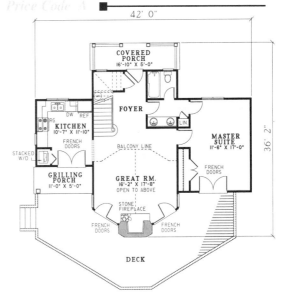

FIRST FLOOR

SECOND FLOOR

Vaulted Ceilings

Design by Frank Betz Associates, Inc.

■ *Total living area 1,198 sq. ft.* ■ *Price Code A* ■

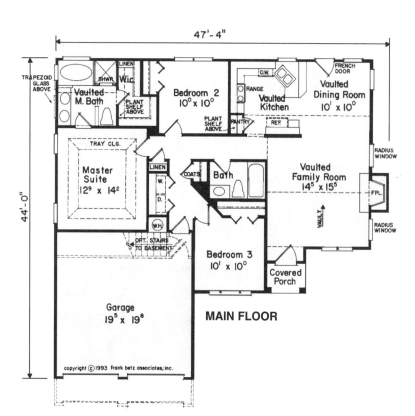

MAIN FLOOR

copyright © 1993 frank betz associates, inc.

No. 97256 BL

■ **This plan features:**

— Three bedrooms

— Two full baths

■ The Family Room, the Dining Area and the efficient L-shaped Kitchen all have vaulted ceilings

■ The Master Suite has a tray ceiling and a vaulted ceiling is over the Master Bath

■ The Laundry Center is near the Bedrooms and the Garage entrance

■ An optional basement or crawl space foundation is available — please specify when ordering

■ No materials list is available for this plan

Main floor — 1,198 sq. ft.
Basement — 1,216 sq ft.
Garage — 410 sq. ft.

Appealing Master Suite

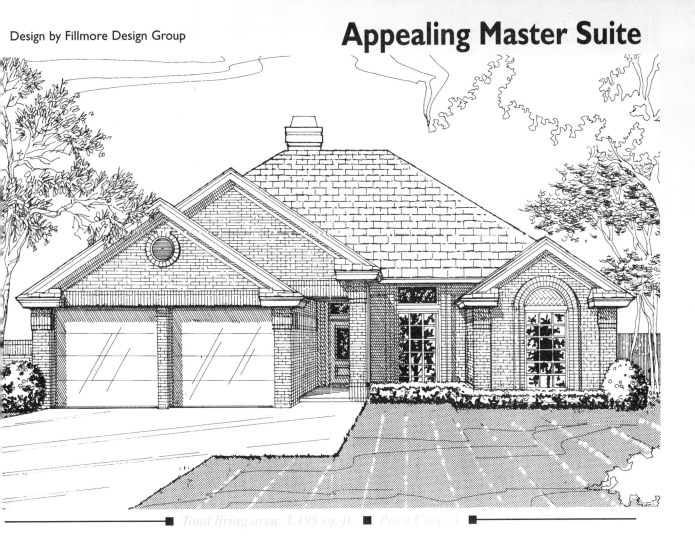

■ *Total living area 1,198 sq. ft.* ■ *Price Code A* ■

No. 92239

■ This plan features:

— Three bedrooms

— Two full baths

■ The sheltered Entry opens to the spacious Living Room with a corner fireplace and Patio access

■ The efficient Kitchen has a serving counter for the Dining Area and is near the Utility Room/Garage entry

■ The private Master Bedroom has a vaulted ceiling and plush Bath with two vanities, walk-in closets and a garden window tub

■ The two additional Bedrooms have ample closets and share a full Bath

■ No materials list is available for this plan

Main floor — 1,198 sq. ft.

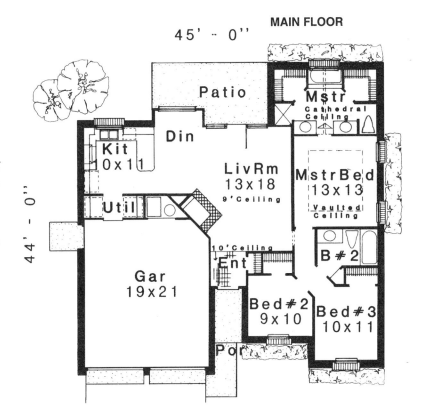

MAIN FLOOR

45' - 0''

44' - 0''

Patio

Mstr
Cathedral Ceiling

Din

Kit
10 x 11

LivRm
13 x 18
9' Ceiling

MstrBed
13 x 13
Vaulted Ceiling

Util

B # 2

10' Ceiling

Ent

Gar
19 x 21

Bed # 2
9 x 10

Bed # 3
10 x 11

Por

Illusion of Spaciousness

Design by Donald A. Gardner Architects, Inc.

G. NATHAN.

© 1997 Donald A. Gardner Architects, Inc.

■ *Total living area 1,246 sq. ft.* ■ *Price Code C* ■

No. 96484

■ **This plan features:**

— Three bedrooms

— Two full baths

■ The Great Room has a fireplace and is open to the Dining Room

■ The Kitchen features a skylight and breakfast bar opening to the screened Porch

■ The Master Suite is privately located and has a full Bath

■ The two additional Bedrooms share a full Bath

Main floor — 1,246 sq. ft.
Garage — 420 sq. ft.

FLOOR PLAN

DECK

GARAGE
19-4 x 20-4

SCREEN PORCH
10-0 x 12-0

KIT.
10-0 x 11-0

skylight

walk-in closet

MASTER BED RM.
14-0 x 11-8
(cathedral ceiling)

DINING
12-4 x 9-4

UTIL.
d w

master bath

GREAT RM.
15-8 x 15-0
fireplace
(cathedral ceiling)

BED RM.
13-4 x 10-0

bath

PORCH

BED RM./ STUDY
11-0 x 11-4
(cathedral ceiling)

10-0

48-0

60-0

© 1997 Donald A Gardner Architects, Inc.

Tremendous Curb Appeal

No. 99806

This plan features:

- Three bedrooms
- Two full baths
- The Great Room has a cathedral ceiling and is enhanced by a fireplace
- The Great Room, the Dining Room and the Kitchen open to each other for a feeling of spaciousness
- The Pantry, skylight and peninsula counter add to the comfort and efficiency of the Kitchen
- The Master Suite has a cathedral ceiling, walk-in and linen closets, and a luxurious private Bath
- The Bedroom/Study is topped by a cathedral ceiling
- A skylight in the full Bath naturally illuminates the room

Main floor — 1,246 sq. ft.
Garage — 420 sq. ft.

Total living area 1,246 sq. ft. ■ Price Code C1

FLOOR PLAN

© 1995 Donald A Gardner Architects, Inc.

Design by Nelson Design Group

Surprising Amenities

No. 82065

This plan features:

- Three bedrooms
- Two full and one half baths
- The entrance into the Dining Room from the Great Room is enhanced by columns
- The Great Room has an optional gas fireplace
- The efficient Kitchen is separated from the Dining Room by a peninsula counter
- The Dining Room opens to a grilling Porch
- No materials list is available for this plan
- An optional basement, slab or crawl space foundation — please specify when ordering

First floor — 609 sq. ft.
Second floor — 642 sq. ft.
Garage — 207 sq. ft.

Total living area 1,251 sq. ft. ■ Price Code A

FIRST FLOOR

SECOND FLOOR

41

Great Place To Start

Design by Nelson Design Group

■ *Total living area 1,281 sq. ft.* ■ *Price Code A* ■

No. 82042

This plan features:

— Three bedrooms

— Two full baths

■ The Great Room has a ten-foot boxed ceiling and a gas fireplace

■ The Dining Room is open to the Great Room and the Kitchen

■ The Kitchen includes a small peninsula counter and Eating Nook

■ The Master Bedroom has a boxed ceiling and private Bath

■ A Laundry Center is located in the hall outside the Bedrooms

■ No materials list is available for this plan

■ An optional slab or crawl space foundation — please specify when ordering

Main floor — 1,281 sq. ft.

MAIN FLOOR

44' 0"

54' 8"

MASTER SUITE
11'-0" X 14'-8"
10' BOXED CEILING

BEDROOM 2
10'-6" X 11'-3"

GARAGE
17'-8" X 20'-0"

BEDROOM 3 / OFFICE
10'-6" X 9'-3"

LIN

WH

8' BOXED COLUMNS

DINING RM.
10'-2" X 11'-10"

GREAT RM.
14'-6" X 17'-0"
GAS FIREPLACE

10' BOXED CEILING

PAN

REF

FOYER

DW

KIT
10'-6" X 15'-10"

RG

NOOK

COVERED PORCH
15'-0" X 8'-0"

Design by Larry E.Belk

Sensational Single

No. 93021 **BL**

This plan features:

- Three bedrooms
- Two full baths
- The unusual angled Foyer opens to the Living Room with a fireplace
- The Kitchen opens to both the Living and Dining Room
- The Dining Room is suitable for both formal and informal occasions
- The Master Bedroom has a large walk-in closet and a private Bath with a dual vanity, a linen closet and whirlpool tub/shower combination
- The two additional Bedrooms share a full Bath
- No materials list is available for this plan

Main floor — 1,282 sq. ft.
Garage — 501 sq. ft.

MAIN FLOOR

Design by The Garlinghouse Company

Delightful Doll House

No. 20161 **BL** ✖ ▨ **Я** ⊡

This plan features:

- Three bedrooms
- Two full baths
- The Living Room has a focal point fireplace and a sloped ceiling
- The efficient Kitchen has a peninsula counter and a built-in Pantry
- The Dining Room features a decorative ceiling and sliding glass doors to the Deck
- The Master Suite has a decorative ceiling, ample closet space and a private full Bath
- The two additional Bedrooms share a full Bath in the hall

Main area — 1,307 sq. ft.
Basement — 1,298 sq. ft.
Garage — 462 sq. ft.

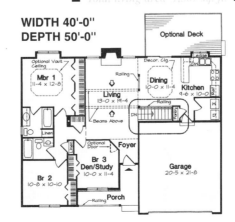

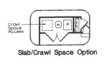

Slab/Crawl Space Option

Fabulous Facade

Design by The Garlinghouse Company

■ *Total living area 1,312 sq. ft.* ■ *Price Code A* ■

No. 24700 BL ✕ 🗺

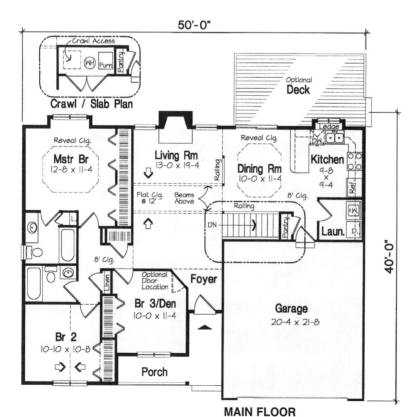

Crawl Access
WH | Furn | Pantry
Crawl / Slab Plan

50'-0"

Optional **Deck**

Reveal Clg.

Mstr Br
12-8 x 11-4

Living Rm
13-0 x 19-4

Reveal Clg.

Railing

Dining Rm
10-0 x 11-4

Ledge

Kitchen
9-8
x
9-4

Ref.

Flat Clg. @ 12' | Beams Above

8' Clg.

Railing

DN

Pantry

Laun. | D.

8' Clg.

Linen

Optional Door Location

Foyer

40'-0"

Br 3/Den
10-0 x 11-4

Garage
20-4 x 21-8

Br 2
10-10 x 10-8

Porch

MAIN FLOOR

■ **This plan features:**

— Three bedrooms

— Two full baths

■ The covered front Porch and the Foyer lead into the open Living Room accented by a hearth fireplace

■ The efficient Kitchen has a peninsula counter and is convenient to the Laundry, the Garage, the Dining Area and the Deck

■ The Master Bedroom features a decorative ceiling and a private Bath

■ The two additional Bedrooms have decorative windows and share a full Bath

Main floor — 1,312 sq. ft.
Basement — 1,293 sq. ft.
Garage — 459 sq. ft.

Design by Studer Residential Design, Inc.

No. 97730

This plan features:

— Three bedrooms

— Two full baths

- This plan has a drive under Garage and Basement

- The Master Bedroom has a tray ceiling and Deck access

- The Great Room and Dining area are topped by a sloped ceiling

- The L-shaped Kitchen is open to the Dining Area and near the Laundry

- The secondary Bedrooms share a full Bath

- No materials list is available for this plan

Main floor —1,315 sq. ft.
Basement — 1,315 sq. ft.
Porch — 155 sq. ft.

Drive-Under Garage

Total living area 1,315 sq. ft. ■ Price Code A

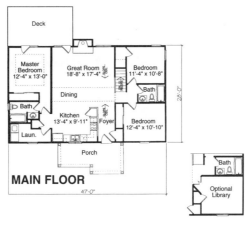

Deck

Master Bedroom 12'-4" x 13'-0"

Great Room 18'-8" x 17'-4"

Dining

Bath

Kitchen 13'-4" x 9'-11"

Foyer

Laun.

Porch

Bedroom 11'-4" x 10'-8"

Bath

Bedroom 12'-4" x 10'-10"

MAIN FLOOR

47'-0"

28'-0"

Bath

Optional Library

Design by Nelson Design Group

No. 82044

This plan features:

— Three bedrooms

— Two full baths

- The Great Room and Dining Room of this home are open to each other

- The Kitchen has an Eating Nook that has access to the Grilling Porch

- There is additional storage in the Garage

- The Master Bedroom is crowned in a box ceiling

- An optional basement, crawl space or slab foundation is available — please specify when ordering

- No materials list is available for this plan

Main floor — 1,317 sq. ft.
Garage — 412 sq. ft.
Porch — 163 sq. ft.

Open Living Space

Total living area 1,317 sq. ft. ■ Price Code A

46' 0"

GRILLING PORCH

NOOK

STORAGE

BED RM. 2 10'-0" x 13'-4"

KIT. 10'-4" x 14'-8"

GARAGE 17'-8" x 20'-4"

REF.

BED RM. 3 10'-8" x 10'-8"

DINING 10'-0" x 9'-0"

OPT. GAS FIREPLACE

GREAT RM. 14'-0" x 20'-0"

MASTER SUITE

COVERED PORCH 14'-4" x 6'-0"

54'-10"

MAIN FLOOR

A Good Traffic Pattern

Design by Frank Betz Associates, Inc.

■ *Total living area 1,321 sq. ft.* ■ *Price Code A* ■

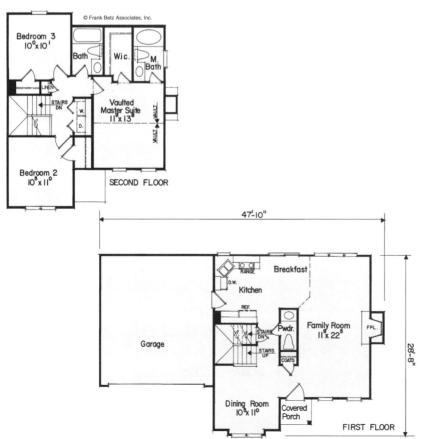

© Frank Betz Associates, Inc.

Bedroom 3
10⁶x10¹

Bath

Wic.

M. Bath

LINEN

STAIRS DN

W.

D.

Vaulted Master Suite
11'x13'

VAULT

VAULT

Bedroom 2
10⁵x11⁰

SECOND FLOOR

47'-10"

28'-8"

Breakfast

RANGE

D.W.

Kitchen

REF.

Garage

STAIRS DN

STAIRS UP

Pwdr.

COATS

Family Room
11⁵x22⁵

FPL.

Dining Room
10⁵x11⁰

Covered Porch

FIRST FLOOR

No. 98433

■ This plan features:

— Three bedrooms

— Two full and one half baths

■ The Dining Room has a boxed window

■ The large Family Room has a focal point fireplace

■ The U-shaped Kitchen is open to the Breakfast Area

■ The Bedrooms and the Laundry Area are on the second floor

■ The Master Suite includes a vaulted ceiling and a private Bath

■ An optional basement, slab, or crawl space foundation — please specify when ordering

First floor — 670 sq. ft.
Second floor — 651 sq. ft.
Basement — 670 sq. ft.
Garage — 404 sq. ft.

Design by Donald A. Gardner Architects, Inc.

Economical Three-Bedroom

No. 99849

This plan features:

— Three bedrooms

— Two full baths

■ Dormers above the covered Porch cast light into the Foyer and the Great Room

■ The spacious open Great Room/Dining Room has a shared cathedral ceiling and a bank of operable skylights

■ The Kitchen, with a breakfast counter, is open to the Dining Area

■ The private Master Bedroom suite has a tray ceiling and a luxurious bath with a double vanity, a separate shower, and skylights over the whirlpool tub

Main floor — 1,322 sq. ft.
Garage & Storage — 413 sq. ft.

© 1993 Donald A. Gardner Architects, Inc.

FLOOR PLAN

Design by Donald A. Gardner Architects, Inc.

For A Narrow Lot

No. 99868

This plan features:

— Three bedrooms

— Two full baths

■ The Great Room features a cathedral ceiling and a focal point fireplace

■ The galley Kitchen is convenient to the Dining Room and Great Room

■ The luxurious Master Suite includes a walk-in closet and a private Bath with a separate shower and garden tub

■ The two additional Bedrooms share a full Bath

Main floor — 1,350 sq. ft.
Garage & storage — 309 sq. ft.

© 1996 Donald A. Gardner Architects, Inc.

FLOOR PLAN

Arched Window

Design by Nelson Design Group

Total living area 1,355 sq. ft. ■ *Price Code A*

No. 82066 BL

■ This plan features:

— Three bedrooms

— Two full baths

■ A large arched window adds to the curb appeal

■ The Dining Room has a vaulted ceiling

■ The Kitchen is separated from the Great Room by a peninsula counter/snack bar

■ The Great Room includes a cozy fireplace as a focal point

■ A rear covered Porch is accessed from the Great Room

■ No materials list is available for this plan

■ An optional slab or crawl space foundation — please specify when ordering

Main floor — 1,355 sq. ft.
Garage/storage — 417 sq. ft.
Porches — 102 sq. ft.

39' 2"

53' 6"

BEDROOM 3
12'-0" X 11'-2"

BEDROOM 2
11'-4" X 9'-6"

8" COLUMN

COVERED PORCH
12'-0" X 4'-0"

HVAC

BATH

GREAT ROOM
9' BOX CEILING
17'-2" X 15'-2"

LIN WH

MASTER SUITE
9' BOX CEILING
15'-0" X 11'-6"

PAN

KITCHEN
10'-0" X 11'-2"

FOYER
7'-0" X 8'-8"

LAU

D
W

M. BATH
14'-6" X 5'-6"

RG

DW REF

PORCH
7'-0" X 5'-0"

8" COLUMNS

GARAGE
20'-10" X 20'-0"

DINING ROOM
10'-0" X 10'-6"

VAULTED CEILING

MAIN FLOOR

© 1999 NELSON DESIGN GROUP, LLC.

No. 61007 BL

This plan features:

- Three bedrooms

- Two full baths

- The galley Kitchen has an efficient work triangle

- The Dining Area is separated from the Great Room by columns

- Choose the French Doors option to create a Study instead of a Bedroom

- The Master Suite is privately located and has a full Bath

- A door in the rear of the Garage can be used for a golf cart or lawn equipment

- No materials list is available for this plan

Main floor — 1,359 sq. ft.

MAIN FLOOR

46' 0"

60' 4"

GRILLING PORCH
14'-6" X 8'-0"

MASTER SUITE
11'-4" X 15'-0"

FRENCH DOORS

FRENCH DOORS
10' BOX CEILING

GREAT ROOM
13'-8" X 17'-6"

10' BOX CEILING

LIN.

M.BATH
11'-4" X 12'-4"

GLASS SHWR

WHP TUB

GLASS BLOCKS

W LAU.
8'-10" X 6'-6"

GOLF CART
8'-0" X 6'-10"

8X8 BOXED COLUMNS

DINING
13'-8" X 10'-0"

OPT. FRENCH DOORS

BEDROOM 3 / DEN / STUDY
11'-4" X 11'-0"

GARAGE
19'-8" X 20'-0"

KIT.
8'-10" X 13'-0"

PAN

FOYER
4'-8" X 8'-3"

RG

DW

REF

PAN

PORCH

BEDROOM 2
11'-4" X 11'-0"

49

Compact Plan

© 1996 Donald A. Gardner Architects, Inc

■ *Total living area 1,372 sq. ft.* ■ *Price Code C* ■

No. 99830

■ **This plan features:**

— Three bedrooms

— Two full baths

■ The Great Room is topped by a cathedral ceiling over a decorative window

■ A bay window enlarges the Dining Area

■ The efficient U-shaped Kitchen has a cooktop peninsula counter

■ The Master Suite is enhanced by ample closet space and a private skylit Bath

Main floor — 1,372 sq. ft.
Garage & Storage — 537 sq. ft.

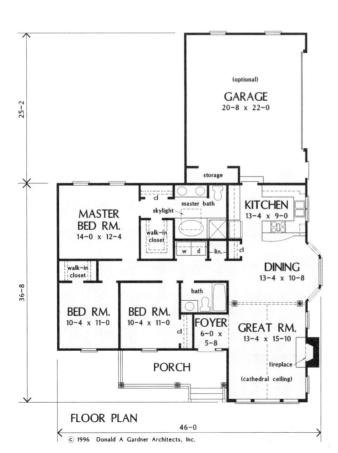

(optional)
GARAGE
20-8 x 22-0

25-2

storage

cl
master bath
skylight
KITCHEN
13-4 x 9-0

MASTER
BED RM.
14-0 x 12-4

walk-in
closet

w   d   lin.   cl

walk-in
closet

DINING
13-4 x 10-8

36-8

bath

BED RM.
10-4 x 11-0

BED RM.
10-4 x 11-0

cl
FOYER
6-0 x
5-8

GREAT RM.
13-4 x 15-10

PORCH

fireplace

(cathedral ceiling)

FLOOR PLAN
46-0

© 1996 Donald A Gardner Architects, Inc.

Design by Frank Betz Associates, Inc.

No. 98411

This plan features:

– Three bedrooms

– Two full and one half baths

– Large front windows, dormers and an old-fashioned Porch add style to this home

– A vaulted ceiling tops the Foyer which opens into the Family Room that is highlighted by a fireplace

– The Dining Room extends from the Family Room for easy entertaining

– An efficient Kitchen is enhanced by a Pantry, a pass-through to the Family Room and direct access to the Dining Room and Breakfast Room

– A decorative tray ceiling, a private Master Bath and a walk-in closet are found in the Master Suite

– Two additional Bedrooms, roomy in size, share the full Bath in the hall

– An optional basement or crawl space foundation — please specify when ordering

Main floor — 1,373 sq. ft.
Basement — 1,386 sq. ft.

Style and Convenience

© Frank Betz Associates, Inc.

FLOOR PLAN

Design by Nelson Design Group

No. 82067

This plan features:

– Three bedrooms

– Two full baths

– A fireplace warms the Great Room

– The Master Bedroom and the Great Room have boxed ceilings

– The Kitchen has a convenient work triangle

– There are large walk-in closets in all the Bedrooms

– A gas fireplace warms the Great Room

– No materials list is available for this plan

– An optional basement or crawl space foundation — please specify when ordering

Main floor — 1,381 sq. ft.
Garage — 416 sq. ft.

Split Bedroom Plan

MAIN FLOOR

Boxed Ceilings

Design by Nelson Design Group

Total living area 1,382 sq. ft. ■ Price Code A

No. 82068 **BL**

■ This plan features:

— Three bedrooms

— Two full baths

■ The front Porch shelters entry into this comfortable home

■ Both the Master Bedroom and the Great Room have boxed ceilings

■ Columns separate the Dining Room from the Great Room

■ The Kitchen is designed in a convenient U-shape

■ The Master Bedroom has twin walk-in closets

■ No materials list is available for this plan

■ An optional slab or crawl space foundation — please specify when ordering

Main floor — 1,382 sq. ft.
Garage — 417 sq. ft.

MAIN FLOOR

Sunny Dormer

No. 99812

This plan features:

- Three bedrooms
- Two full baths
- This plan offers todays comforts with cost effective construction
- The open layout of the Great Room, the Dining Room, and the Kitchen provides convenience and comfort
- The adjoining Deck provides extra living space outdoors
- The Master Bedroom is crowned by a cathedral ceiling and has a private Bath with garden tub, double vanity and a walk-in closet
- The skylit Bonus Room above the Garage offers opportunity for growth

Main floor — 1,386 sq. ft.
Garage — 517 sq. ft.
Bonus — 314 sq. ft.

FLOOR PLAN

© 1996 Donald A Gardner Architects, Inc.

Boxed Columns

No. 61008

This plan features:

- Two bedrooms
- Two full baths
- A gas fireplace warms the Great Room
- The Kitchen contains an angled serving bar
- Windows on three sides brighten the Dining Room
- The secondary Bedroom has the option of a vaulted ceiling
- The Master Bath has two vanities and a walk-in closet
- There is a covered Porch in the rear
- No materials list is available for this plan

Main floor — 1,387 sq. ft.

MAIN FLOOR

Open Spaces

Design by Jannis Vann & Associates, Inc.

■ *Total living area 1,388 sq. ft.* ■ *Price Code A* ■

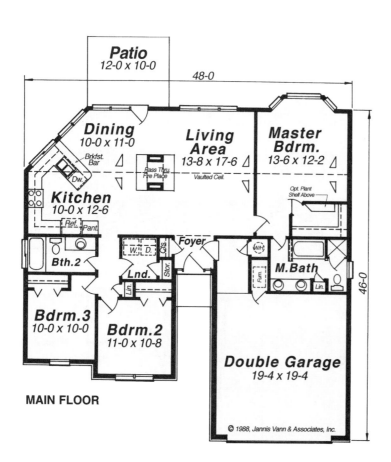

MAIN FLOOR

© 1988, Jannis Vann & Associates, Inc.

No. 93279

■ **This plan features:**

— Three Bedrooms

— Two full Baths

■ The Family Room, the Kitchen and the Breakfast Area form a great space around a pass-thru fireplace

■ The Master Suite includes a walk-in closet, a double vanity, and a separate shower and tub Bath

■ Two additional Bedrooms share a full Bath in the hall

■ The Patio can be accessed from the Dining Area

■ An optional slab or crawl space foundation — please specify when ordering

Main floor — 1,388 sq. ft.
Garage — 400 sq. ft.

Storage Space Surprise

Design by Nelson Design Group

No. 61010

This plan features:

- — Three bedrooms
- — Two full baths
- Though modest in size, this home has a surprising amount of storage space
- The Great Room accesses the covered Porch in the rear
- A serving bar in the Kitchen adds to your convenience
- There is a whirlpool tub in the Master Bath and a boxed ceiling in the Master Bedroom

Main floor — 1,395 sq. ft.

Total living area — 1,395 sq. ft. • Price Code: A

MAIN FLOOR

Easy Family Living

Design by Alan Mascord Design Associates

No. 91549

This plan features:

- — Three bedrooms
- — Two full and one half baths
- The sheltered entry leads into the bright Foyer with a lovely, angled staircase
- The two-story Great Room has a hearth fireplace and an atrium door to backyard
- The convenient Kitchen, with a serving counter/snack bar, opens to the bright Dining Area
- The quiet Master Suite has a walk-in closet and a double vanity Bath
- The two additional Bedrooms have ample closets and share a full Bath

First floor — 663 sq. ft.
Second floor — 740 sq. ft.

Total living area — 1,403 sq. ft. • Price Code: A

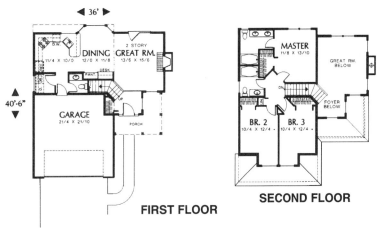

FIRST FLOOR

SECOND FLOOR

Economical Three-Bedroom

Design by Donald A. Gardner Architects, Inc.

B. NATHAN

© 1998 Donald A. Gardner, Inc.

■ *Total living area 1,411 sq. ft.* ■ *Price Code C* ■

No. 98030

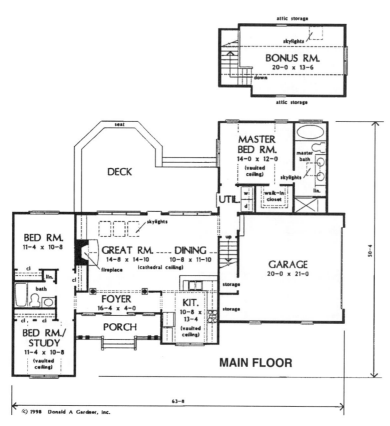

attic storage

skylights

BONUS RM.
20-0 x 13-6

down

attic storage

seat

DECK

MASTER BED RM.
14-0 x 12-0
(vaulted ceiling)

master bath

skylights

UTIL.

w
d

walk-in closet

lin.

skylights

BED RM.
11-4 x 10-8

cl

GREAT RM.
14-8 x 14-10
(cathedral ceiling)

fireplace

DINING
10-8 x 11-10

up

cl

lin.

GARAGE
20-0 x 21-0

bath

storage

FOYER
16-4 x 4-0

KIT.
10-8 x 13-4
(vaulted ceiling)

storage

cl   cl

BED RM./ STUDY
11-4 x 10-8
(vaulted ceiling)

PORCH

MAIN FLOOR

63-8

50-4

© 1998 Donald A Gardner, Inc.

This plan features:

— Three bedrooms

— Two full baths

■ Three bold gables, arched windows and columns frame the entrance to this home

■ From the covered Porch enter the Foyer that is brightened by windows around the door

■ The Foyer is separated from the Great Room by columns

■ The Kitchen is conveniently arranged and has a vaulted ceiling

■ The Master Bedroom has a plush Bath and walk-in closet

■ Two additional Bedrooms are in their own wing and share a Bath

■ No materials list available for this plan

Main floor — 1,411 sq. ft.
Bonus — 330 sq. ft.
Garage — 481 sq. ft.

Design by Donald A. Gardner Architects, Inc.

Cathedral Ceiling

No. 99809

This plan features:

- Four bedrooms
- Two full baths
- A cathedral ceiling expands the Great Room, the Dining Room and the Kitchen
- A versatile Bedroom or Study is topped by a cathedral ceiling over double arched windows
- The Master Suite, complete with a cathedral ceiling, includes a plush Bath and a walk-in closet

Main floor – 1,417 sq. ft.
Garage – 441 sq. ft.

© 1995 Donald A Gardner Architects, Inc.

Total living area 1,417 sq. ft. ■ Price Code 'C'

© 1995 Donald A Gardner Architects, Inc.

Design by Frank Betz Associates, Inc.

Split Bedroom Plan

No. 98415

This plan features:

- Three bedrooms
- Two full baths
- A tray ceiling lends a decorative touch to the Master Bedroom while a vaulted ceiling tops the attached Bath
- A full bath is located between the secondary Bedrooms
- A corner fireplace and a vaulted ceiling highlight the heart of the home, the Family Room
- A wetbar, a serving bar, and a built-in Pantry add convenient touches to the Kitchen
- The formal Dining Room is crowned with an elegant, high ceiling and decorative window
- An optional basement, slab or crawl space foundation — please specify when ordering

Main floor — 1,429 sq. ft.
Basement — 1,472 sq. ft.
Garage — 438 sq. ft.

Total living area 1,429 sq. ft. ■ Price Code 'A'

Striking Style

Design by Frank Betz Associates, Inc.

■ *Total living area 1,432 sq. ft.* ■ *Price Code A* ■

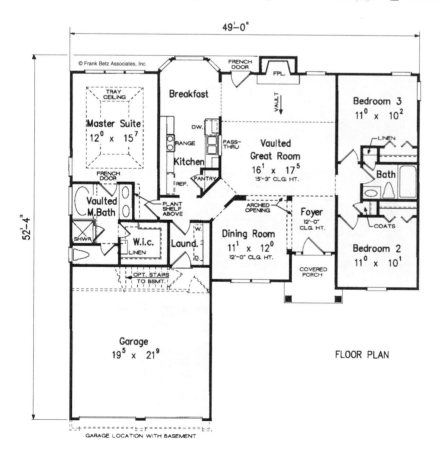

FLOOR PLAN

GARAGE LOCATION WITH BASEMENT

No. 97274

■ This plan features:

— Three bedrooms

— Two full baths

■ Windows and exterior detailing create a striking elevation

■ From the covered front Porch enter the Foyer which has a twelve-foot ceiling

■ The Dining Room has a front window wall and arched openings

■ The secondary Bedrooms are located in their own wing and share a Bath

■ The Master Suite features a tray ceiling, a walk-in closet and a private Bath

■ An optional basement or crawl space foundation — please specify when ordering

Main floor — 1,432 sq. ft.
Basement — 1,454 sq. ft.
Garage — 440 sq. ft.

Design by Frank Betz Associates, Inc.

No. 98422

■ This plan features:

— Three bedrooms

— Two full and one half baths

■ There is a convenient pass-through from the Kitchen into the Family Room

■ A fireplace highlights the spacious Family Room

■ The Kitchen opens to the Breakfast Room which has a French door that accesses the rear yard

■ A decorative ceiling treatment highlights the Master Bedroom while a vaulted ceiling tops the Master Bath

■ Two additional Bedrooms share the use of the full Bath in the hall

■ An optional basement or crawl space foundation — please specify when ordering

First floor — 719 sq. ft.
Second floor — 717 sq. ft.
Bonus — 290 sq. ft.
Basement — 719 sq. ft.
Garage — 480 sq. ft.

Covered Porch

© Frank Betz Associates, Inc.

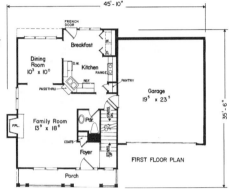

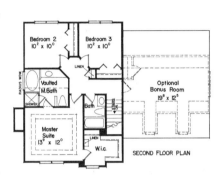

Design by Donald A. Gardner Architects, Inc.

No. 96418

■ This plan features:

— Three bedrooms

— Two full baths

■ The contemporary interior of this home is punctuated by elegant columns

■ Dormers above the covered Porch light the Foyer and the dramatic Great Room which is crowned by a cathedral ceiling and enhanced by a fireplace

■ The Great Room opens to the spacious Kitchen/Breakfast Area with access to the rear Deck

■ Tray ceilings adding interest to the Bedroom/Study, the Dining Room and the Master Bedroom

■ The luxurious Master Bedroom is highlighted by a walk-in closet and the Master Bath with dual vanity, a separate shower and a whirlpool tub

Main floor — 1,452 sq. ft.
Garage and Storage — 427 sq. ft.

Compact Three-Bedroom

© 1990 Donald A. Gardner Architects, Inc.

© 1990 Donald A. Gardner Architects, Inc.

Comfortable Environment

Design by Studer Residential Design, Inc.

■ *Total living area 1,453 sq. ft.* ■ *Price Code A* ■

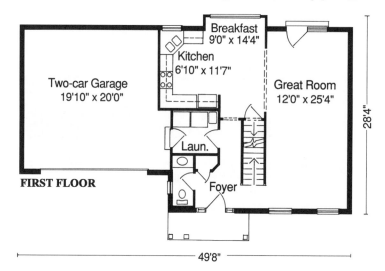

FIRST FLOOR

Breakfast
9'0" x 14'4"

Kitchen
6'10" x 11'7"

Two-car Garage
19'10" x 20'0"

Great Room
12'0" x 25'4"

Laun.

Foyer

28'4"

49'8"

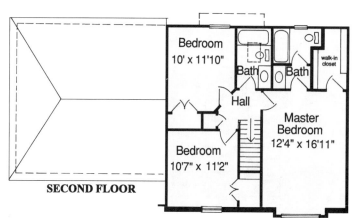

SECOND FLOOR

Bedroom
10' x 11'10"

Bath

Bath

walk-in closet

Hall

Master Bedroom
12'4" x 16'11"

Bedroom
10'7" x 11'2"

No. 92639

■ **This plan features:**

— Three bedrooms

— Two full and one half baths

■ The covered Entry and boxed window enhance the exterior

■ The spacious Great Room, with backyard access is open to the Breakfast Area

■ The U-shaped Kitchen has ample counter and storage space

■ The Master Bedroom has a walk-in closet and a plush Bath

■ Two additional Bedrooms share a full Bath with a skylight

■ A full Basement provides the option of an expanded play area in the lower level

■ No materials list is available for this plan

First floor — 748 sq. ft.
Second floor — 705 sq. ft.
Basement — 744 sq. ft.

Design by The Garlinghouse Company

Easy Living

No. 20164

BL X ☆ R

■ **This plan features:**

– Three bedrooms

– Two full baths

■ A dramatic sloped ceiling and a massive fireplace enhance the Living Room

■ The Dining Room is crowned by a sloping ceiling over a plant shelf and sliding doors to the Deck

■ The U-shaped Kitchen has an abundance of cabinets, a window over the sink and a walk-in Pantry

■ The Master Suite has a private full Bath, a decorative ceiling and a walk-in closet

■ Two additional Bedrooms share a full Bath

First floor — 1,456 sq. ft.
Basement — 1,448 sq. ft.
Garage — 452 sq. ft.

50' - 0"

45' - 4"

(Optional) Deck

Dining 12-0 x 9-9

Plant Shelf Above

Sink

Kitchen 9-4 x 13-4

Desk

Living Rm 12-2 x 14-4

Decor. Clg. (Optional)

MBR #1 11-8 x 14-0

Garage

Crawl Space Access

Slab/Crawl Space Option

Garage 19-4 x 23-6

Foyer

Den/BR #3 10-5 x 11-6

BR #2 10-5 x 10-5

First Floor Plan

Design by Nelson Design Group

Secluded Master Suite

No. 82069

BL

■ **This plan features:**

– Three bedrooms

– Two full baths

■ A peninsula counter that seats five comfortably highlights the open Kitchen

■ The Dining Room has access to the rear yard

■ The Master Suite has a secluded location, a private Bath and a walk-in closet

■ The Laundry Room is off the Kitchen

■ The two additional Bedrooms have a full Bath located between them

■ No materials list is available for this plan

Main floor — 1,466 sq. ft.
Garage/Storage — 380 sq. ft.

49' 2"

44' 2"

BEDROOM 2 11'-6" x 10'-0"

DINING ROOM 14'-4" x 7'-8"

MASTER SUITE 15'-10" X 13'-4"

WHIP TUB/SHWR

M.BATH 6'-0" X 10'-4"

BATH

KITCHEN 17'-4" X 11'-4"

LAU. 7'-6" X 6'-6"

GARAGE 19'-0" X 20'-0"

BEDROOM 3 9'-6" X 10'-0"

FOYER

GREAT ROOM 15'-0" X 18'-0"

© 1999 Nelson Design Group, LLC.

PORCH

MAIN FLOOR

Heart of the Home

Design by Nelson Design Group

■ *Total living area 1,474 sq. ft.* ■ *Price Code A* ■

MAIN FLOOR

46' 10"

56' 4"

BED RM. 3
11'-0" X 10'-6"

GREAT RM.
18'-0" X 16'-0"
9' BOXED CEILING

M.BED RM.
16'-6" X 12'-4"
9' BOXED CEILING

HVAC

LIN

FOYER

DINING RM.
10'-6" X 10'-10"

DW

I.IN

M.BATH

RG

KIT.

REF

BED RM. 2
11'-0" X 10'-0"

PRCH.

W

PAN.

D

WH

GARAGE
20'-10" X 20'-0"

No. 82032

■ **This plan features:**

— Three bedrooms

— Two full baths

■ The Great Room is topped by a nine-foot, boxed ceiling and is accented by a focal point fireplace

■ The Master Suite is located on the opposite side of the home from the additional Bedrooms for privacy

■ The formal Dining Room has direct access to the Kitchen

■ The entrance from the Garage into the Laundry Room creates a desirable Mud Room

■ No materials list is available for this plan

■ An optional basement, slab or crawl space foundation — please specify when ordering

Main floor — 1,474 sq. ft.
Garage — 417 sq. ft.

Design by Design Basics, Inc.

Arched Front Porch

No. 99490 BL X

■ **This plan features:**

— Three bedrooms

— Two full baths

■ The cozy front Porch of this home gives an attractive Country appearance

■ The tiled Foyer leads into the Great Room, which is accented by a fireplace with transom windows to either side

■ The Kitchen includes a snack bar/island, and a Pantry and is open to the Breakfast Room

■ A bright bay window highlights the Breakfast Room

■ The Master Suite includes a whirlpool Bath and a walk-in closet

■ The secondary Bedroom is in proximity to the full Bath in the hall

■ The Den or third Bedroom is enhanced by a double door entry

■ An optional basement or slab foundation — please specify when ordering

Main floor — 1,479 sq. ft.

Total living area 1,479 sq. ft. ■ Price Code A

MAIN FLOOR

Design by Studer Residential Design, Inc.

Easy Living

No. 97724 BL

■ **This plan features:**

— Three bedrooms

— Two full baths

■ The Great Room combines with the Dining area to create an open, spacious effect

■ An atrium door leads to a raised Deck creating a favorable indoor/outdoor relationship

■ The Master Bedroom has a large walk-in closet and a deluxe Bath

■ The rear walkout basement creates the opportunity for more living space

■ No material list is available for this plan

Main floor — 1,488 sq. ft.
Basement — 1,488 sq. ft.
Garage — 417 sq. ft.

Total living area 1,488 sq. ft. ■ Price Code B

MAIN FLOOR

Elegant Window Treatment

Design by The Garlinghouse Company

■ *Total living area 1,492 sq. ft.* ■ *Price Code A* ■

No. 34150 ⬛BL ✖ 🗺 ᴙR

■ This plan features:

— Three bedrooms

— Two full baths

■ The expansive Living Room has a sloped ceiling above a hearth fireplace and Deck access

■ An efficient Kitchen has easy access to the Dining Room

■ The Master Bedroom features a private Master Bath and a roomy walk-in closet

■ The Den/Bedroom can be a homey, well-lit Office

Main floor — 1,492 sq. ft.
Basement — 1,486 sq. ft.
Garage — 462 sq. ft.

MAIN FLOOR

Design by Nelson Design Group

Stylish Details

No. 82070

This plan features:

– Three bedrooms

– Two full baths

Arched openings and decorative ceiling treatments give this home a custom look

The Foyer has a ten-foot ceiling and opens to the Gallery Area

Columns identify the opening from the Gallery into the Great Room

The Kitchen is open to the Breakfast Room and highlighted by a peninsula counter

The secondary Bedrooms have a full Bath located between them

An optional basement, slab or crawl space foundation — please specify when ordering

No materials list is available with this plan

Main floor — 1,496 sq. ft.
Garage/Storage — 417 sq. ft.

MAIN FLOOR

Design by Nelson Design Group

Open Spaces

No. 82027

This plan features:

– Three bedrooms

– Two full baths

The Great Room creates a terrific first impression with a boxed ceiling and a focal point fireplace

The Dining Room is open to both the Great Room and the Kitchen for easy meals

The peninsula counter in the Kitchen doubles as a snack bar for meals on the run

The Master Suite is crowned by a pan ceiling adding a touch of elegance to the room

Bedroom two includes a vaulted ceiling and an arched window

An optional basement, slab or crawl space foundation — please specify when ordering

No materials list is available with this plan

Main floor — 1,500 sq. ft.
Garage/storage — 417 sq. ft.

MAIN FLOOR

Today's Homeowner in Mind

Design by Larry E. Belk

Total living area 1,500 sq. ft. ■ Price Code A

No. 93027 BL

This plan features:

- Three bedrooms

- Two full baths

■ The formal Dining Room opens off the Foyer and has a classic bay window

■ The Kitchen is notable for its angled eating bar which opens to the Living Room

■ A cozy fireplace in the Living Room, can be enjoyed from the Kitchen

■ The Master Suite includes a whirlpool tub/shower combination, and a walk-in closet

■ Ten-foot ceilings provide volume in the active living areas

■ No materials list is available for this plan

Main floor — 1,500 sq. ft.
Garage — 437 sq. ft.

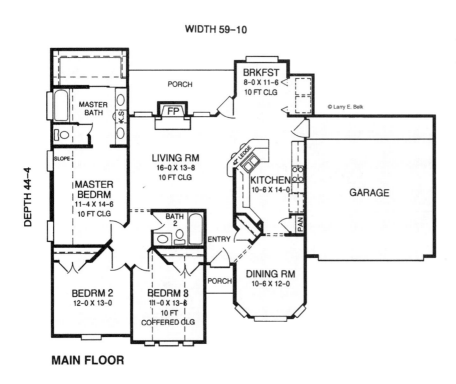

WIDTH 59-10

DEPTH 44-4

PORCH

BRKFST
8-0 X 11-6
10 FT CLG

FP

MASTER BATH

K.S.

© Larry E. Belk

LIVING RM
16-0 X 13-8
10 FT CLG

42" LEDGE

KITCHEN
10-6 X 14-0

GARAGE

SLOPE

MASTER BEDRM
11-4 X 14-6
10 FT CLG

BATH 2

ENTRY

PAN

BEDRM 2
12-0 X 13-0

BEDRM 8
11-0 X 13-6
10 FT COFFERED CLG

PORCH

DINING RM
10-6 X 12-0

MAIN FLOOR

Design by Frank Betz Associates, Inc.

High Ceilings & Arched Windows

No. 98441

This plan features:

- Three bedrooms

- Two full baths

- Natural illumination streams into the Dining Room and the Sitting Area of the Master Suite through large arched windows

- The Kitchen has a convenient pass-through to the Great Room and a serving bar for the Breakfast Room

- The Great Room is topped by a vaulted ceiling and accented by a fireplace

- Decorative columns accent the entrance of the Dining Room

- A tray ceiling over the Master Suite and vaulted ceilings over the Sitting Room and the Master Bath add a feeling of elegance

- No materials list is available for this plan

- An optional basement or crawl space foundation — please specify when ordering

Main floor — 1,502 sq. ft.
Basement — 1,555 sq. ft.
Garage — 448 sq. ft.

Total living area 1,502 sq. ft.   Price Code B

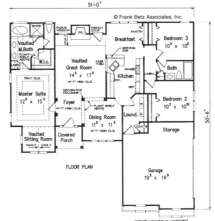

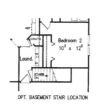

Design by Nelson Design Group

Bedroom Wing

No. 61009

This plan features:

- Three bedrooms

- Two full baths

- There are covered Porches in both the front and the rear of this home

- Boxed ceilings grace the Dining and the Great Rooms

- The Kitchen is well-planned for convenient meal preparation

- Plenty of extra space is available in the Garage

- All of the Bedrooms are spacious as well as the closets

- No materials list is available for this plan

Main floor — 1,504 sq. ft.

Total living area 1,504 sq. ft.   Price Code B

MAIN FLOOR

Fireplace-Equipped

Design by The Garlinghouse Company

Total living area 1,505 sq. ft. ■ Price Code B ■

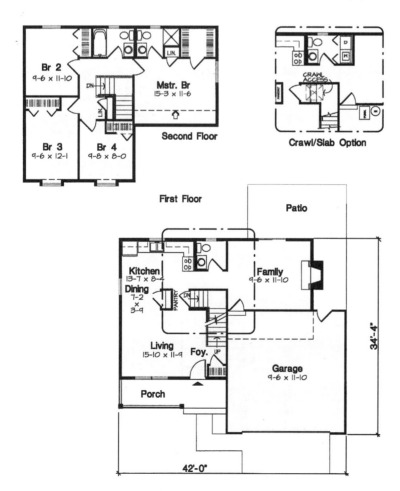

Br 2
9-6 x 11-10

Mstr. Br
15-3 x 11-6

DN

LIN.

Second Floor

Br 3
9-6 x 12-1

Br 4
9-8 x 8-0

Crawl/Slab Option

CRAWL ACCESS

First Floor

Patio

Kitchen
13-7 x 8-4

Dining
7-2 x 3-9

PANTRY

DN

Family
9-6 x 11-10

Living
15-10 x 11-9

Foy.

UP

Garage
9-6 x 11-10

34'-4"

Porch

42'-0"

No. 24326

This plan features:

— Four bedrooms

— Two full, one three-quarter and one half baths

■ A lovely front Porch shades the entrance

■ The spacious Living Room opens into the Dining Area and then into the efficient Kitchen

■ The Family Room is equipped with a cozy fireplace and sliding glass doors to the Patio

■ The Master Suite has a large walk-in closet and a private Bath with a step-in shower

■ Three additional Bedrooms share a full Bath in the hall

First floor — 692 sq. ft.
Second floor — 813 sq. ft.
Basement — 699 sq. ft.
Garage — 484 sq. ft.

Cozy Front Porch

No. 92649

This plan features:

– Three bedrooms

– Two full baths

Multiple gables and a cozy front Porch make this house appealing

The Foyer leads to the bright and cheery Great Room capped by a sloped ceiling and highlighted by a fireplace

The Dining Area includes an alcove of windows adding light and dimension to the room

The functional Kitchen provides an abundance of counter space plus a snack bar

The rear Porch is accessed from the Dining Area

The Master Bedroom Suite includes a walk-in closet and a private Bath

Two additional Bedrooms share a full Bath

Main floor — 1,508 sq. ft.
Basement — 1,439 sq. ft.
Garage — 440 sq. ft.

MAIN FLOOR

Porch

Dining Area
11'6" x 14'2"

Great Room
16'6" x 17'

Master Bedroom
14' x 11'9"

Kitchen
18' x 10'10"

Bath

Foyer

Bath

Hall

Two-car Garage
20' x 22'

Laun.

Porch

Bedroom
10'6" x 10'6"

Bedroom
11' x 10'6"

47'

60'

Charm & Convenience

No. 96458

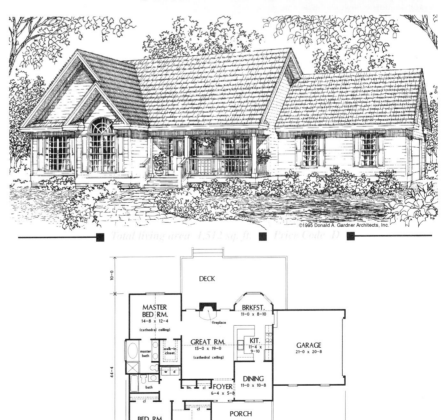

This plan features:

– Three bedrooms

– Two full baths

The open design pulls the Great Room, Kitchen and Breakfast Bay into one common area

Cathedral ceilings add volume in the Great Room, the Master Bedroom and a secondary Bedroom

The rear Deck expands the living and entertaining space to the outdoors

The Dining Room provides a quiet place for relaxing family dinners

Two additional Bedrooms share a full Bath

Main floor — 1,512 sq. ft.
Garage & Storage — 455 sq. ft.

DECK

MASTER BED RM.
14-8 x 12-4
(cathedral ceiling)

master bath

walk-in closet

BRKFST.
11-0 x 8-10

fireplace

GREAT RM.
15-0 x 19-0
(cathedral ceiling)

KIT.
11-4 x 9-10

GARAGE
21-0 x 20-8

bath

w d

DINING
11-0 x 10-8

FOYER
6-4 x 5-8

BED RM.
12-0 x 11-0

BED RM.
11-0 x 11-0
(cathedral ceiling)

PORCH

FLOOR PLAN

64-4

44-4

10-0

© 1995 Donald A Gardner Architects, Inc.

Private Master Suite

Design by Donald A. Gardner Architects, Inc.

B. NATHAN

■ Total living area 1,515 sq. ft. ■ Price Code D ■

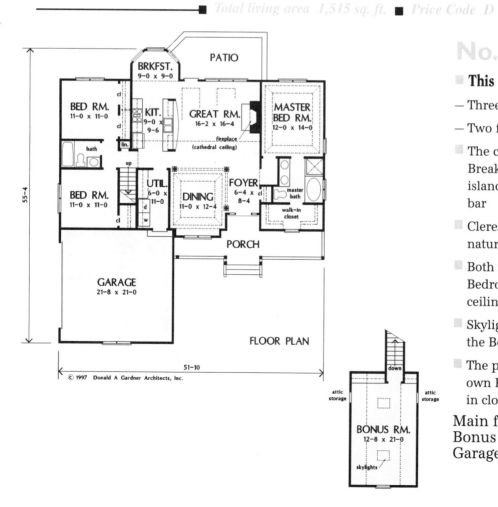

FLOOR PLAN

No. 99835

■ This plan features:

— Three bedrooms

— Two full baths

■ The convenient Kitchen has a Breakfast alcove and an extended island with a sink and a serving bar

■ Clerestory dormers provides natural light for the Great Room

■ Both the Dining Room and Master Bedroom are enhanced by tray ceilings

■ Skylights flood natural light into the Bonus space

■ The private Master Suite has its own Bath and an expansive walk-in closet

Main floor — 1,515 sq. ft.
Bonus — 288 sq. ft.
Garage — 476 sq. ft.

Design by The Garlinghouse Company

No. 20204

Abundance of Closet Space

■ **This plan features:**

– Three bedrooms

– Two full baths

■ Roomy walk-in closets are featured in all the Bedrooms

■ The Master Bedroom has a decorative ceiling and a private Bath

■ The Living Room is enhanced with a sloped ceiling and sliders to the Deck

■ The efficient Kitchen has plenty of cupboard space and a Pantry

Main area — 1,532 sq. ft.
Garage — 484 sq. ft.

MAIN FLOOR

Design by Nelson Design Group

No. 82033 BL

Perfect for Entertaining

■ **This plan features:**

– Three bedrooms

– Two full baths

■ The Kitchen opens to the Dining Room, which adjoins the Great Room creating a perfect arrangement for entertaining

■ The Great Room includes a boxed ceiling and a cozy fireplace

■ The Master Bedroom is topped by a pan ceiling and pampered by a lavish Bath with two walk-in closets

■ The two additional Bedrooms have a double vanity Bath located between them

■ No materials list is available with this plan

Main floor — 1,538 sq. ft.
Garage/storage — 441 sq. ft.

MAIN FLOOR

Dormers and Covered Porch

Design by Nelson Design Group

■ *Total living area 1,541 sq. ft.* ■ *Price Code B* ■

FIRST FLOOR

- 34' 8"
- 61' 10"
- GARAGE 18'-4" X 20'-0"
- STRG.
- PATIO
- WHP TUB
- KITCHEN 16'-9" X 11'-6"
- M.BATH 16'-10" X 11'-6"
- GREAT RM. 14'-6" X 15'-0"
- M.BED RM. 13'-0" X 15'-0"
- OPT. GAS FIREPLACE
- COVERED PORCH 32'-0" X 8'-0"

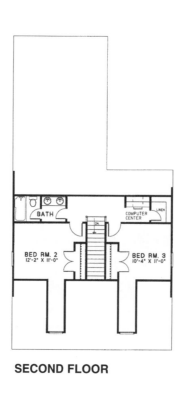

SECOND FLOOR

- BATH
- COMPUTER CENTER
- LINEN
- BED RM. 2 12'-2" X 11'-0"
- BED RM. 3 10'-4" X 11'-0"

No. 82030

■ This plan features:

— Three bedrooms

— Two full baths

■ An easy entrance through the Garage and the Laundry Room cuts down on tracked-in dirt

■ The Master Suite includes two walk-in closets and a whirlpool Bath

■ The two additional Bedrooms are located on the second floor

■ There is a built-in computer center in the hallway

■ An optional basement, slab or crawl space foundation — please specify when ordering

■ No materials list is available for this plan

First floor — 990 sq. ft.
Second floor — 551 sq. ft.
Garage — 367 sq. ft.

Design by Donald A. Gardner Architects, Inc.

Arched Windows

No. 98005

This plan features:

– Three bedrooms

– Two full baths

■ Privacy and openness are balanced in this efficient house designed with expansion in mind

■ The combined Great Room and Dining Area features a cathedral ceiling, a fireplace, and access to the Deck

■ An efficient, U-shaped Kitchen is convenient to the Dining and Utility Areas

■ Crowned with a tray ceiling, the Master Bedroom includes a walk-in closet and a fully appointed Bath

■ Two secondary Bedrooms, one an optional Study with a tray ceiling, share the second full Bath

Main floor — 1,542 sq. ft.
Bonus — 352 sq. ft.
Garage — 487 sq. ft.

©1997 Donald A. Gardner Architects, Inc.

Total living area 1,542 sq. ft. ■ Price Code D

© 1997 Donald A Gardner Architects, Inc.

Design by James Fahy, P.E., P.C.

Small, But Not Lacking

No. 94116

This plan features:

– Three bedrooms

– Two full baths

■ The Great Room adjoins the Dining Room for ease in entertaining

■ The Kitchen is equipped with a peninsula counter/snack bar extending the work space and offering convenience in serving informal meals

■ The split Bedroom plan allows privacy for the Master Bedroom Suite with a private Bath and a walk-in closet

■ Two additional Bedrooms share the full Bath in the hall

■ The Garage entry is convenient to the Kitchen

Main floor — 1,546 sq. ft.
Garage — 440 sq. ft.
Basement — 1,530 sq. ft.

Total living area 1,546 sq. ft. ■ Price Code C

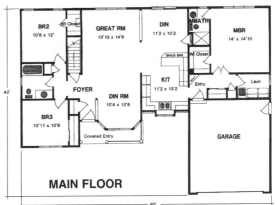

MAIN FLOOR

Traditional Two-Story

Design by Donald A. Gardner Architects, Inc.

Total living area 1,558 sq. ft. ■ *Price Code D*

SECOND FLOOR PLAN

BED RM.
11-0 x 10-8

attic storage

cl

attic storage

cl

BED RM.
10-10 x 11-8

bath

down

cl

cl

great room below

FIRST FLOOR PLAN

master bath

MASTER BED RM.
13-2 x 13-0

walk-in closet

w   d

lin.

DECK

KITCHEN
9-0 x 11-8

UTIL.

cl

GARAGE
14-4 X 20-8

DINING
11-4 x 12-0

pd. rm.

GREAT RM.
14-8 x 16-0
(cathedral ceiling)

fireplace

FOYER
7-0 x 6-9

up

PORCH

49-0

52-0

No. 99883

■ **This plan features:**

— Three bedrooms

— Two full and one half baths

■ The two-story Foyer welcomes guests into the Great Room crowned with a cathedral ceiling and highlighted by a fireplace

■ A pass-through above the Kitchen sink makes both serving and cleaning up a snap

■ The secluded Master Suite is highlighted by a generous walk-in closet and a private Bath with a corner garden tub

First floor — 1,116 sq. ft.
Second floor — 442 sq. ft.
Garage & storage — 313 sq. ft.

Casually Elegant

Design by Donald A. Gardner Architects, Inc.

No. 96417

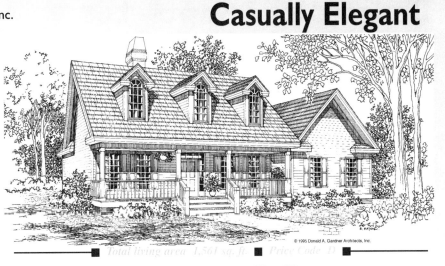

© 1995 Donald A. Gardner Architects, Inc.

Total living area 1,561 sq. ft. ■ Price Code D

This plan features:

— Three bedrooms

— Two full baths

■ Arched windows, dormers and charming front and back Porches create a Country flavor for this home

■ The central Great Room has a cathedral ceiling, a fireplace and a clerestory window

■ The Breakfast Bay is for casual dining and is easily served by the Kitchen peninsula counter

■ Columns accent the entrance to the formal Dining Room

■ A cathedral ceiling crowns the Master Bedroom

■ The Master Bath has skylights, a whirlpool tub and a double vanity

■ The two additional Bedrooms share a Bath located between the rooms

Main floor — 1,561 sq. ft.
Garage & Storage — 346 sq. ft.

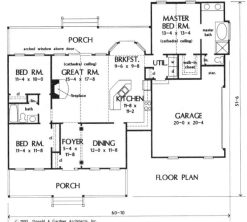

© 1995 Donald A. Gardner Architects, Inc.

Traditional Ranch

Design by The Garlinghouse Company

No. 20220

Total living area 1,568 sq. ft. ■ Price Code B

This plan features:

— Three bedrooms

— Two full baths

■ A large palladian window gives this home great curb appeal, and illuminates the Living Room

■ A vaulted ceiling in the Living Room adds to the architectural interest and space to the room

■ Sliding glass doors in the Dining Room lead to the Deck

■ A built-in Pantry, a double sink and a breakfast bar help create the efficient Kitchen

■ The Master Suite includes a walk-in closet and a private Bath with a double vanity

■ Two additional Bedrooms share a full Bath in the hall

Main floor — 1,568 sq. ft.
Basement — 1,568 sq. ft.
Garage — 509 sq. ft.

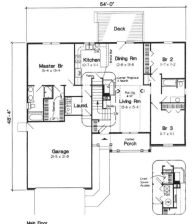

Main Floor

Designed for a Narrow Lot

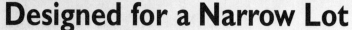

Design by Studer Residential Design, Inc.

■ *Total living area 1,575 sq. ft.* ■ *Price Code B* ■

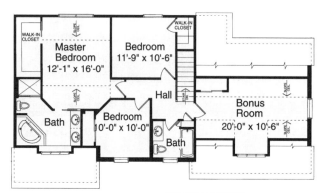

Second Floor Plan

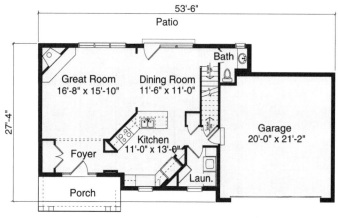

First Floor Plan

No. 97712

■ **This plan features:**

— Three bedrooms

— Two full and one half baths

■ Superior exterior detailing characterizes this narrow lot home

■ The gracious entrance to this home is highlighted by transom and sidelight windows

■ The Great Room, with its corner fireplace, is just steps beyond the Foyer

■ The Dining Room accesses the rear Patio for outdoor meals

■ The Bedrooms are all on the second floor and have ample closets

■ No materials list is available for this plan

First floor — 798 sq. ft.
Second floor — 777 sq. ft.
Bonus — 242 sq. ft.
Basement — 798 sq. ft.

Design by Donald A. Gardner Architects, Inc.

No Wasted Space

No. 99834 BL ✕ ℛ

This plan features:

— Three bedrooms

— Two full baths

▪ The Great Room with a fireplace and built-in cabinets shares a cathedral ceiling with the angled Kitchen

▪ The separate Dining Room allows for more formal entertaining

▪ The Master Bedroom is topped by a cathedral ceiling, and has a walk-in closet, and a well-appointed Bath

▪ The front and rear covered Porches encourage relaxation

▪ The skylit Bonus Room makes a great Recreation Room or Office in the future

Main floor — 1,575 sq. ft.
Second floor — 276 sq. ft.
Garage — 536 sq. ft.

© 1994 Donald A. Gardner Architects, Inc.

Total living area 1,575 sq. ft. ▪ Price Code D

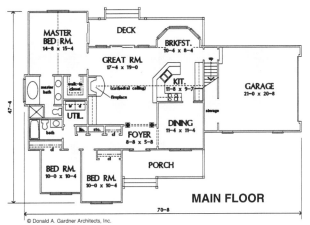

MAIN FLOOR

© Donald A. Gardner Architects, Inc.

Design by Donald A. Gardner Architects, Inc.

Traditional Beauty

No. 99802 BL ✕ 🗺 ℛ

This plan features:

— Three bedrooms

— Two full baths

▪ This traditional beauty has large arched windows, round columns, a covered Porch, brick veneer and an open floor plan

▪ The clerestory dormers above the covered Porch light the Foyer

▪ A cathedral ceiling enhances the Great Room along with a cozy fireplace

▪ The Kitchen has a center island and a Breakfast Area with access to the large Deck and an optional Spa

▪ Tray ceilings are over the Master Bedroom, the Dining Room and the Bedroom/Study

▪ A dual vanity, separate shower and a whirlpool tub are in the Master Bath

Main floor — 1,576 sq. ft.
Garage — 465 sq. ft.

© 1993 Donald A Gardner Architects, Inc.

Total living area 1,576 sq. ft. ▪ Price Code D

FLOOR PLAN

© 1993 Donald A Gardner Architects, Inc.

Friendly Front Porch

Design by James Fahy, P.E., P.C.

■ *Total living area 1,576 sq. ft.* ■ *Price Code C* ■

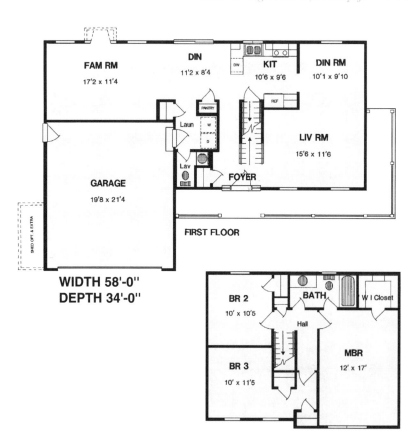

FAM RM
17'2 x 11'4

DIN
11'2 x 8'4

KIT
10'6 x 9'6

DIN RM
10'1 x 9'10

PANTRY

Laun

REF

LIV RM
15'6 x 11'6

Lav

FOYER

GARAGE
19'8 x 21'4

SHED OPT. & EXTRA

FIRST FLOOR

WIDTH 58'-0"
DEPTH 34'-0"

BR 2
10' x 10'5

BATH

W I Closet

Hall

BR 3
10' x 11'5

MBR
12' x 17'

SECOND FLOOR

No. 94138

■ **This plan features:**

— Three bedrooms

— One full and one half baths

■ This design creates a Country feeling with a wrap-around Porch

■ The efficient Kitchen easily serves the Dining Area with an extended counter and a built-in Pantry

■ The spacious Family Room has an optional fireplace and access to the Laundry/Garage entry

■ The large Master Bedroom, with a walk-in closet, has access to a full Bath

■ No materials list is available for this plan

First floor — 900 sq. ft.
Second floor — 676 sq. ft.
Basement — 900 sq. ft.
Garage — 448 sq. ft.

Design by Design Basics, Inc.

No. 99404

BL ✕ ✦

This plan features:

– Three bedrooms

– Two full and one half baths

– The spacious Great Room is enhanced by a fireplace and transom windows

– The Breakfast Room has a bow window and direct access to the Kitchen

– A snack bar extends the work space in the Kitchen

– The Master Suite is enhanced by a boxed, nine-foot ceiling, a whirlpool Bath and a large walk-in closet

– The second floor balcony overlooks the staircase and tiled Entry

– The two second floor Bedrooms share a full Bath in the hall

First floor — 1,191 sq. ft.
Second floor — 405 sq. ft.
Basement — 1,191 sq. ft.
Garage — 454 sq. ft.

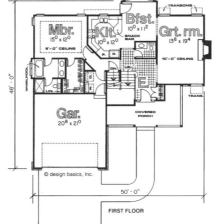

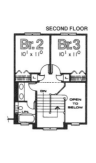

Bathed in Natural Light

Design by Frank Betz Associates, Inc.

No. 98416

BL ✕

This plan features:

– Three bedrooms

– Two full and one half baths

– A high arched window illuminates the Foyer and adds style to the exterior of the home

– Vaulted ceilings in the formal Dining Room, the Breakfast Room and the Great Room create volume

– The Master Suite is crowned with a decorative tray ceiling

– The Master Bath has a double vanity and a walk-in closet

– The Loft, with the option of becoming a fourth Bedroom, highlights the second floor

– An optional basement or crawl space foundation — please specify when ordering

First floor — 1,133 sq. ft.
Second floor — 486 sq. ft.
Basement — 1,133 sq. ft.
Bonus — 134 sq. ft.
Garage — 406 sq. ft.

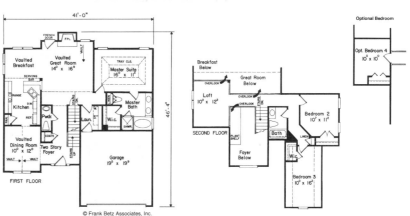

79

Convenient Floor Plan

Design by The Garlinghouse Company

■ *Total living area 1,625 sq. ft.* ■ *Price Code B* ■

Main Floor

Alternate Foundation Plan

No. 24701

■ This plan features:

— Three bedrooms

— Two full baths

■ The central Foyer leads to the Den/Guest with an arched window below a vaulted ceiling and the Living Room accented by a two-sided fireplace

■ The efficient, U-shaped Kitchen has a peninsula counter/breakfast bar serving the Dining Room and is adjacent to the Utility/Pantry

■ The Master Suite features a large walk-in closet and a private Bath with a double vanity and a whirlpool tub

■ Two additional Bedrooms with ample closet space share a full Bath

Main floor — 1,625 sq. ft.
Basement — 1,625 sq. ft.
Garage — 455 sq. ft.

Design by Donald A. Gardner Architects, Inc.

An Air of Sophistication

No. 98036

This plan features:

- Three bedrooms

- Two full baths

- Gables, with arch-topped windows and keystone accents, add an air of class to this home's exterior

- The covered Porch reveals the front door with a transom and sidelights

- Inside, the Foyer has a ten-foot ceiling

- Just beyond is the Great Room with a fireplace and a cathedral ceiling

- The U-shaped Kitchen has a counter that serves the Dining Room

- The Dining Room is bathed in light with windows on three sides

- There is a Deck at the rear of the home

- The Master Bedroom has a cathedral ceiling and a walk-in closet

- Two other Bedrooms have bright front wall windows

Main floor — 1,629 sq. ft.

Design by Lifestyle Home Design

Single-Level Living

No. 99329

This plan features:

- Three bedrooms

- Two full baths

- A fireplace between the windows is the focus of the Living Room

- An angled counter in the Kitchen serves the sunny Breakfast Room, the Dining Area and the Deck

- A vaulted ceiling tops the Master Suite which also has a skylit Bath and a walk-in closet

- Two additional Bedrooms are served by a full Bath in the hall

Main floor — 1,642 sq. ft.
Basement — 1,642 sq. ft.
Garage — 448 sq. ft.

Charm and Personality

Design by Donald A. Gardner Architects, Inc.

© 1996 Donald A. Gardner Architects, Inc.

■ *Total living area 1,655 sq. ft.* ■ *Price Code D* ■

No. 99871

■ **This plan features:**

— Three bedrooms

— Two full baths

■ Space and light radiate throughout this Country home

■ Interior columns dramatically open the Foyer and the Kitchen to the spacious Great Room

■ The Great Room offers a cathedral ceiling and a fireplace as well as Deck access

■ The Master Suite, with a tray ceiling, combines privacy with a skylit Bath and outdoor access to the rear Deck with spa

■ Tray ceilings with arched windows bring a special elegance to the Dining Room and the front Study

Main floor — 1,655 sq. ft.
Garage — 434 sq. ft.

FLOOR PLAN

© 1996 Donald A Gardner Architects, Inc.

Design by Nelson Design Group

Brick Beauty

No. 82039 BL

This plan features:

- Three bedrooms

- Two full baths

- The Great Room includes a ten-foot boxed ceiling and a fireplace

- The Dining Room is open to the Kitchen for a more spacious feeling

- The Kitchen includes a peninsula counter/breakfast bar for meals on the go

- The Dining Room and the Master Bedroom have access to the Courtyard

- No materials list is available for this plan

- An optional slab or crawl space foundation — please specify when ordering

Main floor — 1,660 sq. ft.
Garage — 390 sq. ft.
Porch — 143 sq. ft.

MAIN FLOOR

Design by Fillmore Design Group

Easy Everyday Living

No. 92238 BL

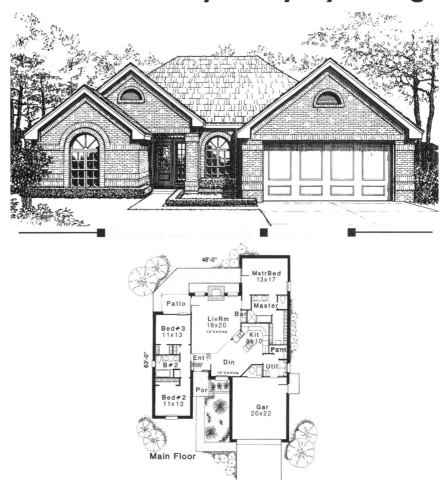

This plan features:

- Three bedrooms

- Two full baths

- The front facade is accented by segmented arches, and sidelight and transom windows

- The open Living Room, with a focal point fireplace and wet bar, has access to the Patio

- The Dining Area opens to both the Living Room and the Kitchen

- The efficient Kitchen has a cooktop island, a walk-in Pantry and a Utility Area with a Garage entry

- A large walk-in closet, a double vanity Bath and access to the Patio are featured in the Master Bedroom

- Two additional Bedrooms share a double vanity Bath

Main floor — 1,664 sq. ft.
Basement — 1,600 sq. ft.
Garage — 440 sq. ft

Main Floor

83

Carefree Comfort

Design by Sun-tel

■ *Total living area 1,665 sq. ft.* ■ *Price Code B* ■

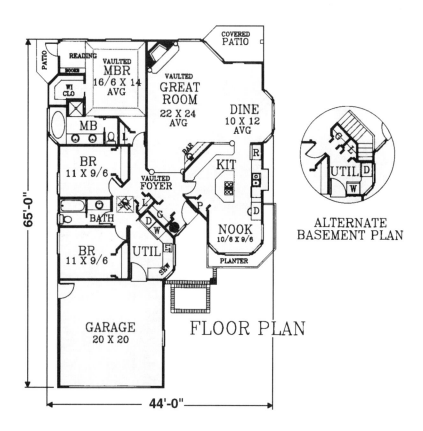

FLOOR PLAN

ALTERNATE
BASEMENT PLAN

No. 91418 BL ✕

■ **This plan features:**

— Three bedrooms

— Two full baths

■ The Foyer has a dramatic vaulted ceiling and provides access to all areas of this home

■ The Kitchen provides easy meal preparation for the sunny eating Nook and the adjacent Dining Area

■ A vaulted ceiling tops the Great Room which also has a corner fireplace

■ A Master Bedroom has a private Reading Nook, a vaulted ceiling, a walk-in closet, and a private Bath

■ Two additional Bedrooms share a full Bath in the hall

■ An optional basement, slab or crawl space foundation — please specify when ordering

Main area — 1,665 sq. ft.
Garage — 400 sq. ft.

Design by Design Basics, Inc.

Keystone Arches

No. 94923

This plan features:

– Three bedrooms

– Two full baths

■ Brick and stucco enhance the dramatic front elevation and volume entrance

■ An inviting Entry leads into the expansive Great Room with a hearth fireplace framed by transom windows

■ The Dining Room has a bay window and a decorative ceiling

■ The corner Master Suite enjoys a tray ceiling, a roomy walk-in closet and a plush Bath with a double vanity and whirlpool, window tub

■ Two additional Bedrooms, with large closets, share a full Bath

Main floor — 1,666 sq. ft.
Basement — 1,666 sq. ft.
Garage — 496 sq. ft.

Total living area 1,666 sq. ft. ■ Price Code B

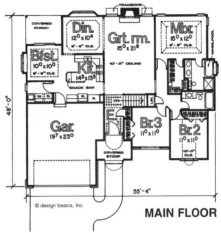

© design basics, Inc.

MAIN FLOOR

Design by Donald A. Gardner Architects, Inc.

Perfect Home for Narrow Lot

No. 96487

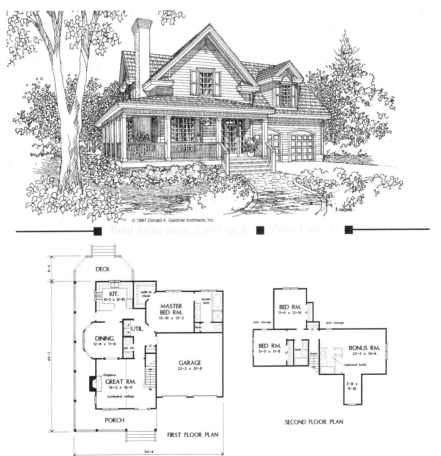

This plan features:

– Three bedrooms

– Two full and one half baths

■ The wrap-around Porch and the two-car Garage are unusual features for a narrow lot floor plan

■ An alcove of windows and columns add distinction to Dining Room

■ A cathedral ceiling and an inviting fireplace accent the spacious Great Room

■ The efficient Kitchen, with a peninsula counter, accesses the side Porch and Deck

■ The Master Suite is located on first floor; the two additional Bedrooms and the Bonus Room are on second floor

First floor — 1,219 sq. ft.
Second floor — 450 sq. ft.
Bonus — 406 sq. ft.
Garage — 473 sq. ft.

© 1997 Donald A. Gardner Architects, Inc.

Total living area 1,669 sq. ft. ■ Price Code C

FIRST FLOOR PLAN

SECOND FLOOR PLAN

Keystones & Arched Windows

Design by Frank Betz Associates, Inc.

■ *Total living area 1,670 sq. ft.* ■ *Price Code B* ■

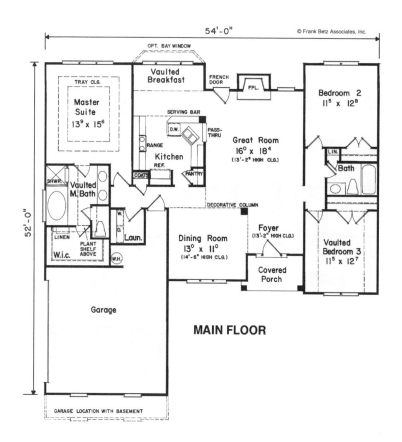

MAIN FLOOR

No. 98432

■ This plan features:

— Three bedrooms

— Two full baths

■ Large arched windows in the Dining Room and Bedroom three offer eye-catching appeal

■ A decorative column helps to define the Dining Room

■ A fireplace and a French door to the rear yard can be found in the Great Room

■ The efficient Kitchen includes a serving bar, a Pantry and a pass-through to the Great Room

■ The plush Master Suite includes a private Bath and a walk-in closet

■ An optional basement, slab or crawl space foundation — please specify when ordering

Main floor — 1,670 sq. ft.
Garage — 240 sq. ft.

Design by The Garlinghouse Company

Sunny Master Bedroom

Total living area 1,686 sq. ft. ■ Price Code B

No. 34029

This plan features:

— Three bedrooms

— Two full baths

■ The covered Porch shelters the entrance

■ The Foyer separates the Dining Room from the Breakfast Area and the Kitchen

■ The Living Room is enhanced by a vaulted, beam ceiling and a fireplace

■ The Master Bedroom has a decorative ceiling and a skylight in the private Bath

■ An optional Deck is accessible through sliding doors off the Master Bedroom

Main floor — 1,686 sq. ft.
Basement — 1,676 sq. ft.
Garage — 484 sq. ft.

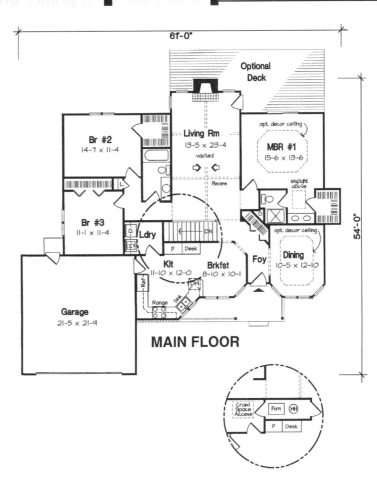

MAIN FLOOR

Slab/Crawl Space Option

Simplicity at it's Finest

Design by Design Basics, Inc.

Total living area 1,694 sq. ft. ■ Price Code B

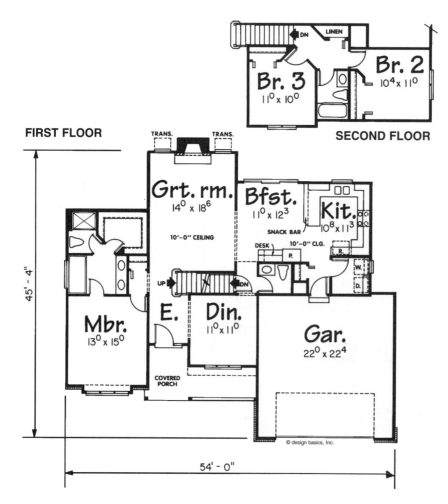

FIRST FLOOR

SECOND FLOOR

No. 99420

■ **This plan features:**

— Three bedrooms

— Two full and one half baths

■ The covered Porch gives this home a nostalgic feel

■ The volume Great Room offers a fireplace with transom windows on either side

■ A built-in planning desk and a Pantry are in the Breakfast Area

■ A snack bar, for informal meals adds to the efficient Kitchen

■ The formal Dining Room has a decorative window that overlooks the Porch

■ The isolated Master Suite has a comfortable Bath and a walk-in closet

First floor — 1,298 sq. ft.
Second floor — 396 sq. ft.
Basement — 1,298 sq. ft.
Garage — 513 sq. ft.

Design by The Garlinghouse Company

No. 10677

This plan features:

— Three bedrooms

— Two full and one half baths

■ A built-in planter separates the Living Room from the Family Room

■ A convenient, angled serving counter separates the Kitchen from the Family Room

■ Double sinks and a built-in vanity are in the Master Bath

First floor — 932 sq. ft.
Second floor — 764 sq. ft.
Basement — 920 sq. ft.
Garage — 430 sq. ft.

Arches Grace Facade

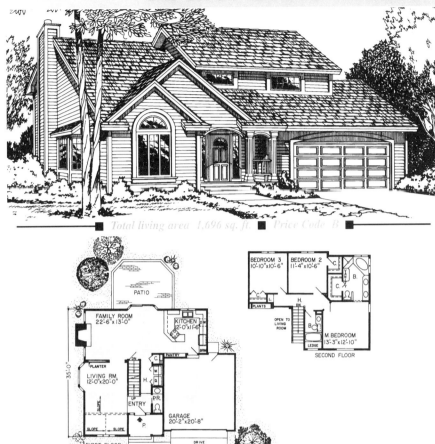

Total living area 1,696 sq. ft. ■ Price Code B

Design by Fillmore Design Group

No. 92290 BL

This plan features:

— Four bedrooms

— Two full baths

■ The gracious Entry has columns framing the Living and Breakfast Rooms

■ The Living Room is enhanced by a cathedral ceiling, palladian window and a hearth fireplace between built-in bookshelves

■ The efficient Kitchen has a corner Pantry, a peninsula counter serving the Breakfast Area and a nearby Utility/Garage entry

■ The corner Master Bedroom offers a cozy Sitting Area, Patio access, a walk-in closet and a lavish Bath

■ The three additional Bedrooms with over-sized closets, share a double vanity Bath

■ No materials list is available for this plan

Main floor — 1,696 sq. ft.
Garage — 389 sq. ft.

Elegant Palladian Window

Total living area 1,696 sq. ft. ■ Price Code B

Floor Plan

Simple Classic

Design by Studer Residential Design, Inc.

■ *Total living area 1,698 sq. ft.* ■ *Price Code B* ■

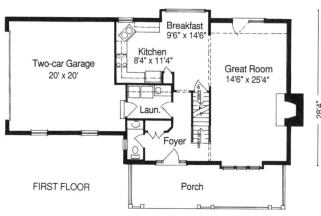

FIRST FLOOR

Two-car Garage
20' x 20'

Breakfast
9'6" x 14'6"

Kitchen
8'4" x 11'4"

Great Room
14'6" x 25'4"

Laun.

Foyer

Porch

28'4"

54'4"

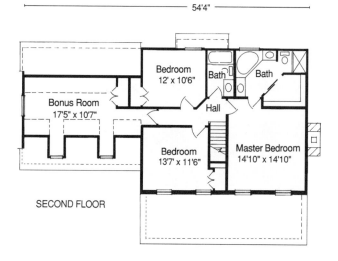

SECOND FLOOR

Bedroom
12' x 10'6"

Bath

Bath

Bonus Room
17'5" x 10'7"

Hall

Bedroom
13'7" x 11'6"

Master Bedroom
14'10" x 14'10"

No. 92690

■ This plan features:

— Three bedrooms

— Two full and one half baths

■ The expansive Great Room incorporates a cozy fireplace

■ The Breakfast Room and the Kitchen adjoin to each other

■ The practical Laundry Room has a counter for folding clothes

■ The second floor Master Suite includes a private whirlpool Bath and a walk-in closet

■ There is a Bonus Room over the Garage for future expansion

■ No materials list is available for this plan

First floor — 868 sq. ft.
Second floor — 830 sq. ft.
Bonus — 269 sq. ft.
Basement — 850 sq. ft.
Garage — 417 sq. ft.

European Sophistication

No. 99831

This plan features:

- Three bedrooms
- Two full baths

- Keystone arches, gables, and stucco give this home's exterior a European feeling

- The large Great Room with a fireplace shares Porch access with the Dining Room

- The open, efficient Kitchen has a serving counter as well as a Utility Room and Garage entry

- An octagonal tray ceiling dresses up the Dining Area

- Special ceiling treatments include a cathedral ceiling in the Great Room and tray ceilings in the Master Bedroom and a front Bedroom

- The indulgent Master Bath has a garden tub, a shower and twin vanities

- The Bonus Room over the Garage adds space and flexibility

Main floor — 1,699 sq. ft.
Bonus — 386 sq. ft.
Garage — 637 sq. ft.

© 1996 Donald A Gardner Architects, Inc.

Total living area 1,699 sq. ft. ■ Price Code D

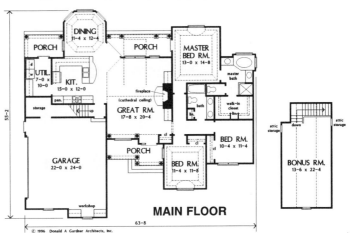

MAIN FLOOR

© 1996 Donald A Gardner Architects, Inc.

Streaming Natural Light

No. 91514

This plan features:

- Three bedrooms
- Two full and one half baths

- The outstanding, two-story Great Room has an unusual floor-to-ceiling, corner window and a cozy, hearth fireplace

- The formal Dining Room extends the Great Room and makes entertaining easy

- The efficient Kitchen has a work island, a Pantry, and a pass-thru to the Great Room

- The quiet Master Suite has a vaulted ceiling and a plush Bath with a double vanity, a spa tub and a walk-in closet

- On the second floor, two additional Bedrooms share a full Bath and a Bonus Area

First floor — 1,230 sq. ft.
Second floor — 477 sq. ft.
Bonus — 195 sq. ft.

Total living area 1,707 sq. ft. ■ Price Code B

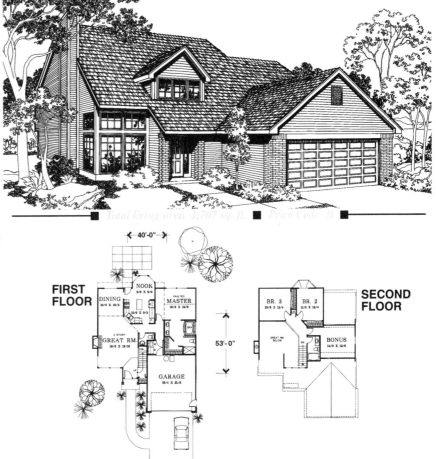

FIRST FLOOR

SECOND FLOOR

Wide Open and Convenient

Design by The Garlinghouse Company

Total living area 1,737 sq. ft. ■ Price Code B ■

No. 20100

■ This plan features:

— Three bedrooms

— Two full baths

■ Vaulted ceilings enhance the Dining Room and the Master Bedroom

■ A sloped ceiling over an inviting fireplace adds appeal to the Living Room

■ A skylight illuminates the Master Bath and complements the Master Bedroom

■ Two additional Bedrooms share a double vanity Bath

Main floor — 1,737 sq. ft.
Basement — 1,727 sq. ft.
Garage — 484 sq. ft.

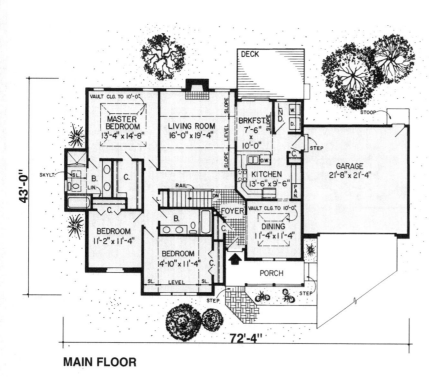

MAIN FLOOR

Design by Donald A. Gardner Architects, Inc.

Clever Use of Interior Space

No. 99844

This plan features:

– Three bedrooms

– Two full baths

– An efficient layout with cathedral and tray ceilings creates a feeling of space

– The Great Room has a cathedral ceiling above a cozy fireplace, built-in shelves and columns

– The octagonal Dining Room and the Breakfast Alcove have abundant windows

– The open Kitchen features an island counter sink and a Pantry

– The Master Bedroom is enhanced by a tray ceiling and a plush Bath

Main floor — 1,737 sq. ft.
Garage & storage — 517 sq. ft.

© 1994 Donald A. Gardner Architects, Inc.

■ Total living area 1,737 sq. ft. ■ Price Code D

MAIN FLOOR

© Donald A. Gardner Architects, Inc.

Design by The Garlinghouse Company

Perfect Compact Ranch

No. 10839

This plan features:

– Two bedrooms

– Two full baths

– The large, sunken Great Room, with a cozy fireplace, is the center of the home

– The Master Bedroom has a wonderful private Bathroom with a skylight

– The huge, three-car Garage includes a work area for the family carpenter

– The U-shaped Kitchen includes a Breakfast Nook for informal gatherings and an angled serving bar for the Great Room gatherings

Main floor — 1,738 sq. ft.
Basement — 1,083 sq. ft.
Garage — 796 sq. ft.

■ Total living area 1,738 sq. ft. ■ Price Code B

93

Secluded Master Suite

Design by The Garlinghouse Company

■ *Total living area 1,741 sq. ft.* ■ *Price Code B* ■

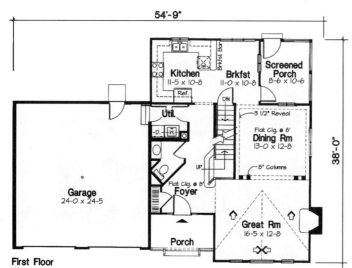

First Floor

Crawl/Slab Plan
NOTE: Mechanicals to be placed in Utility Room with this option.

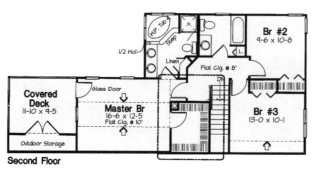

Second Floor

No. 24720

■ **This plan features:**

— Three bedrooms

— Two full and one half baths

■ The arched Porch shelters entry into the open Foyer with a cascading staircase

■ Columns frame the entrance to the formal Dining Room from the Great Room

■ The efficient Kitchen has a breakfast bar, the Breakfast Area with Screened Porch access, and a nearby Utility/Garage entry

■ The Master Bedroom offers a private Deck, a large walk-in closet and a plush Bath

■ Two additional Bedrooms, with ample closets, share a full Bath

First floor —900 sq. ft.
Second floor — 841 sq. ft.
Basement —891 sq. ft.
Garage — 609 sq. ft.

Design by Studer Residential Design, Inc.

For the Discriminating Buyer

No. 92625

This plan features:

– Three bedrooms

– Two full baths

This plan offers an attractive, classic brick design with multiple gables, and wing walls

A sloped ceiling adds elegance to the formal Dining Room

A sloped ceiling and a corner fireplace enhance the Great Room

The Kitchen has a garden window above the double sink and a curved serving bar

The Master Suite is equipped with a large walk-in closet and a private Bath with an oval corner tub, a separate shower and a double vanity

Two additional Bedrooms share a full Bath

Main floor — 1,746 sq. ft.
Basement — 1,560 sq. ft.
Garage — 455 sq. ft.

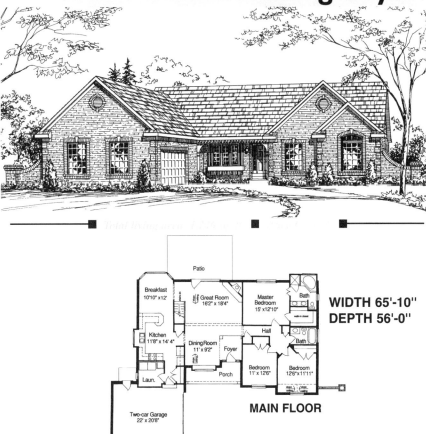

WIDTH 65'-10''
DEPTH 56'-0''

MAIN FLOOR

Design by Studer Residential Design, Inc.

Appealing Arches

No. 92658

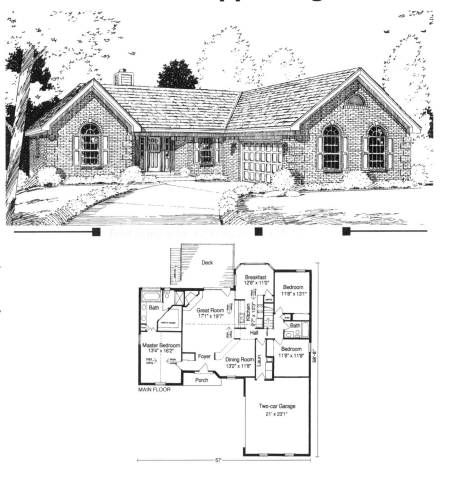

This plan features:

– Three bedrooms

– Two full baths

The brick exterior is accented by quoins and arched windows

The Foyer opens to the formal Dining Room and the spacious Great Room

Sloped ceiling above a corner fireplace, and an atrium door to the Deck enhance Great Room

The efficient Kitchen has a serving counter, a bright Breakfast Area, Pantry and nearby Laundry/Garage entry

The secluded Master Bedroom offers a sloped ceiling above an arched window, a large walk-in closet and a lavish Bath with a garden window tub

Two additional Bedrooms, with ample closets, share a full Bath

No materials list is available for this plan

Main floor — 1,756 sq. ft.
Garage — 485 sq. ft.

Convenience and Forethought

Design by Nelson Design Group

■ *Total living area 1,758 sq. ft.* ■ *Price Code B* ■

No. 82035

■ This plan features:

— Three bedrooms

— Two full baths

■ The Foyer is separated from the Dining Room by boxed columns

■ The Great Room is open to the Breakfast Room and has access to the Grilling Porch

■ The ideal Kitchen has an angled counter for easy serving and cleaning up

■ The Master Suite is enhanced by a pan ceiling and a pampering Master Bath

■ An optional slab or crawl space foundation — please specify when ordering

■ No materials list is available for this plan

Main floor — 1,812 sq. ft.
Garage/storage — 417 sq. ft.

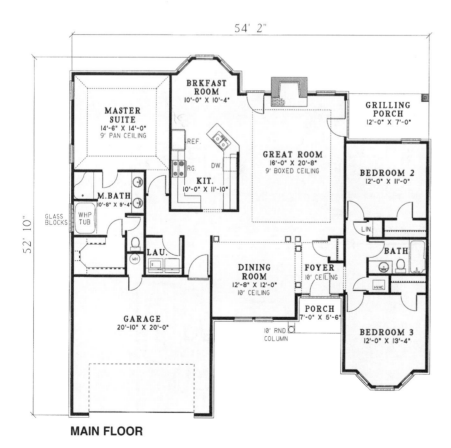

MAIN FLOOR

Design by Ahmann Design, Inc.

No. 93133 BL X 🦅 ЯR

This plan features:

- Three bedrooms

- Two full baths

- The Foyer opens to the spacious Living Room highlighted by a wall of windows

- The country-size Kitchen has a work island, an Eating Nook with backyard access, and is near the Laundry/Garage entry

- French doors open to a luxurious Master Bedroom with window alcove, walk-in closet and double vanity Bath

- The two additional Bedrooms' with large closets, share a full Bath

Main floor —1,761 sq. ft.
Garage — 658 sq. ft.
Basement— 1,761 sq. ft.

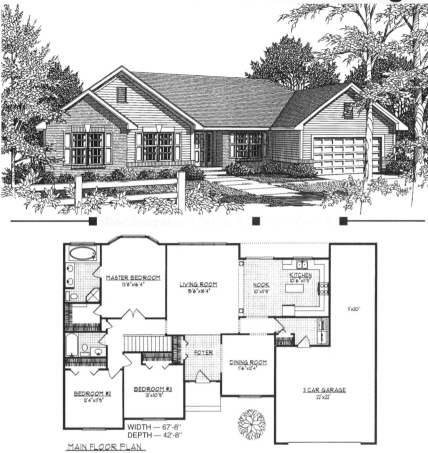

MASTER BEDROOM 13'8"x16'4"
LIVING ROOM 15'6"x18'4"
NOOK 10'x11'9"
KITCHEN 10'6"x11'9"
11'x20'
FOYER
DINING ROOM 11'6"x12'4"
3 CAR GARAGE 22'x22'
BEDROOM #2 12'4"x11'9"
BEDROOM #3 13'x10'9"
WIDTH — 67'-8"
DEPTH — 42'-8"
MAIN FLOOR PLAN

Design by Donald A. Gardner Architects, Inc.

No. 98035 BL X ЯR

This plan features:

- Three bedrooms

- Two full baths

- Front and rear covered Porches add outdoor living space

- The Dining Room has a decorative ceiling and is open to the Foyer and the Great Room

- The Great Room has a fireplace set between built-in shelves

- The Kitchen and Great Room have cathedral ceilings

- The Breakfast Nook is brightened by windows and a French door to the rear Porch

- The Master Bedroom has a decorative ceiling and dual walk-in closets

- The two secondary Bedrooms and a full Bath are located on the opposite side of the home

Main floor — 1,762 sq. ft.
Bonus — 316 sq. ft.
Garage — 520 sq. ft.

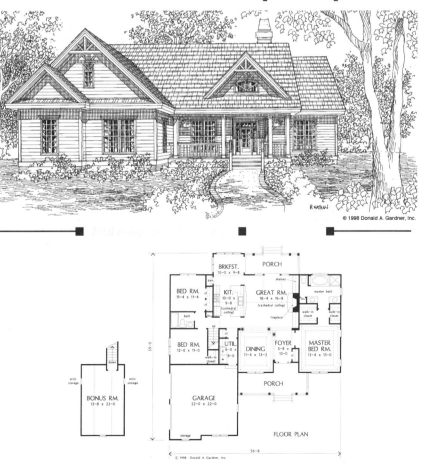

B. NATHAN
© 1998 Donald A. Gardner, Inc.

BRKFST. 10-0 x 9-8
PORCH
BED RM. 11-4 x 11-4
KIT. 10-0 x 9-8 (cathedral ceiling)
GREAT RM. 18-4 x 16-8 (cathedral ceiling) fireplace
master bath
shelves
walk-in closet
walk-in closet
bath
BED RM. 12-0 x 11-0
UTIL 6-0 x 8-0
DINING 11-4 x 13-2
FOYER 5-8 x 10-0
MASTER BED RM. 13-4 x 15-0
walk-in closet
59-0
attic storage
attic storage
BONUS RM. 13-8 x 22-0
GARAGE 22-0 x 22-0
PORCH
storage
56-8
FLOOR PLAN
© 1998 Donald A. Gardner, Inc.

A Little Drama

Design by Studer Residential Design, Inc.

■ *Total living area 1,768 sq. ft.* ■ *Price Code B* ■

Breakfast
10 x 13-4

Kitchen
8-6 x 11

Porch

Bath

Laundry

Sunken
Great Room
13 x 17-4

stairs up

stairs dn

walk-in
closet

Foyer

Dining Room
11-4 x 12

WIDTH 55'-4"
DEPTH 40'-4"

Porch

furniture
alcove

Two-car Garage
20-4 x 20

FIRST FLOOR

Bedroom
11-4 x 11-4

Bath

Hall

Master
Bedroom
12 x 16

Great Room
Below
12' ceiling

Foyer
Below
12' ceiling

stairs dn

Bath

Bedroom
11-4 x 9-6

tray ceiling

walk-in closet

SECOND FLOOR

No. 92609

■ **This plan features:**

— Three bedrooms

— Two full and one half baths

■ The 12-foot high Entry is highlighted by a transom window and sidelights,

■ The sunken Great Room has a fireplace and access to a rear Porch

■ The Breakfast Bay is open to the Kitchen and has access to the rear Porch

■ The Master Bedroom features a tray ceiling, walk-in closet and a private Master Bath

■ No materials list is available for this plan

First floor — 960 sq. ft.
Second floor — 808 sq. ft.
Basement — 922 sq. ft.
Garage — 413 sq. ft.

Design by Donald A. Gardner Architects, Inc.

Casual Country Charmer

No. 96493

This plan features:

- Three bedrooms
- Two full baths
- Columns and arches frame the front Porch
- The open floor plan combines the Great Room, Kitchen, and the Dining Room
- The Kitchen offers a convenient Breakfast bar for quick meals
- The Master Suite features a luxurious Bath
- The secondary Bedrooms share a full Bath with a dual vanity

Main floor — 1,770 sq. ft.
Bonus — 401 sq. ft.
Garage — 630 sq. ft.

© 1997 Donald A. Gardner Architects, Inc.

Total living area 1,770 sq. ft. ■ Price Code D

FLOOR PLAN

© 1997 Donald A. Gardner Architects, Inc.

Design by The Garlinghouse Company

Energy Efficient Entry

No. 24714

This plan features:

- Two bedrooms
- Two full baths
- The attractive covered Porch adds curb appeal to this charming home
- A cozy window seat and a vaulted ceiling enhance the private Den
- The sunken Great Room is accented by a fireplace located between windows
- The screened Porch, accessed from the Dining Room, extends the living space to the outdoors
- The Master Bath features a garden tub, separate shower, dual walk-in closets and a skylight
- No materials list is available for this plan

Main floor — 1,771 sq. ft.
Basement — 1,194 sq. ft.
Garage — 517 sq. ft.

Total living area 1,771 sq. ft. ■ Price Code B

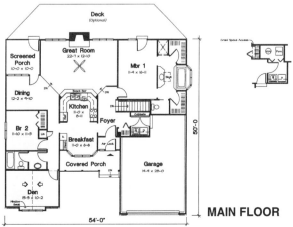

MAIN FLOOR

Quaint, Cozy Exterior

Design by Design Basics, Inc.

© design basics, inc.

■ *Total living area 1,771 sq. ft.* ■ *Price Code B* ■

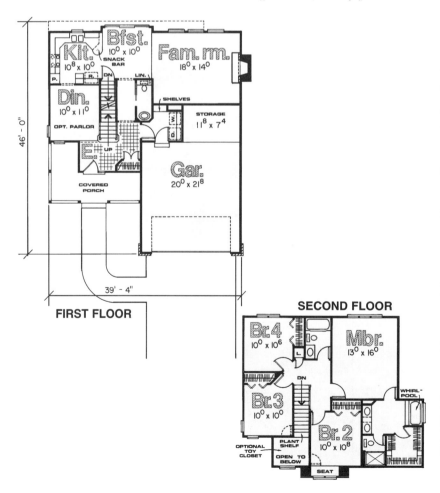

FIRST FLOOR

39' - 4"

46' - 0"

Bfst.
10⁰ x 10⁰

Kit.
10⁸ x 10⁰

SNACK BAR

Fam. rm.
18⁰ x 14⁰

P.

R.

DN

LIN.

SHELVES

Din.
10⁰ x 11⁰

OPT. PARLOR

STORAGE
11⁸ x 7⁴

W

D

UP

COVERED PORCH

Gar.
20⁰ x 21⁸

SECOND FLOOR

Br. 4
10⁰ x 10⁶

Mbr.
13⁰ x 16⁰

Br. 3
10⁰ x 10⁰

DN

WHIRL-POOL

Br. 2
10⁰ x 10⁸

OPTIONAL TOY CLOSET

PLANT SHELF

OPEN TO BELOW

SEAT

No. 94949

This plan features:

— Four bedrooms

— Two full and one half baths

■ The covered Porch leads into the tiled Entry with banister staircase

■ The formal Dining Room could also be a Parlor

■ The compact Kitchen has a counter/snackbar, Pantry and Breakfast Area with backyard access

■ The spacious Family Room has an inviting fireplace and triple windows

■ The corner Master Bedroom features a roomy walk-in closet and a plush Bath

First floor — 866 sq. ft.
Second floor — 905 sq. ft.
Basement — 866 sq. ft.
Garage — 541 sq. ft.

Design by Design Basics, Inc.

No. 99488

Handsome Detailing

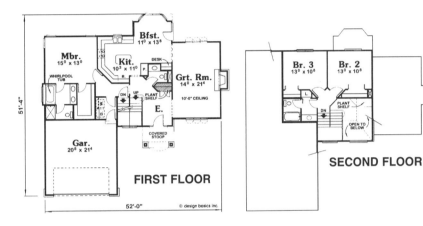

Total living area 1,772 sq. ft. ■ *Price Code B*

This plan features:

- Three bedrooms
- Two full and one half baths
- Unique windows highlight the front elevation of this design
- The expansive Great Room has a fireplace and triple windows on two walls
- The Kitchen has a work island and is open to the Breakfast Area
- The Master Bath has a walk-in closet and a private Bath and is near the Laundry Area
- The spacious secondary Bedrooms share a full Bath on the second floor

First floor — 1,314 sq. ft.
Second floor — 458 sq. ft.
Garage — 454 sq. ft.

FIRST FLOOR

SECOND FLOOR

Design by Studer Residential Design, Inc.

No. 92630

Charming Brick Ranch

Total living area 1,782 sq. ft. ■ *Price Code B*

This plan features:

- Three bedrooms
- Two full baths
- The Foyer, Great Room and Dining Room open to each other and have vaulted ceilings
- The efficient Kitchen has Laundry and Pantry easily serves Dining Room, Breakfast Area and Screened Porch
- The luxurious Master Bedroom features a tray ceiling and French doors to private bath with a double vanity, walk-in closet and whirlpool tub
- The two additional Bedrooms, one easily converted to a Study, share a full Bath
- No materials list is available for this plan

Main floor — 1,782 sq. ft.
Garage — 407 sq. ft.
Basement — 1,735 sq. ft.

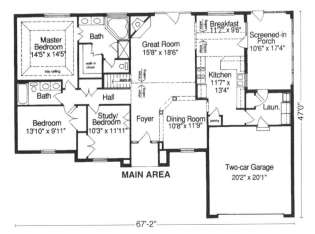

MAIN AREA

101

Second Floor Balcony

Design by The Garlinghouse Company

■ *Total living area 1,785 sq. ft.* ■ *Price Code B* ■

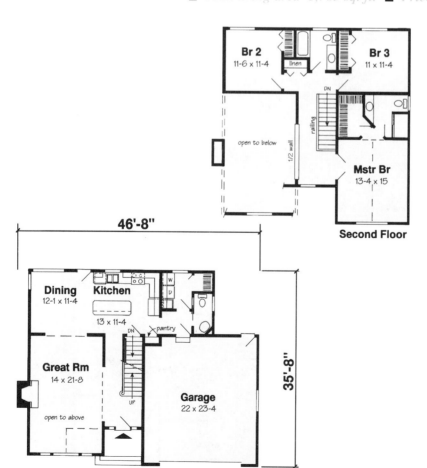

Second Floor

First Floor

No. 24610

■ **This plan features:**

— Three bedrooms

— Two full and one half baths

■ The Great Room has a focal point fireplace and a two-story ceiling

■ The efficient Kitchen has a work island, double sink, a built-in Pantry and ample storage and counter space

■ The convenient first floor Laundry Room is near the kitchen and Garage Entry

■ The Master Suite has a private Bath and a walk-in closet

■ The two additional Bedrooms share a full Bath

First floor — 891 sq. ft.
Second floor — 894 sq. ft.
Garage — 534 sq. ft.
Basement — 891 sq. ft.

Design by Nelson Design Group

No. 82038

This plan features:

- Three bedrooms
- Two full baths
- Eight-inch boxed columns accent the Dining Room
- A boxed ceiling and a fireplace decorate the Great Room
- The Kitchen and Breakfast Room are open to each other and a angled counter extends work space in the Kitchen
- The Master Suite is privately located and has a luxurious Bath
- The side grilling Porch extends living space outdoors
- An optional basement, slab or crawl space foundation – please specify when ordering
- No materials list is available for this plan

Main floor – 1,787 sq. ft.
Garage – 417 sq. ft.

Surprisingly Spacious

Total living area 1,787 sq. ft.   Price Code B

MAIN FLOOR

Design by James Fahy, P.E., P.C.

No. 94105

This plan features:

- Three bedrooms
- Two full and one half baths
- The two-story Foyer has a dramatic landing
- The spacious combined Living/Dining Room has a hearth fireplace and decorative windows
- The large Kitchen has a built-in Pantry and informal Dining Area with a sliding glass door to the rear yard
- The first floor Master Bedroom features a walk-in closet, Dressing Area and full Bath
- The two additional Bedrooms on the second floor share a full Bath
- No materials list is available for this plan

First floor – 1,281 sq. ft.
Second floor – 511 sq. ft.
Garage – 467 sq. ft.

Classic Style and Comfort

Total living area 1,792 sq. ft.   Price Code B

WIDTH 58'-0"
DEPTH 44'-0"   **FIRST FLOOR**

SECOND FLOOR

Style and Practicality

© 1998 Donald A. Gardner, Inc.

B. NATHAN

■ *Total living area 1,795 sq. ft.* ■ *Price Code D* ■

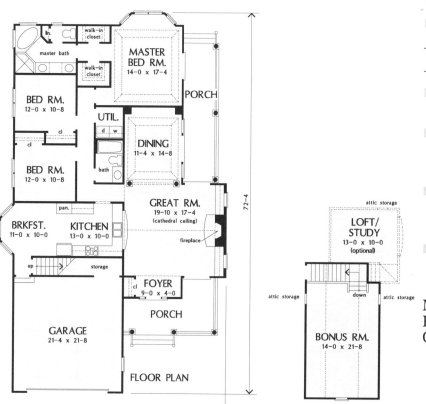

FLOOR PLAN

© 1998 Donald A Gardner, Inc.

No. 98020

■ **This plan features:**

— Three bedrooms

— Two full baths

■ This design easily fits on a narrow lot and has front and side Porches

■ The efficient Kitchen has a Pantry, Breakfast Area and is near the Garage Entry

■ The Great Room has a fireplace and is open to the formal Dinning Room

■ The Master Suite features a tray ceiling, two walk-in closets and a plush Bath

Main floor — 1,795 sq. ft.
Bonus — 368 sq. ft.
Garage — 520 sq. ft.

No. 82072

This plan features:

- Three bedrooms

- Two full baths

■ The Great Room is highlighted by a fireplace flanked by windows

■ The Kitchen includes a center work island and easy access to the formal Dining Room and the Breakfast Room

■ In the hall outside of the Master Suite, there is a built-in computer center

■ A pan ceiling adds elegance to the Master Bedroom

■ An optional basement, slab or crawl space foundation — please specify when ordering

■ No materials list is available for this plan

Main floor —1,800 sq. ft.
Garage/storage — 462 sq. ft.
Porches — 198 sq. ft.

Total living area 1,800 sq. ft. ■ Price Code B

MAIN FLOOR

Wonderful One Level Living

Design by Ahmann Design, Inc.

No. 93193

This plan features:

- Three bedrooms

- Two full and one half baths

■ The charming front Porch opens to the tiled Entry and arched entrance to Dining Room

■ The Great Room enhanced by a cathedral ceiling and a cozy fireplace set in a wall of windows

■ The large and convenient Kitchen has a work island/snackbar, Eating Nook with sliding glass doors to backyard, and is near the Laundry/Garage entry

■ The Master Bedroom features a walk-in closet and plush Bath with a double vanity and spa tub

■ The two additional Bedroom's with ample closets and double windows, share a full Bath

■ No materials list is available for this plan

Main floor — 1,802 sq. ft.
Basement — 1,802 sq. ft.

Total living area 1,802 sq. ft. ■ Price Code C

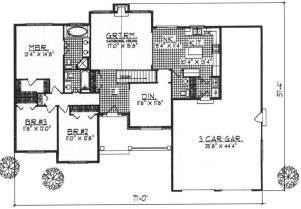

MAIN FLOOR PLAN

Columns & Arched Windows

Design by Design Basics, Inc.

© design basics inc.

■ *Total living area 1,806 sq. ft.* ■ *Price Code C* ■

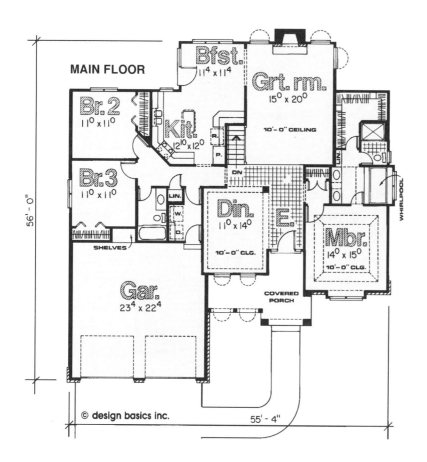

MAIN FLOOR

Bfst.
11⁴ x 11⁴

Grt. rm.
15⁰ x 20⁰
10'-0" CEILING

Br. 2
11⁰ x 11⁰

Kit.
12¹⁰ x 12⁰

Br. 3
11⁰ x 11⁰

56' - 0"

LIN.

W.

SHELVES

Din.
11⁰ x 14⁰
10'-0" CLG.

E.

Mbr.
14⁰ x 15⁰
10'-0" CLG.

WHIRLPOOL

Gar.
23⁴ x 22⁴

COVERED PORCH

© design basics inc.

55' - 4"

No. 99487 BL ✕

■ This plan features:

— Three bedrooms

— Two full baths

■ The Great Room and formal Dining Room are open to the tiled entry

■ A brick fireplace and arched windows highlight the Great Room

■ The Kitchen has a work island angled range and a built-in Pantry

■ The Master Suite has a sloped ceiling, private Bath and large walk-in closet

■ An optional basement or slab foundation — please specify when ordering

Main floor — 1,806 sq. ft.
Garage — 548 sq. ft.

Design by Design Basics, Inc.

No. 94928

This plan features:

– Three bedrooms

– Two full and one half baths

■ Arches accent the front porch

■ The tiled Foyer and Great Room have ten-foot ceilings

■ The sunny Breakfast Nook has a convenient planning desk

■ The Great Room and the Kitchen share a two-way fireplace

■ The large Master Suite includes a walk-in closet and a whirlpool Bath

■ The Kitchen has a snack bar and a corner sink

■ The secondary Bedrooms share a full Bath

Main floor — 1,808 sq. ft.
Basement — 1,808 sq. ft.
Garage — 551 sq. ft.

Lovely Arches

■ Total living area 1,808 sq. ft. ■ Price Code C ■

MAIN FLOOR

Design by Nelson Design Group

No. 82073

This plan features:

– Three bedrooms

– Two full and one half baths

■ A vaulted ceiling adds style to the Foyer of this home

■ The Great Room has a cozy fireplace for cooler evenings

■ The efficient Kitchen includes a peninsula counter

■ The Breakfast Area has a bright and sunny bay window

■ There is Bonus Area on the second floor for future expansion

■ An optional basement, slab or crawl space foundation — please specify when ordering

■ No materials list is available for this plan

First floor — 921 sq. ft.
Second floor — 920 sq. ft.
Garage/storage — 529 sq. ft.
Bonus — 233 sq. ft.

Planning Ahead

■ Total living area 1,841 sq. ft. ■ Price Code C ■

FIRST FLOOR

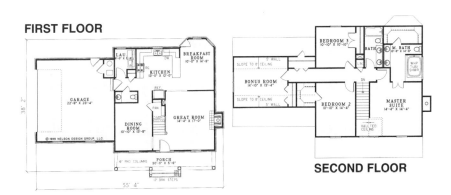

SECOND FLOOR

Appealing Front Porch

Design by Design Basics, Inc.

■ *Total living area 1,842 sq. ft.* ■ *Price Code C* ■

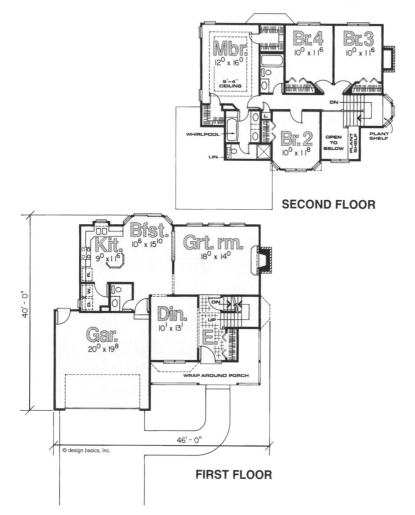

SECOND FLOOR

FIRST FLOOR

No. 94935

■ **This plan features:**

— Four bedrooms

— Two full and one half baths

■ An appealing wrap around Porch graces this home

■ The light and airy two-story Entry has a side-light, plant shelf and a closet

■ A wall of windows and fireplace are featured in the Great Room

■ The Kitchen has easy access to the Breakfast Area, Dining Room and the Garage

■ The lovely Master Bedroom Suite features a tiered ceiling, two walk-in closets and a deluxe Bath

First floor — 919 sq. ft.
Second floor — 923 sq. ft.
Basement — 919 sq. ft.
Garage — 414 sq. ft.

Design by Design Basics, Inc.

Friendly Front Porch

No. 94901 BL ✕

This plan features:

– Three bedrooms

– Two full and one half baths

– The formal Living Room has transom windows

– The Dining Room is open to the Living Room for easy entertaining

– The efficient, U-shaped Kitchen, and Pantry, snack bar counter, adjoins the Breakfast Area with access to backyard

– The sunken Family Room has a handsome fireplace and a wall of windows

– The Master Bedroom features a boxed ceiling, walk-in closet and a plush Bath with double vanity and whirlpool tub

– The two additional Bedrooms share a full Bath

First floor — 1,042 sq. ft.
Second floor — 803 sq. ft.
Basement — 1,042 sq. ft.
Garage — 486 sq. ft.

■ Total living area 1,845 sq. ft. ■ Price Code C ■

FIRST FLOOR

SECOND FLOOR

Design by Design Basics, Inc.

Porch Adds Style

No. 99491 BL ✕

This plan features:

– Four bedrooms

– Two full and one half baths

■ The tiled two-story Entry includes a large coat closet

■ Triple windows and a fireplace highlight the Great Room

■ The Kitchen has a boxed window over the sink and is open to the Breakfast Area

■ The Laundry Room is conveniently located off the Kitchen

■ The volume ceiling and arched window in the front Bedroom add a touch of elegance

■ The large Master Suite has dual walk-in closets, corner windows and a private Bath with a double vanity and whirlpool tub

■ An optional basement or slab foundation — please specify when ordering

First floor — 919 sq. ft.
Second floor — 927 sq. ft.
Garage — 414 sq. ft.

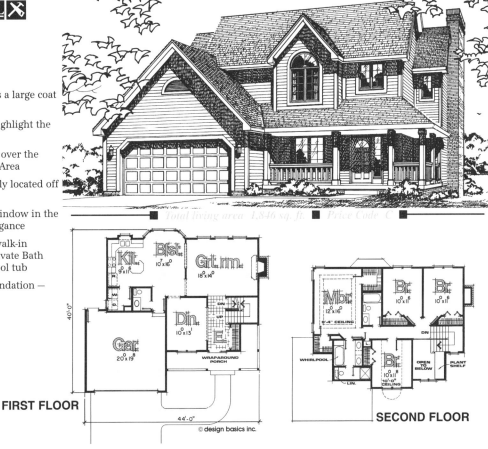

■ Total living area 1,846 sq. ft. ■ Price Code C ■

FIRST FLOOR

SECOND FLOOR

109

Terrific Kid's Nook

Design by Nelson Design Group

■ *Total living area 1,848 sq. ft.* ■ *Price Code C* ■

MAIN FLOOR

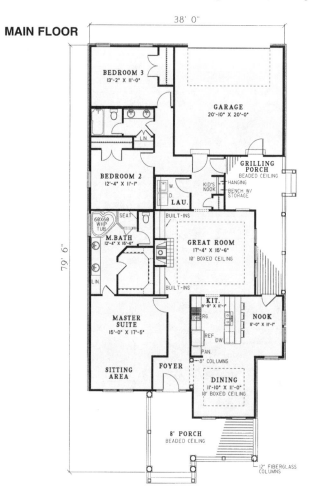

No. 82021

■ This plan features:

— Three bedrooms

— Two full baths

■ The combination Dining Room, Kitchen and Nook provides a great area for family interaction

■ The Great Room includes a fireplace and built-in shelves

■ A terrific kid's Nook has storage space for sports gear, hats and gloves or outdoor toys

■ The Master Suite includes a Sitting Area, Bedroom, and a private Bath with a walk-in closet

■ An optional basement, slab or crawl space foundation — please specify when ordering

■ No materials list is available for this plan

Main floor — 1,848 sq. ft.
Garage — 429 sq. ft.
Porches — 430 sq. ft.

Attractive Styling

No. 93427 BL

This plan features:

– Three bedrooms

– Two full baths

■ Windows, sidelights and transoms combine to create a dramatic entrance

■ The formal Dining Room, off the Foyer, enjoys a view of the front yard and access to the Family Room

■ A grand fireplace, with windows to either side, serves as a focal point of the Family Room

■ The Breakfast Room/Kitchen is open to the Family Room

■ The secluded Master Suite has a walk-in closet, a recessed ceiling and a five-piece Bath

■ The two additional Bedrooms share a full Bath

■ No materials list is available for this plan

Main floor — 1,849 sq. ft.

Garage — 555 sq. ft.

Total living area 1,849 sq. ft. ■ Price Code B

Appealing Roofline

No. 99434 BL

This plan features:

– Three bedrooms

– Two full baths

■ The covered Porch provides space and shelter from the elements

■ The tiled Entry is illuminated by the front doors sidelights

■ A hutch space and a large front window accent the Dining Room

■ The Great Room has a fireplace set between a pair of windows with transoms above them

■ The U-shaped Kitchen has a center island and is open to the Breakfast Area

■ The Master Bedroom has a large walk-in closet and a Bath with a skylight

■ The two secondary Bedrooms each have a distinctive front wall window

Main floor — 1,850 sq. ft.

Garage — 487 sq. ft.

Total living area 1,850 sq. ft. ■ Price Code B

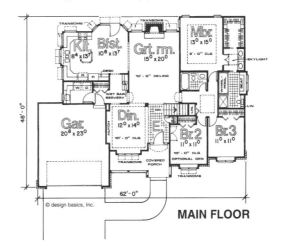

© design basics, inc.

MAIN FLOOR

Totally Modern

Design by Nelson Design Group

Total living area 1,851 sq. ft. ■ Price Code C

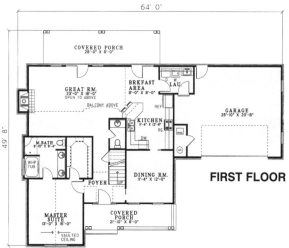

FIRST FLOOR

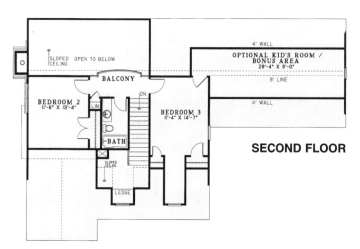

SECOND FLOOR

No. 82074

■ This plan features:

— Three bedrooms

— Two full and one half baths

■ The covered front and rear Porches add outdoor living space to this home

■ The two-story Great Room has a balcony above, a cozy fireplace and is open to the Breakfast Area

■ The Master Suite is topped with a vaulted ceiling and includes a walk-in closet and a whirlpool Bath

■ An optional basement, slab or crawl space foundation — please specify when ordering

■ No materials list is available for this plan

First floor – 1,311 sq. ft.
Second floor – 540 sq. ft.
Bonus – 276 sq. ft.
Garage – 534 sq. ft.

Design by Nelson Design Group

No. 82075

Four Bedrooms

This plan features:

- Four bedrooms

- Two full baths

- The Kitchen is open to the Breakfast Room and the formal Dining Room are laid out for easy interaction between the rooms

- A terrific fireplace highlights the Great Room with French doors to either side accessing the rear Porch

- The privately located Master Suite has a luxurious Bath and two walk-in closets

- The secondary Bedrooms have ample closet space

- The side entry Garage opens to the laundry/Mud Room

- An optional basement, slab or crawl space foundation — please specify when ordering

- No materials list is available for this plan

Main floor – 1,854 sq. ft.
Garage/Storage – 498 sq. ft.
Porches – 197 sq. ft.

MAIN FLOOR

Design by Greg Marquis & Associates

No. 93410

Demonstrative Detail

This plan features:

- Three bedrooms

- Two full and one half baths

- Keystone arched windows, stone and stucco combine with shutters and a flower boxes to create an eye-catching elevation

- The Foyer has access to the Dining Room, Family Room or the Master Suite

- The Family Room has a sloped ceiling and is accented by a fireplace with windows to either side

- The Kitchen/Breakfast Area has easy access to the rear Porch

- The two roomy Bedrooms on the second floor share the full Bath in the hall

- An optional Bonus Area over the Garage offers possibilities for future expansion

First floor – 1,317 sq. ft.
Second floor – 537 sq. ft.
Bonus – 312 sq. ft.
Basement – 1,317 sq. ft.
Garage – 504 sq. ft.

Family Room with Skylights

Design by Greg Marquis & Associates

■ Total living area 1,856 sq. ft. ■ Price Code B ■

No. 93420 BL

■ This plan features:

- – Three bedrooms
- – Two full and one half baths
- ■ In the center of this home is the skylit Family room
- ■ The Kitchen has a convenient work triangle
- ■ A wall of windows brightens the Breakfast Nook
- ■ The first floor Master Bedroom has a private Bath and large walk-in closet
- ■ Balcony overlooks the Family Room below
- ■ The two secondary Bedrooms share a full Bath on the second floor
- ■ No materials list is available for this plan

First floor — 1,299 sq. ft.
Second floor — 557 sq. ft.
Bonus — 272 sq. ft.
Basement — 1,299 sq. ft.
Garage — 494 sq. ft.

Design by Design Basics, Inc.

Fieldstone Facade

No. 94911 BL ✗ 🗺 ℛ

This plan features:

- Three bedrooms
- Two full baths
- Inviting covered Porch shelters entrance
- The expansive Great Room is enhanced by a cozy fireplace and three transom windows
- The Breakfast Area adjoins the Great Room to create an open spacious area
- The efficient Kitchen has a counter snack bar is near the Laundry and Garage entry
- The first floor Master Bedroom Suite has an arched window, sloped ceiling and a double vanity Bath
- Two additional Bedrooms share a Bonus Area and a full Bath on the second floor

First floor — 1,405 sq. ft.
Second floor — 453 sq. ft.
Bonus — 300 sq. ft.
Basement — 1,405 sq. ft.
Garage — 490 sq. ft.

Total living area 1,858 sq. ft. ■ Price Code C

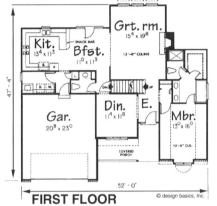

FIRST FLOOR
© design basics, inc.

SECOND FLOOR

Design by Donald A. Gardner Architects, Inc.

Classic Cottage

No. 98014 BL ✗ ℛ

This plan features:

- Three Bedrooms
- Two full and one half baths
- This economical design is perfect for a narrow lot
- Twin dormers and a gabled Garage provide substantial curb appeal
- The dramatic Great Room is enhanced by two clerestory dormers and a balcony
- Crowned in an elegant tray ceiling, the first floor Master Suite has a private Bath and a walk-in closet

First floor — 1,336 sq. ft.
Second floor — 523 sq. ft.
Bonus — 225 sq. ft.

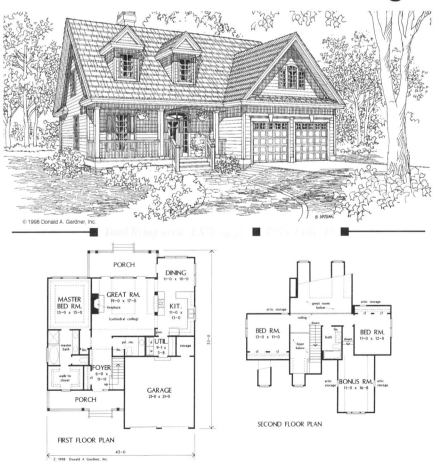

© 1998 Donald A. Gardner, Inc.

Total living area 1,859 sq. ft. ■ Price Code B

FIRST FLOOR PLAN

SECOND FLOOR PLAN

Upstairs Options

Total living area 1,860 sq. ft. ■ Price Code C

FIRST FLOOR

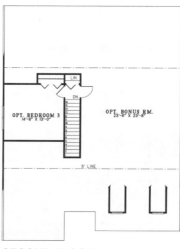

SECOND FLOOR

No. 61014 BL

■ This plan features:

— Two bedrooms

— Two full baths

■ The large Dining Room is open to the Foyer and the Kitchen

■ The U-shaped Kitchen has a bar for quick meals

■ Columns mark the entrance to the Great Room

■ The Master Bedroom has a large walk-in closet

■ The second floor has expansion space for a third bedroom and Bonus Room

■ An optional basement, slab, or crawl space foundation — please specify when ordering

■ No materials list is available for this plan

Main floor — 1,860 sq. ft.
Bonus — 247 sq. ft.
Garage — 377 sq. ft.

Design by Studer Residential Design, Inc.

Curb Appeal

No. 97743

■ **This plan features:**

- Three bedrooms
- Two full baths
- Three windows that brighten the Dining Room
- The efficient Kitchen is opened to the Breakfast Room
- The Great Room has a unique ceiling treatment
- The Master Bedroom features a large walk-in closet
- The Laundry Room has plenty of counter space
- No materials list is available for this plan

Main floor – 1,860 sq. ft.
Basement – 1,860 sq. ft.
Garage – 444 sq. ft.

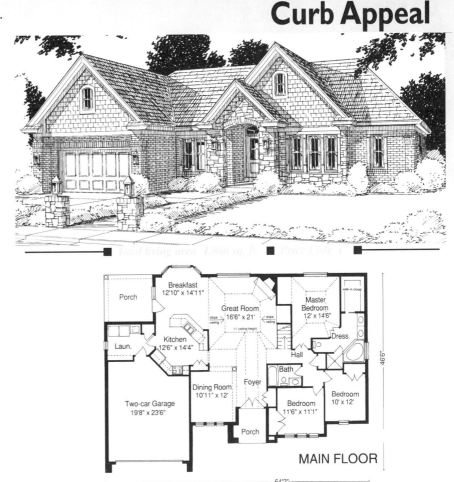

MAIN FLOOR

Design by Donald A. Gardner Architects, Inc.

Dramatic Windows and Gables

No. 99851

■ **This plan features:**

- Three bedrooms
- Two full and one half baths
- The barrel vaulted entrance Foyer has a coat closet
- Interior columns add elegance and visually divide the Foyer from the Dining Room and the Great Room from the Kitchen
- The Great Room has a cathedral ceiling and a bank of windows
- A boxed bay window adds space to the formal Dining Room
- An angled center island and breakfast counter separate the Kitchen from the breakfast Area
- The first floor Master Suite has dual closets plus a garden tub with skylight above
- The two Bedrooms upstairs share a Bath

First floor – 1,416 sq. ft.
Second floor – 445 sq. ft.
Bonus – 284 sq. ft.
Garage – 485 sq. ft.

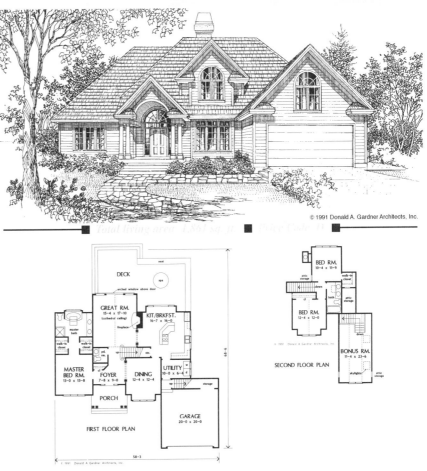

© 1991 Donald A. Gardner Architects, Inc.

Attractive Details

Total living area 1,867 sq. ft. ■ *Price Code B* ■

MAIN FLOOR

© 1998 NELSON DESIGN GROUP, LLC.

No. 82036 [BL]

■ **This plan features:**

— Four bedrooms

— Two full baths

■ Decorative columns divide the Dining Room from the Foyer and the Great room

■ The Great Room includes a fireplace a built-in cabinet and a boxed ceiling

■ The Breakfast Area has direct access to the Master Suite and three-sided bay window

■ The Master Bedroom has a pan ceiling and large private Bath

■ An optional basement, slab or crawl space foundation — please specify when ordering

■ No materials list is available for this plan

Main floor – 1,817 sq. ft.
Garage/storage – 377 sq. ft.

Design by Ahmann Design, Inc.

Charming Brick Home

No. 93107 BL Я R

This plan features:

- Three bedrooms

- Two full baths

- The Foyer opens to a spacious Living Room with a fireplace and an airy Dining Room with access to the Patio

- The Kitchen, with a work island and ample storage space, is open to the Dining Room

- The Master Bedroom with a walk-in closet, access to the Patio and a plush Bath with a window tub, a step-in shower and a double vanity

- The two additional Bedrooms, with decorative windows, share a full Bath

- No materials list is available for this plan

Main floor — 1,868 sq. ft.
Basement — 1,868 sq. ft.
Garage — 782 sq. ft.

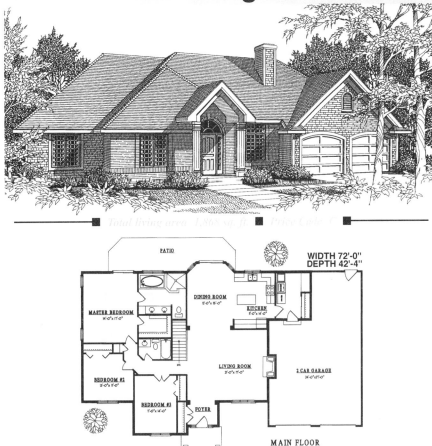

WIDTH 72'-0"
DEPTH 42'-4"

MAIN FLOOR

Appealing Gables

Design by James Fahy, P.E., P.C.

No. 94139 BL

This plan features:

– four bedrooms

– Two full and one half baths

- The two-story Foyer is highlighted by sidelights and a banister staircase

- The formal Living Room accented by a lovely bay window

- The expansive Family Room has a cozy fireplace framed by windows

- The efficient Kitchen with work island, Pantry and Dining Area with backyard access, and is near the Dining Room and Laundry/Garage entry

- The Master Bedroom offers a walk-in closet and private Bath

- The additional Bedrooms share a full Bath

- No materials list is available for this plan

First floor — 1,009 sq. ft.
Second floor — 862 sq. ft.
Basement — 994 sq. ft.
Garage — 506 sq. ft.

FIRST FLOOR

SECOND FLOOR

European Styling

Design by Rick Garner

■ Total living area 1,873 sq. ft. ■ Price Code D ■

No. 92552

■ **This plan features:**

— Four bedrooms

— Two full baths

■ An Arch top window, quoins shutters and a columned covered front Porch combine for an impressive facade

■ The formal Foyer has access to the Dining Room and the spacious Den

■ The Kitchen is open to the informal Eating Area and is separated from the Den by an angled counter eating bar

■ The Master Suite is privately located

■ An optional slab or crawl space foundation — please specify when ordering

Main floor — 1,873 sq. ft.
Bonus — 145 sq. ft.
Garage — 613 sq. ft.

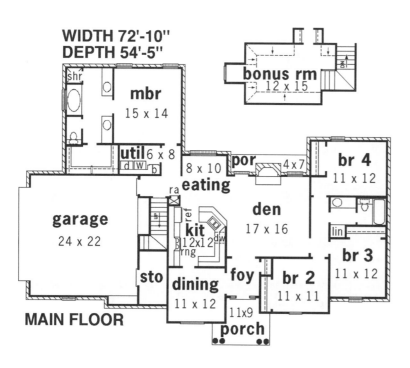

WIDTH 72'-10"
DEPTH 54'-5"

bonus rm
12 x 15

mbr
15 x 14

shr

util 6 x 8

eating
8 x 10

por
4 x 7

br 4
11 x 12

garage
24 x 22

kit
12x12

den
17 x 16

lin

br 3
11 x 12

sto

dining
11 x 12

foy
11x9

br 2
11 x 11

MAIN FLOOR

porch

Design by Frank Betz Associates, Inc.

Family-Sized Accommodations

No. 98454

This plan features:

— Four bedrooms

— Two full and one half baths

■ The Foyer and the Family Room have vaulted ceilings

■ A fireplace in an alcove of windows is in Family Room

■ The angled Kitchen with a work island and a Pantry is open to the Breakfast Area

■ The Master Bedroom is has a tray ceiling, a lavish Bath and a walk-in closet

■ The three additional Bedrooms share a double vanity Bath and there is a optional Bonus Room

■ An optional basement or crawl space foundation — please specify when ordering

First floor — 1,320 sq. ft.
Second floor — 554 sq. ft.
Bonus — 155 sq. ft.
Basement — 1,320 sq. ft.
Garage — 406 sq. ft.

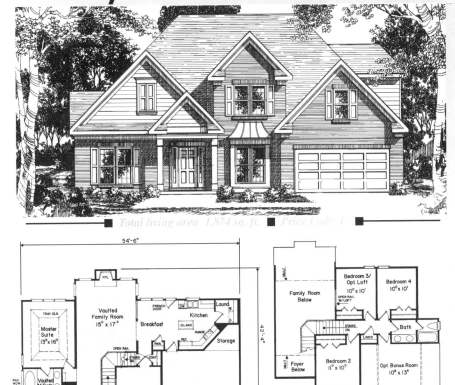

Total living area 1,874 sq. ft. ■ Price Code C

Design by Frank Betz Associates, Inc.

Spectacular Front Window

No. 97253

This plan features:

— Three bedrooms

— Two full baths

■ The spectacular front window highlights the formal Dining Room

■ The Living Room has a bay window

■ The Family Room has a vaulted ceiling and a fireplace with windows to either side

■ The Kitchen includes a walk-in Pantry, and a serving bar expanding storage space

■ The Master Suite features a tray ceiling in the bedroom and a vaulted ceiling in the Bath

■ The secondary Bedrooms are on the opposite side of the home from the Master Suite and share the full Bath in the hall

■ An optional basement, slab or crawl space foundation — please specify when ordering

■ No materials list is available for this plan

Main floor — 1,875 sq. ft.
Basement — 1,891 sq. ft.
Garage — 475 sq. ft.

Total living area 1,875 sq. ft. ■ Price Code C

MAIN FLOOR

Great Room With Columns

Design by Donald A. Gardner Architects, Inc.

© 1995 Donald A Gardner Architects, Inc.

■ *Total living area 1,879 sq. ft.* ■ *Price Code D* ■

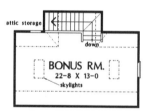

attic storage

down

BONUS RM.
22-8 X 13-0
skylights

No. 99807 BL X 🗺 R

■ **This plan features:**

— Three bedrooms

— Two full baths

■ The Great Room has a cathedral ceiling, a fireplace and is open to the breakfast Area

■ Tray ceilings and circle top picture windows accent the front Bedroom and the Dining Room

■ The secluded Master Suite, has a tray ceiling, and includes a Bath with skylight, a garden tub and spacious walk-in closet

■ The two additional Bedrooms share a full Bath

Main floor — 1,879 sq. ft.
Garage — 485 sq. ft.
Bonus — 360 sq. ft.

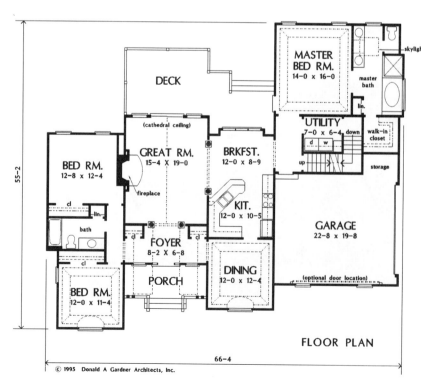

DECK

(cathedral ceiling)

GREAT RM.
15-4 x 19-0

fireplace

BED RM.
12-8 x 12-4

cl

lin.

bath

BRKFST.
12-0 x 8-9

KIT.
12-0 x 10-5

MASTER BED RM.
14-0 x 16-0

master bath

lin.

skylight

UTILITY
7-0 x 6-4

d w

down

up

walk-in closet

storage

GARAGE
22-8 x 19-8

FOYER
8-2 X 6-8

cl

cl

BED RM.
12-0 x 11-4

PORCH

DINING
12-0 x 12-4

(optional door location)

55-2

66-4

FLOOR PLAN

© 1995 Donald A Gardner Architects, Inc.

Design by Frank Betz Associates, Inc.

With All the Amenities

No. 98430

This plan features:

– Three bedrooms

– Two full and one half baths

■ The Foyer has a sixteen-foot high ceiling

■ Arched openings highlight the hallway into the Great Room which has a fireplace and a French door to the rear yard

■ The Dining Room, convenient to both the Great Room and the Kitchen, has a vaulted ceiling

■ The expansive Kitchen features a center work island, a built-in Pantry and a Breakfast Area with a tray ceiling

■ The Master Suite has a tray ceiling and includes a lavish private Bath and a huge walk-in closet

■ The secondary Bedrooms have private access to a full Bath

■ An optional basement, slab or crawl space foundation — please specify when ordering

Main floor — 1,884 sq. ft.
Basement — 1,908 sq. ft.
Garage — 495 sq. ft.

Total living area 1,884 sq. ft. ■ Price Code C

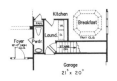

OPT. BASEMENT STAIRS LOCATION

Main floor

Design by Design Basics, Inc.

Easy Traffic Flow

No. 94909

This plan features:

– Four bedrooms

– Two full and one half baths

■ The formal Dining Room has a boxed window

■ A fireplace and a wall of windows accent the Family Room

■ The Breakfast Area with bay window is a part of the efficient Kitchen

■ The Kitchen has a Laundry Area

■ The Master Bedroom Suite features two walk-in closets and a double vanity Bath

■ The three additional Bedrooms share a full Bath

First floor — 925 sq. ft.
Second floor — 960 sq. ft.
Basement — 925 sq. ft.
Garage — 455 sq. ft.
Bonus — 258 sq. ft.

Total living area 1,885 sq. ft. ■ Price Code C

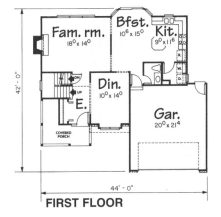

FIRST FLOOR

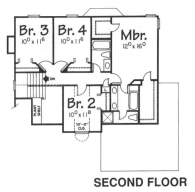

SECOND FLOOR

French Influenced Design

Design by Larry E. Belk

Total living area 1,890 sq. ft. ■ Price Code C

MAIN FLOOR

WIDTH 65'-10"
DEPTH 53'-5"

No. 96601 BL

This plan features:

— Three bedrooms

— Two full baths

■ The formal Dining Room has a ten-foot coffered, decorative ceiling

■ The oversized Living Room includes built-in bookcases on either side of the fireplace

■ An angled bar separates the Kitchen and Breakfast Room and opens the Kitchen to the Living Room beyond

■ The Master Bedroom includes a luxurious Master Bath with a huge walk-in closet, dual vanities, and separate whirlpool tub and shower

■ No materials list is available for this plan

Main floor — 1,890 sq. ft.
Garage — 565 sq. ft.

Design by Nelson Design Group

In Perfect Balance

No. 82041

This plan features:

- Three bedrooms

- Two full baths

- The Kitchen opens to the Great Room and Breakfast Room to create spacious living area

- The Kitchen includes wrap around counters and a snack bar

- The spacious Great Room has a boxed ceiling and access to the Grilling Porch

- The Master Suite has direct access to the Grilling Porch and a lavish Master Bath

- An optional basement, slab or crawl space foundation – please specify when ordering

- No materials list is available for this plan

Main floor —1,892 sq. ft.
Garage — 374 sq. ft.
Porch — 198 sq. ft.

Total living area 1,892 sq. ft. ■ Price Code C

MAIN FLOOR

Design by Studer Residential Design, Inc.

Distinctive Detail and Design

No. 92644

This plan features:

- Three bedrooms

- Two full and one half baths

- The Foyer is highlighted by decorative windows

- The Great Room is accented by a hearth fireplace, French doors with an arched window above and a high ceiling

- The formal Dining Room is enhanced by a furniture alcove and decorative window

- The efficient, L-shaped Kitchen has a work island, walk-in Pantry, bright Breakfast Area, an adjoins the Laundry, half Bath and Garage entry

- The Master Bedroom features a walk-in closet, and plush Bath with two vanities and whirlpool tub

- The two additional Bedrooms share a full Bath and computer desk

- The second floor features a computer desk and window seat

First floor — 1,036 sq. ft.
Second floor — 861 sq. ft.

Total living area 1,897 sq. ft. ■ Price Code C

Beautiful Arched Window

Design by Design Basics, Inc.

■ *Total living area 1,911 sq. ft.* ■ *Price Code C* ■

No. 94966

■ This plan features:

— Three bedrooms

— Two full baths

■ The Entry and the Great Room have ten-foot ceilings

■ A see-through fireplace is between the Great Room and the Hearth Room

■ A built-in entertainment center and a bay window highlight the Hearth Room

■ The Breakfast Room and Hearth Room are open to the Kitchen

■ The privately located Master Suite includes a decorative ceiling, private Bath and a large walk-in closet

Main floor — 1,911 sq. ft.
Garage — 481 sq. ft.

MAIN FLOOR

© design basics, inc.

Design by Donald A. Gardner Architects, Inc.

Pretty as a Picture

No. 98008

BL X R

This plan features:

- Three bedrooms

- Two full baths

- The wraparound front Porch is beautiful and functional

- The Great Room has a cathedral ceiling and a fireplace

- The Dining Room has windows that overlook the front Porch, plus and a tray ceiling

- The convenient Kitchen has a good work triangle

- The Master Bedroom is privately located and features a galley Bath and a walk-in closet

- The two-car Garage is conveniently located in the rear of the home

- There is a Bonus Room over the Garage to be finished to suit your needs

Main floor — 1,911 sq. ft.
Bonus — 406 sq. ft.
Garage — 551 sq. ft.

MAIN FLOOR

Design by Donald A. Gardner Architects, Inc.

Great as a Mountain Retreat

No. 99815

BL X R

This plan features:

- Three bedrooms

- Two full baths

- Board and batten siding, stone, and stucco combine to give this popular plan a casual appearance

- The open, user-friendly Kitchen has an island counter, and huge pantry and breakfast Area

- The Dining Area is separated from the foyer and Great Room by decorative columns

- The Master Suite has a deep tray ceiling, a large walk-in closet, an extravagant private Bath and access to the back Porch

Main floor — 1,912 sq. ft.
Garage — 580 sq. ft.
Bonus — 398 sq. ft.

© 1996 Donald A Gardner Architects, Inc.

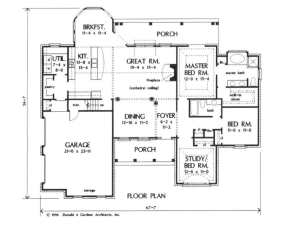

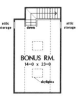

FLOOR PLAN

Beautiful Stucco & Stone

Design by Frank Betz Associates, Inc.

■ *Total living area 1,913 sq. ft.* ■ *Price Code C* ■

FIRST FLOOR PLAN

© Frank Betz Associates, Inc.

SECOND FLOOR PLAN

No. 98445

■ This plan features:

— Three bedrooms

— Two full and one half baths

■ This home is accented by keystone arches and a turret styled roof

■ The two-story Foyer includes a half Bath

■ The vaulted Family Room is highlighted by a fireplace and a French door to the rear yard

■ An optional basement, slab or crawl space foundation — please specify when ordering

■ No materials list is available for this plan

First floor — 1,398 sq. ft.
Second floor — 515 sq. ft.
Bonus — 282 sq. ft.
Basement — 1,398 sq. ft.
Garage — 421 sq. ft.

Plenty of Storage

■ *Total living area 1,925 sq. ft.* ■ *Price code* ■

No. 82076 BL

This plan features:

- Four bedrooms

- Two full baths

- All of the Bedrooms have walk-in closets

- The Great Room has a fireplace set between French doors opening to the rear Porch

- The Kitchen opens to the Breakfast Room

- Columns delineate the Dining Room

- There is a Storage Room in the rear of the Garage

- An optional basement or slab foundation — please specify when ordering

- No materials list is available for this plan

Main floor — 1,926 sq. ft.
Garage — 417 sq. ft.

MAIN FLOOR

Traditional Gem

Design by The Garlinghouse Company

■ *Total living area 1,930 sq. ft.* ■ *Price Code C* ■

FIRST FLOOR

Optional Deck

Kit 11 x 12

Brkfst 10 x 11-6

Family Rm 16 x 13

pan

W D

DN

Dining Rm 11 x 14

slope slope

Garage 20-8 x 20

UP

Living Rm 11 x 12

Entry

38'-0"

44'-10"

Slab/Crawlspace Option

Br 2 10 x 12-8

Br 3 10 x 11

DN

MBr 1 14-4 x 15

slope

open to below

SECOND FLOOR

No. 34851 BL

■ This plan features:

— Three bedrooms

— Two full and one half baths

■ The Living/Dining Room combination has a sloped ceiling and decorative windows

■ The Family Room has a cozy fireplace and direct access to the Deck

■ The efficient Kitchen has a Pantry, a work island and a Laundry closet, and is adjacent to the Breakfast Area and the formal Dining Room

■ The Master Suite, with a sloped ceiling, has a private Master Bath and a walk-in closet

■ The two additional Bedrooms have direct access to a full Bath

First floor — 1,056 sq. ft.
Second floor — 874 sq. ft.
Basement — 1,023 sq. ft.
Garage — 430 sq. ft.

Front Porch of Yesteryear

■ *Total living area 1,930 sq. ft.* ■ *Price Code C* ■

No. 93290

■ **This plan features:**

- Three bedrooms

- Two full and one half baths

■ The open Foyer is flanked by the formal Living and Dining Rooms

■ The Breakfast Nook has a bay window overlooking the rear yard and spacious Deck

■ The luxurious Master Bedroom has a decorative tray ceiling, an oversized walk-in closet and a plush Bath

■ The secondary Bedrooms include generous closet space and share a full Bath

First floor — 981 sq. ft.
Second floor — 899 sq. ft.
Staircase — 50 sq. ft.
Basement — 425 sq. ft.
Garage — 588 sq. ft.

SECOND FLOOR

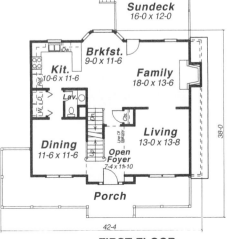

FIRST FLOOR

Windows for Natural Lighting

Design by Design Basics, Inc.

■ *Total living area 1,931 sq. ft.* ■ *Price Code C* ■

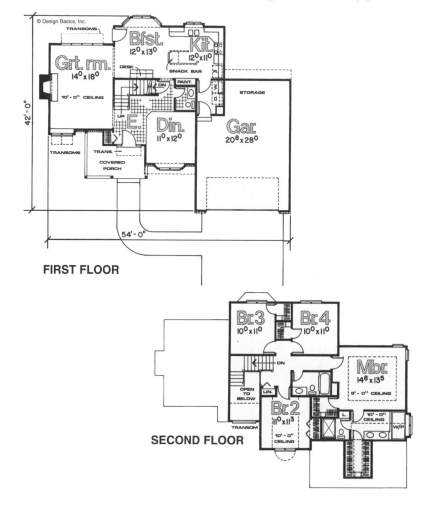

FIRST FLOOR

SECOND FLOOR

No. 94902

■ **This plan features:**

— Four bedrooms

— Two full and one half baths

■ A covered front Porch, sidelights and a transom window highlight the Entry to this home

■ The Great Room features a hearth fireplace, transom windows and a ten-foot ceiling

■ The Kitchen has a convenient center island and is open to the Breakfast Room

■ The Master Bedroom Suite features a decorative ceiling, two walk-in closets and a double vanity Bath with a whirlpool tub

■ The secondary Bedrooms share a full Bath

First floor — 944 sq. ft.
Second floor — 987 sq. ft.
Basement — 944 sq. ft.
Garage — 557 sq. ft.

Double Arches Add Elegance

■ *Total living area 1,932 sq. ft.* ■ *Price Code C* ■

No. 93098

This plan features:

- Three bedrooms

- Two full baths

- Double arches and two palladian windows add distinction to this elegant design

- The Foyer opens to the formal Dining Room and Living Room

- Ten-foot ceilings in all major living areas give the home an expansive feeling

- The Kitchen features an angled eating bar and is open to both the Breakfast Room and Living Room

- The Master Suite includes a Master Bath and a huge walk-in closet

- No materials list is available for this plan

Main floor — 1,932 sq. ft.
Garage — 552 sq. ft.

MAIN FLOOR

Spectacular Sophistication

Design by Design Basics, Inc.

■ *Total living area 1,933 sq. ft.* ■ *Price Code C* ■

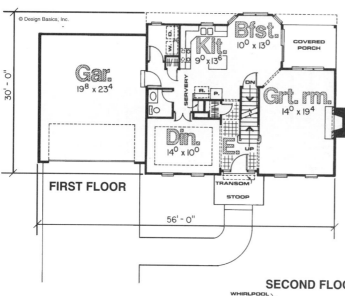

FIRST FLOOR

56' - 0"

SECOND FLOOR

No. 94944

■ **This plan features:**

— Four bedrooms

— Two full and one half baths

■ The tiled Foyer has a coat closet and leads to the formal Dining Room and Great Room

■ An inviting fireplace and windows on two walls highlight the Great Room

■ The Kitchen has a work island and is open to the Breakfast Area

■ The Master Bedroom features a nine-foot boxed ceiling, a walk-in closet and whirlpool bath

■ The three additional Bedrooms share a full Bath with a double vanity

First floor — 941 sq. ft.
Second floor — 992 sq. ft.
Basement — 941 sq. ft.
Garage — 480 sq. ft.

Design by Frank Betz Associates, Inc.

Outstanding Four Bedroom

■ *Total living area 1,945 sq. ft.* ■ *Price Code C* ■

No. 98435

■ This plan features:

— Four bedrooms

— Two full baths

■ The Foyer opens to the Great Room and the formal Dining Room

■ The efficient Kitchen has a Pantry, a serving bar, and is open to the Breakfast Room

■ A fireplace with windows on each side highlights the expansive Great Room

■ The Master Bedroom features a tray ceiling and a plush Bath

■ The three secondary Bedrooms share a full Bath

■ An optional basement or crawl space foundation — please specify when ordering

Main floor — 1,945 sq. ft.

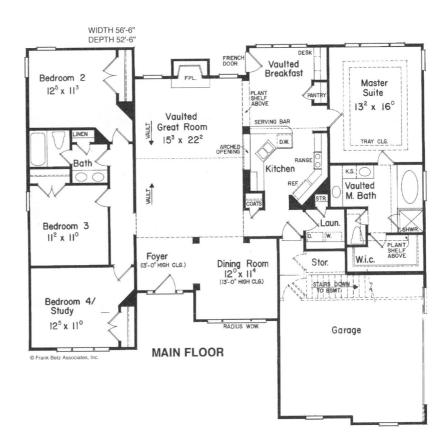

MAIN FLOOR

© Frank Betz Associates, Inc.

Home for Today & Tomorrow

Design by Patrick Morabito A.I.A.

Total living area 1,950 sq. ft. ■ Price Code C

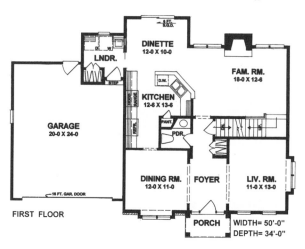

FIRST FLOOR

WIDTH= 50'-0"
DEPTH= 34'-0"

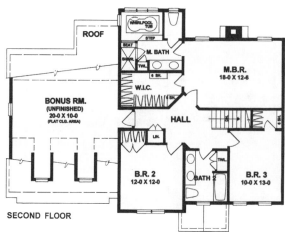

SECOND FLOOR

No. 93342

■ This plan features:

— Three bedrooms

— Two full and one half baths

■ The formal Foyer is flanked by the formal Dining Room and the Living Room

■ The Kitchen, the Dinette and the Family Room have an open layout for easy family interaction

■ The Master Suite includes a walk-in closet, a whirlpool tub, a separate shower and a double vanity

■ The two additional Bedrooms share a full Bath

■ There is a large Bonus Room for future expansion

■ No materials list is available for this plan

First floor — 1,004 sq. ft.
Second floor — 946 sq. ft.
Basement — 1,004 sq. ft.
Garage — 450 sq. ft.

Small Yet Roomy

■ *Total living area 1,950 sq. ft.* ■ *Price Code C* ■

No. 82077 BL

This plan features:

— Three bedrooms

— Two full baths

■ The Great Room is open to the Breakfast Room, the Dining Room and the Foyer

■ The large Master Suite is privately located and has a luxurious Bath and walk-in closet

■ A Grilling Porch and a Deck add outdoor living space

■ An optional basement, slab, or crawl space foundation — please specify when ordering

■ No materials list is available for this plan

Main floor –1,950 sq. ft.
Garage/Storage - 518 sq. ft.

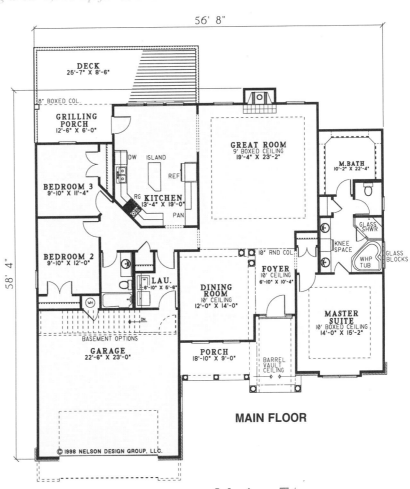

MAIN FLOOR

© 1998 NELSON DESIGN GROUP, LLC.

Elegant Entry

Design by Larry E. Belk

■ *Total living area 1,955 sq. ft.* ■ *Price Code C* ■

No. 93031 [BL]

■ This plan features:

— Three bedrooms

— Two full baths

■ The covered front Porch has distinctive square columns

■ The angled Foyer opens to the large Great Room with a fireplace and the formal Dining Room is defined by columns

■ The Master Bath features an angled whirlpool tub, a separate shower and a dual vanity

■ The Kitchen has a Pantry and ample cabinet and counter space

■ A coffered ceiling treatment highlights the Breakfast Room

■ No materials list is available for this plan

First floor — 1,955 sq. ft.
Bonus — 240 sq. ft.
Garage — 561 sq. ft.

WIDTH 60-10

BRKFST
8-6 X 9-6
10 FT CLG

PORCH

MASTER
BATH

BEDRM 3
11-6 X 12-4

KITCHEN
10-6 X 14-6
10 FT CLG

GREAT ROOM
19-4 X 17-6
11 FT CLG

MASTER BEDRM
13-4 X 14-6
10 FT CLG

BATH 2

DEPTH 65-0

BEDRM 2
14-0 X 10-6

UTIL
8-0 X 6-0

DINING ROOM
12-4 X 12-0
12 FT CLG

FOYER
10 FT CLG

PORCH

GARAGE
21-4 X 23-4

FIRST FLOOR

© Larry E. Belk

BATH 2

STAIRS
UP TO FUTURE
EXP AREA

BEDRM 2
14-0 X 11-4

UTIL

GARAGE

BONUS

■ *Total living area 1,957 sq. ft.* ■ *Price Code C* ■

No. 94906 BL X

■ This plan features:

— Four bedrooms

— Two full and one half baths

■ The covered, front Porch opens to a tiled Entry

■ The formal Dining Room has decorative windows

■ The Family Room opens to the Kitchen and the Breakfast Area, and has a fireplace and a ten-foot ceiling

■ The private Master Bedroom has transom windows, and a plush Bath with a whirlpool tub

First floor — 1,348 sq. ft.
Second floor — 609 sq. ft.
Storage room — 341 sq. ft.
Basement — 1,348 sq. ft.
Garage — 566 sq. ft.

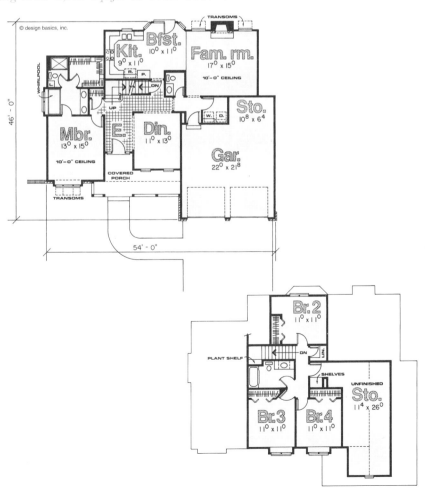

Stylish Trimmings

Design by Nelson Design Group

■ *Total living area 1,957 sq. ft.* ■ *Price Code C* ■

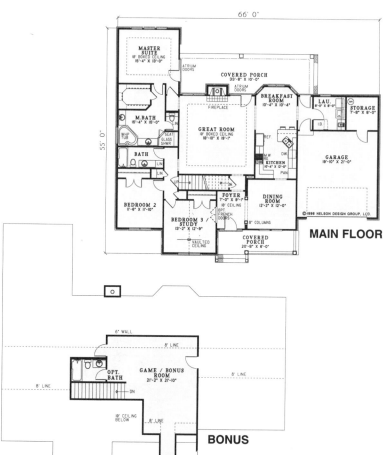

MAIN FLOOR

BONUS

No. 82078

■ This plan features:

— Three bedrooms

— Two full baths

■ The Great Room features a ten-foot boxed ceiling and access to the rear covered Porch

■ The Master Suite, privately located, has a plush Bath

■ The Kitchen opens to the Breakfast Room and the formal Dining Room

■ The Garage opens to the Laundry Area and has a large storage area

■ An optional basement, slab, or crawl space foundation — please specify when ordering

■ No materials list is available for this plan

Main floor – 1,957 sq. ft.
Bonus – 497 sq. ft,
Porches – 203 sq. ft.
Garage/storage – 417 sq. ft.

Elegant and Efficient

■ *Total living area 1,959 sq. ft.* ■ *Price Code D* ■

No. 92515 BL ✕

■ This plan features:

— Three bedrooms

— Two full baths

■ The large Living Room features a hearth fireplace, a decorative ceiling and French doors to the backyard

■ A decorative window and ceiling highlight the formal Dining Room

■ The large Kitchen has double ovens, a cooktop/peninsula snackbar and an Eating Nook

■ The large Master Bedroom Suite has a decorative ceiling, a walk-in closet and a plush Bath with a double vanity and a whirlpool tub

■ An optional slab or crawl space foundation — please specify when ordering

Main floor — 1,959 sq. ft.
Garage — 484 sq. ft.

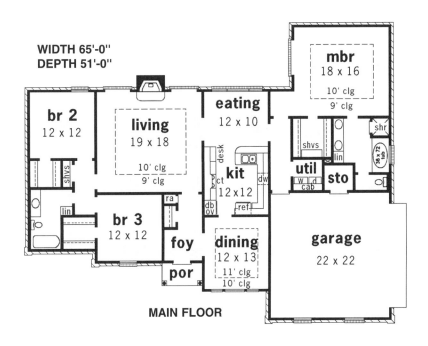

WIDTH 65'-0''
DEPTH 51'-0''

br 2
12 x 12

living
19 x 18
10' clg
9' clg

eating
12 x 10

mbr
18 x 16
10' clg
9' clg

shvs

shvs

lin

shr
36 x 72 tub

kit
12 x 12

util

sto

br 3
12 x 12

foy

dining
12 x 13
11' clg
10' clg

garage
22 x 22

por

MAIN FLOOR

Classic Comfort

Design by Patrick Morabito A.I.A.

■ *Total living area 1,961 sq. ft.* ■ *Price Code C* ■

FIRST FLOOR
WIDTH= 63'-0"
DEPTH= 47'-0"

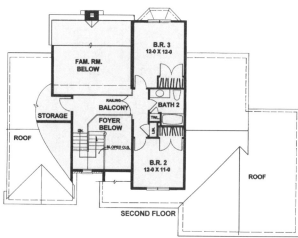

SECOND FLOOR

No. 93349 [BL]

■ **This plan features:**

— Three bedrooms

— Two full and one half baths

■ The spacious Family Room has a vaulted ceiling and a hearth fireplace

■ The efficient Kitchen has an extended counter/eating bar and a bright Dinette Area with a bay window and access to the Deck

■ The first floor Master Bedroom has a walk-in closet and a Master Bath with a double vanity

■ The two additional Bedrooms are on the second floor and share a full Bath

■ No materials list is available for this plan

First floor — 1,454 sq. ft.
Second floor — 507 sq. ft.
Basement — 1,454 sq. ft.
Garage — 642 sq. ft.

Comfortable and Charming

■ *Total living area 1,964 sq. ft.* ■ *Price Code C* ■

No. 92660 **BL**

■ **This plan features:**

– Three bedrooms

– Two full baths

■ The Foyer opens to the spacious Great Room which has a massive fireplace between built-in shelves, and access to the Patio

■ The formal Dining Room has a sloped ceiling and an expansive view of the backyard

■ The Kitchen features a cooktop island, a Pantry and a Breakfast Area which opens to the formal Dining Room

■ The Master Bedroom has a sloped ceiling, a huge walk-in closet and a luxurious Bath

■ No materials list is available for this plan

Main floor — 1,964 sq. ft.
Garage — 447 sq. ft.
Basement — 1,809 sq. ft.

MAIN FLOOR

Exciting Elevation

Design by Studer Residential Design, Inc.

■ *Total living area 1,970 sq. ft.* ■ *Price Code C* ■

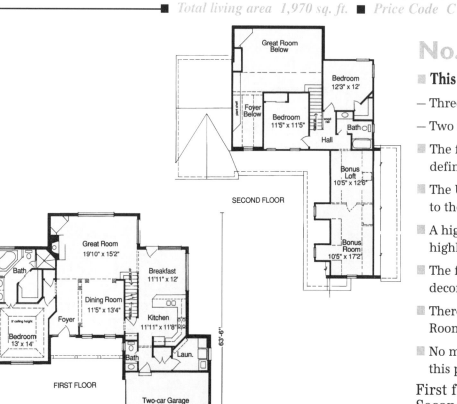

Great Room
Below

Bedroom
12'3" x 12'

Foyer
Below

Bedroom
11'5" x 11'5"

Bath

Hall

plant shelf

wood rail

SECOND FLOOR

Bonus
Loft
10'5" x 12'6"

Bonus
Room
10'5" x 17'2"

Great Room
19'10" x 15'2"

Breakfast
11'11" x 12'

Bath

Dining Room
11'5" x 13'4"

Kitchen
11'11" x 11'8"

Foyer

9' ceiling height

Bedroom
13' x 14'

Bath

Laun.

FIRST FLOOR

Two-car Garage
21' x 23'10"

55'

63'-6"

No. 92668

■ This plan features:

— Three bedrooms

— Two full and one half baths

■ The formal Dining Room is defined by columns

■ The U-shaped Kitchen has access to the Dining Room and the Nook

■ A high ceiling and a fireplace highlight the Great Room

■ The first floor Master Suite has a decorative ceiling

■ There are two separate Bonus Rooms for future consideration

■ No materials list is available for this plan

First floor – 1,497 sq. ft.
Second floor – 473 sq. ft.
Bonus – 401 sq. ft.
Basement – 1,420 sq. ft.
Garage – 468 sq. ft.

Unique and Desirable

© 1996 Donald A Gardner Architects, Inc.

■ *Total living area 1,977 sq. ft.* ■ *Price Code D* ■

No. 99803

This plan features:

- Three bedrooms

- Two full baths

- The private Master Bedroom has a walk-in closet and a skylit bath

- Two additional Bedrooms, one could be used as a Study, share a full Bath

- The Great Room has a cathedral ceiling, a fireplace and built-in shelves

- A skylit screened Porch, and a Deck with built-in seats and a Spa provide outdoor living space

- The Kitchen is conveniently located between the Dining Room and the skylit Breakfast Area

Main floor — 1,977 sq. ft.
Bonus — 430 sq. ft
Garage & storage — 610 sq. ft.

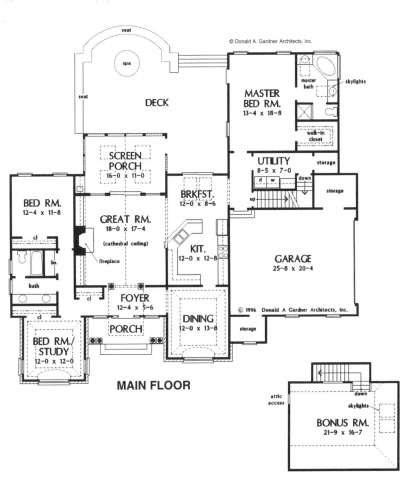

MAIN FLOOR

Compact Yet Cozy

Design by Nelson Design Group

■ *Total living area 1,980 sq. ft.* ■ *Price Code B* ■

No. 82031 BL

■ **This plan features:**

— Three bedrooms

— Two full baths

■ The Kitchen has a breakfast bar and opens to the Dining Area which has a vaulted ceiling

■ The privately located Master Suite has a large walk-in closet and a private Bath

■ The Great Room features a fireplace and direct access to the rear yard

■ Two additional Bedrooms share a full Bath

■ An optional basement, slab, or crawl space foundation — please specify when ordering

■ No materials list is available for this plan

Main floor — 1,980 sq. ft.
Garage/storage — 417 sq. ft.

MAIN FLOOR

51' 6"

52' 4"

MASTER SUITE
13'-0" X 20'-10"
9' PAN CEILING

BEDROOM 2
12'-4" X 10'-0"

GREAT ROOM
17'-0" X 20'-0"
9' PAN CEILING

LAU.
5'-6" X 6'-2"

M.B.
7'-6" X 10'-0"

STRG.

BATH LIN

GARAGE
20'-10" X 20'-0"

REF.

KITCHEN
12'-0" X 12'-0"

FOYER

BEDROOM 3
12'-4" X 11'-8"

DW

PRCH

DINING
12'-0" X 10'-0"

VAULTED CEILING

What a First Impression

■ *Total living area 1,987 sq. ft.* ■ *Price Code C*

No. 97718 [BL]

■ This plan features:

— Three bedrooms

— Two full and one half baths

■ The sunken Great Room with a fireplace opens to both the Solarium and the Breakfast Nook

■ The Kitchen has a work island/eating bar, ample counter space and is convenient to the Laundry Area and the formal Dining Room

■ The Master Bedroom has a decorative high ceiling and a large Bath with a walk-in closet

■ There is a Bonus Room over the Garage for future expansion

■ No materials list is available for this plan

First floor —1,060 sq. ft.
Second floor — 927 sq. ft.
Bonus — 267 sq. ft.

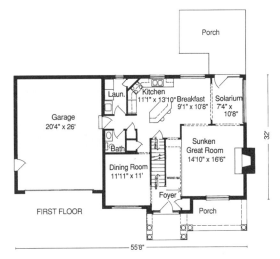

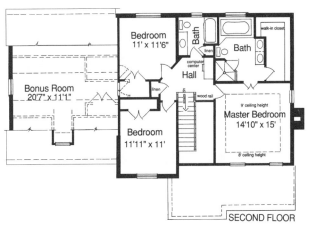

Southern Breezes

Design by Nelson Design Group

■ *Total living area 1,988 sq. ft.* ■ *Price Code C* ■

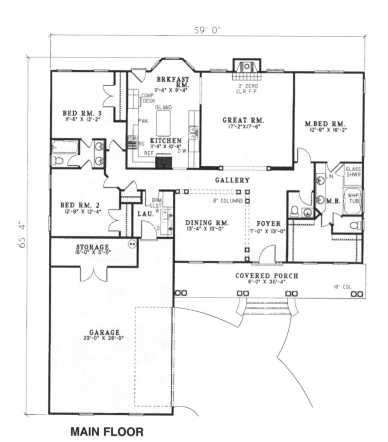

MAIN FLOOR

No. 82028 BL

■ This plan features:

— Three bedrooms

— Two full and one half baths

■ Elegant columns separate the Dining Room and entry into the Great Room from the Gallery

■ The Kitchen has a center work island, a built-in computer desk, and a Breakfast Area with a bay window

■ The Master Suite has a huge walk-in closet and a private Bath

■ An optional slab or crawl space foundation — please specify when ordering

■ No materials list is available for this plan

Main floor — 1,988 sq. ft.
Garage/storage — 598 sq. ft.
Porch — 385 sq. ft.

Design by Nelson Design Group

Great Detailing

■ *Total living area 1,989 sq. ft.* ■ *Price Code C* ■

No. 82079

■ This plan features:

— Four bedrooms

— Three full baths

■ The Great Room features a twelve-foot ceiling and a focal point fireplace

■ The efficient Kitchen has a Pantry, an eating bar and is open to the large Breakfast Room

■ The Master Suite has a large walk-in closet and a whirlpool Bath

■ The secluded Guest Bedroom has a private Bath and a walk-in closet

■ An optional slab or crawl space foundation — please specify when ordering

■ No materials list is available for this plan

Main floor – 1,989 sq. ft.
Garage/storage – 521 sq. ft.

MAIN FLOOR

© 1999 NELSON DESIGN GROUP, LLC.

149

Inviting Welcome

Design by Donald A. Gardner Architects, Inc.

Total living area 1,989 sq. ft. ■ *Price Code D*

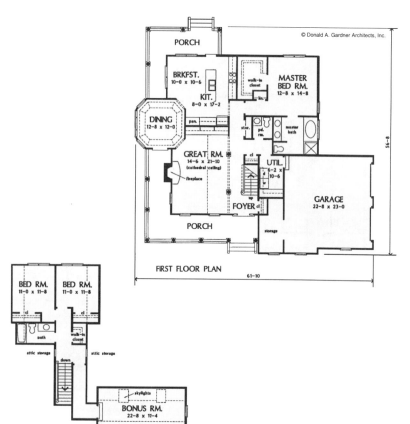

FIRST FLOOR PLAN

SECOND FLOOR PLAN

No. 96472

■ This plan features:

— Three bedrooms

— Two full and one half baths

■ Triple gables and a wrap-around front Porch highlight the front of this home

■ The Great Room has a cathedral ceiling and a cozy fireplace

■ The octagonal Dining Room has a tray ceiling, and easy access to the Porch for outdoor dining

■ The Kitchen features a Pantry, a work island and the Breakfast Area

■ The privately located Master Suite has a roomy walk-in closet and a full Bath

First floor — 1,512 sq. ft.
Second floor — 477 sq. ft.
Bonus — 347 sq. ft.
Garage & storage — 636 sq. ft.

European Influenced

■ *Total living area 1,990 sq. ft.* ■ *Price Code "C"* ■

No. 82052 [BL]

■ This plan features:

- Three bedrooms

- Two full and one half baths

■ The Foyer and the Dining Room of this home have ten-foot ceilings

■ The Kitchen includes a built-in Pantry and a peninsula counter

■ The Master Suite has a whirlpool Bath and a walk-in closet

■ A built-in Media Center and a fireplace highlight the Great Room

■ An optional slab or crawl space foundation — please specify when ordering

■ No materials list is available for this plan

First floor – 1,515 sq. ft.
Second floor – 475 sq. ft.
Garage – 405 sq. ft.

FIRST FLOOR

SECOND FLOOR

Classic Colonial

Design by Design Basics, Inc.

■ *Total living area 1,993 sq. ft.* ■ *Price Code C* ■

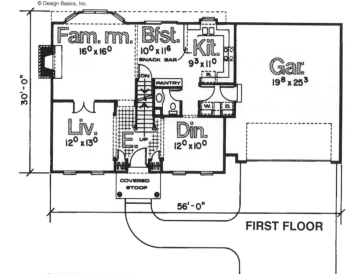

FIRST FLOOR

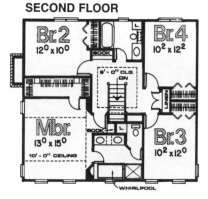

SECOND FLOOR

No. 97411

■ **This plan features:**

— Four bedrooms

— Two full and one half baths

■ This is a classic Colonial style home

■ The Living and Dining Rooms have columned entries from the Foyer

■ The Family Room has a fireplace and a large bay window

■ The U-shaped Kitchen is separated from the Breakfast Nook by a snack bar

■ The Master Bedroom has a huge walk-in closet and a private Bath

■ A two-car Garage completes this design

First floor — 1,000 sq. ft.
Second floor — 993 sq. ft.
Garage — 534 sq. ft.

Private Office

© Michael E. Nelson

Total living area 1,994 sq. ft. ■ *Price Code C*

No. 82080 **BL**

■ This plan features:

— Three bedrooms

— Two full baths

■ The Master Suite includes a private Office with a wall of built-in shelves

■ A fireplace is on the rear wall of the Great Room

■ One of the two secondary Bedrooms has a vaulted ceiling

■ The Kitchen has ample counter space

■ There is a Storage Area in the rear of the Garage

■ An optional basement, slab, or crawl space foundation — please specify when ordering

■ No materials list is available for this plan

Main floor — 1,994 sq. ft.
Garage — 417 sq. ft.

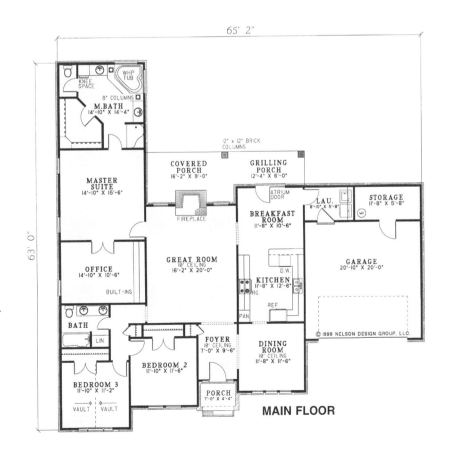

MAIN FLOOR

Skylit Master Bath

Design by Design Basics, Inc.

■ *Total living area 1,996 sq. ft.* ■ *Price Code C* ■

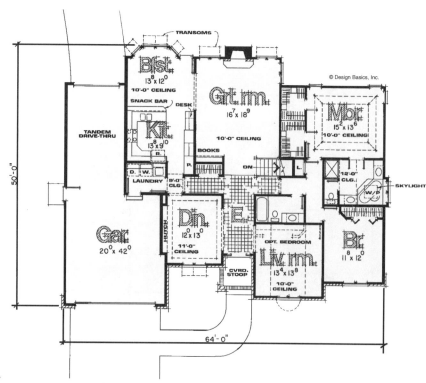

No. 94926 BL

■ **This plan features:**

— Two bedrooms

— Two full baths

■ The Great Room has a large fireplace and transom windows

■ The Living Room, or possible third bedroom, has a 10-foot ceiling and a large front window

■ The formal Dining Room has a hutch space

■ The convenient Kitchen has a snack bar, built-in desk and Pantry

■ The Breakfast Nook has a bay window with transoms and a ten-foot ceiling

■ The Master Bedroom has a decorative ceiling, two walk-in closets and a full Bath

■ The two-car Garage has a third bay in the rear

Main floor — 1,996 sq. ft.

Design by Design Basics, Inc.

Distinctive Design

■ *Total living area 1,998 sq. ft.* ■ *Price Code C* ■

No. 94904

■ **This plan features:**

– Three bedrooms

– Two full and one half baths

■ The Living Room has a bay window and French doors leading into the Family Room

■ A built-in curio cabinet and hutch space highlight the formal Dining Room

■ The Kitchen has an island cooktop and a Breakfast Area

■ The Family Room has a focal point fireplace

■ The spacious Master Bedroom has a vaulted ceiling, a decorative window and a luxurious Bath with a double walk-in closet

First floor — 1,093 sq. ft.
Second floor — 905 sq. ft.
Basement — 1,093 sq. ft.
Garage — 527 sq. ft.

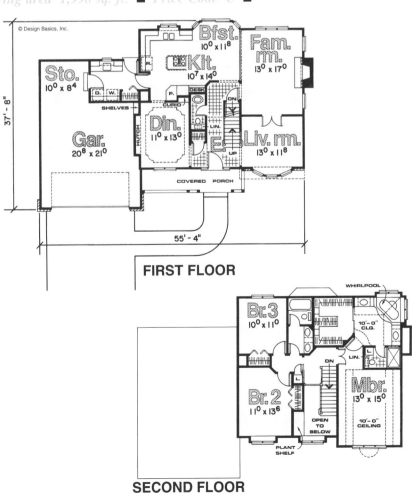

© Design Basics, Inc.

FIRST FLOOR

Sto.
10⁰ x 8⁴

Gar.
20⁸ x 21⁰

Bfst.
10⁰ x 11⁸

Kit.
10⁷ x 14⁰

Fam. rm.
13⁰ x 17⁰

Din.
11⁰ x 13⁰

Liv. rm.
13⁰ x 11⁸

COVERED   PORCH

37'- 8"

55'- 4"

SECOND FLOOR

WHIRLPOOL

Br. 3
10⁰ x 11⁰

10'- 0"
CLG.

Br. 2
11⁰ x 13⁶

Mbr.
13⁰ x 15⁰

10'- 0"
CEILING

OPEN TO BELOW

PLANT SHELF

155

Quaint Front Porch

Design by Design Basics, Inc.

■ *Total living area 1,999 sq. ft.* ■ *Price Code C* ■

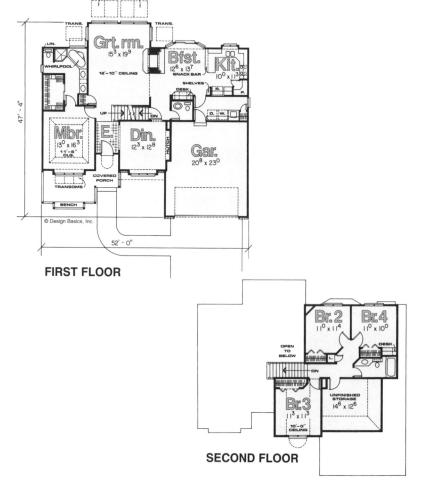

FIRST FLOOR

SECOND FLOOR

No. 94900

■ **This plan features:**

— Four bedrooms

— Two full and one half baths

▦ The covered Porch and Victorian touches create a unique elevation

▦ A one and a half story Entry Hall leads into the formal Dining Room

▦ Abundant windows and a see-through fireplace highlight the Great Room

▦ The Kitchen/Breakfast Area features a snack bar, a built-in desk, a walk-in Pantry and abundant counter space

▦ The Laundry Area has access to the Garage and the side yard

▦ The Master Suite has a vaulted ceiling and a luxurious Bath

First floor — 1,421 sq. ft.
Second floor — 578 sq. ft.
Basement — 1,421 sq. ft.

Design by Donald A. Gardner Architects, Inc.

Stately Arched Entry

No. 98011

This plan features:

- Three bedrooms

- Two full and one half baths

- Columns highlight the stately arched entry Porch

- The Dining Room has a tray ceiling and is defined by columns

- The Great Room has a fireplace and access to the rear Porch/Deck

- The Kitchen has ample cabinet and counter space

- The Master Bedroom has a bay window and a tray ceiling

- The Master Bath features dual vanities and walk-in closets

- There are two secondary Bedrooms, one of which could be used as a Study

- A Bonus Room is located over the two-car Garage

Main floor — 2,024 sq. ft.
Bonus — 423 sq. ft.
Garage — 623 sq. ft.

© 1998 Donald A. Gardner, Inc.

Total living area 2,024 sq. ft. ■ Price Code E

FLOOR PLAN

© 1998 Donald A. Gardner, Inc.

Design by Donald A. Gardner Architects, Inc.

Relaxed Country Living

No. 96402

This plan features:

- Three bedrooms

- Two full baths

- This comfortable Country home features a deluxe Master Suite, front and back Porches and a dual-sided fireplace

- The vaulted Great Room has a vaulted ceiling, two clerestory dormers and a fireplace shared with the Breakfast Area

- The Dining Room and front Bedroom/Study have tray ceilings

- The Master Bedroom features a vaulted ceiling, back Porch access, and a luxurious Bath with an over-sized, walk-in closet

- The skylit Bonus Room over the Garage provides extra room for family needs

Main floor — 2,027 sq. ft.
Bonus — 340 sq. ft.
Garage & storage — 532 sq. ft.

© 1997 Donald A. Gardner Architects, Inc.

Total living area 2,027 sq. ft. ■ Price Code E

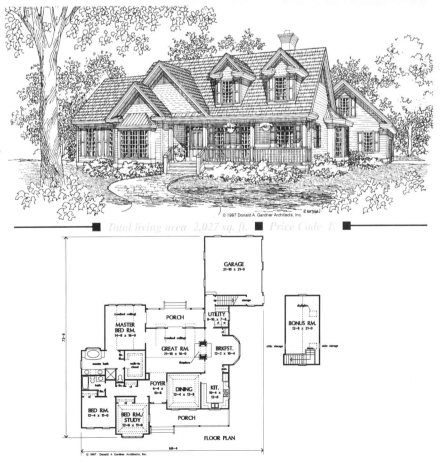

FLOOR PLAN

© 1997 Donald A. Gardner Architects, Inc.

Opposing Sides

Design by Nelson Design Group

■ *Total living area 2,034 sq. ft.* ■ *Price Code C* ■

MAIN FLOOR

No. 82081

■ **This plan features:**

— Four bedrooms

— Two full baths

■ The Great Room has a fireplace and French doors

■ The Dining Room and Foyer have high ceilings

■ The efficient Kitchen opens to the cheerful Breakfast Room

■ The privately located Master Suite has a large Bath with dual, walk-in closets

■ The three additional Bedrooms have ample closet space and share a full Bath

■ An optional basement, slab, or crawl space foundation — please specify when ordering

■ No materials list is available for this plan

Main floor – 2,034 sq. ft.
Garage – 576 sq. ft.

Design by Jannis Vann & Associates, Inc.

Friendly Porch

■ *Total living area 2,036 sq. ft.* ■ *Price Code C* ■

No. 98911 BL ✖

■ This plan features:

- Four bedrooms
- Two full and one half baths
- ■ The formal Living and Dining Rooms are open to each other for easy entertaining
- ■ The efficient Kitchen opens to the Breakfast Area
- ■ The Family Room features a fireplace, built-in cabinets and access to the Patio/Deck
- ■ The Master Bedroom has a decorative ceiling, a large walk-in closet and a double vanity Bath
- ■ An optional basement, slab, or crawl space foundation — please specify when ordering

First floor — 907 sq. ft.
Second floor — 1,129 sq. ft.
Basement — 907 sq.ft.

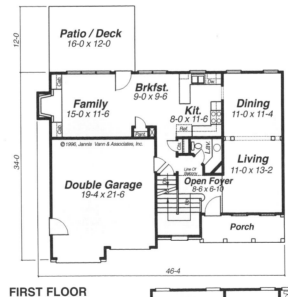

FIRST FLOOR

Patio / Deck
16-0 x 12-0

Family
15-0 x 11-6

Brkfst.
9-0 x 9-6

Kit.
8-0 x 11-6

Dining
11-0 x 11-4

Living
11-0 x 13-2

Double Garage
19-4 x 21-6

Open Foyer
8-6 x 6-10

Porch

© 1996, Jannis Vann & Associates, Inc.

SECOND FLOOR

Master Bdrm.
13-6 x 15-8

Bdrm.2/ Sitting
10-0 x 11-6

Bth.2

Bdrm.3
10-8 x 10-4

M.Bath

Laund.

Open Foyer

Bdrm.4
11-0 x 10-0

Prairie Style Retreat

Design by The Meredith Corporation

■ *Total living area 2,038 sq. ft.* ■ *Price Code C* ■

Photography supplied by The Meredith Corporation

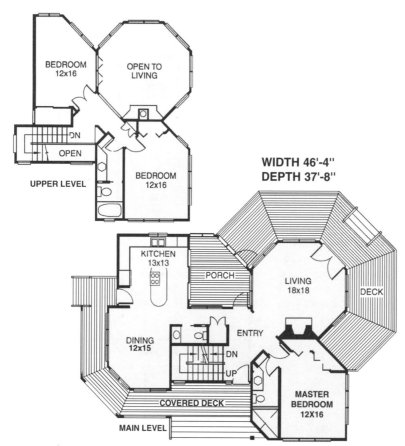

BEDROOM 12x16

OPEN TO LIVING

DN

OPEN

UPPER LEVEL

BEDROOM 12x16

WIDTH 46'-4"
DEPTH 37'-8"

KITCHEN 13x13

PORCH

LIVING 18x18

DECK

DINING 12x15

ENTRY

DN

UP

COVERED DECK

MASTER BEDROOM 12X16

MAIN LEVEL

No. 32109

■ **This plan features:**

— Three bedrooms

— Two full and one half baths

■ Shingle siding, expansive windows and wrap-around Decks accent the exterior of this home

■ The octagonal shaped Living Room has a two-story ceiling and French doors

■ The Kitchen has a cooktop island and is open to the Dining Room

■ The first floor Master Suite has a private Bath

■ The two additional second floor Bedrooms share a full Bath

First floor — 1,213 sq. ft.
Second floor — 825 sq. ft.
Basement — 1,213 sq. ft.

160

Design by Ahmann Design, Inc.

Open Great Room

■ *Total living area 2,044 sq. ft.* ■ *Price Code C* ■

No. 97131

This plan features:

- Four bedrooms

- Two full and one half baths

- The open Great Room has a cozy fireplace

- The Kitchen has ample counter space, an eating bar, and a sunny Breakfast Nook

- The Master Suite has a walk-in closet and a full Bath with Spa tub

- Other amenities include a main floor Laundry Room, Powder Room and attached two-car Garage

- No materials list is available for this plan

First floor — 1,365 sq. ft.
Second floor — 679 sq. ft.

MAIN FLOOR

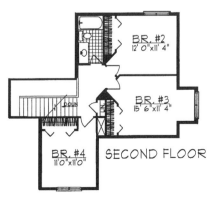

SECOND FLOOR

French Influenced

Design by Donald A. Gardner Architects, Inc.

© 1990 Donald A. Gardner Architects, Inc.

■ *Total living area 2,045 sq. ft.* ■ *Price Code E* ■

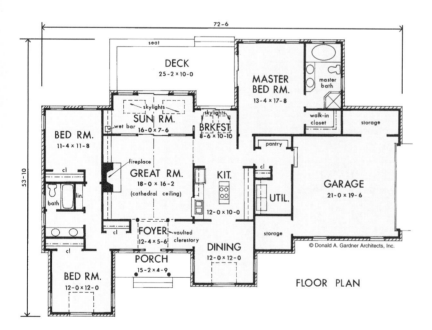

FLOOR PLAN

© Donald A. Gardner Architects, Inc.

No. 96421

■ This plan features:

— Three bedrooms

— Two full baths

■ Arched windows, round columns and rich brick veneer create curb appeal

■ The foyer has natural light from an arched clerestory window

■ The Great Room, with skylight and wetbar, is adjacent to the Sun Room

■ The Kitchen with a cooktop island is centrally located

■ The large Master Bedroom opens to the Deck

Main floor – 2,045 sq. ft.
Garage & storage – 563 sq. ft.

Dream Home

©1995 Donald A. Gardner Architects, Inc.

Total living area 2,050 sq. ft. ■ *Price Code E* ■

No. 96465   BL ✕ Я R

■ This plan features:

– Three bedrooms

– Two full baths

■ The Foyer opens to the Study/Living Room, the formal Dining Room and the Great Room

■ The Kitchen has an angled peninsula bar, a large Breakfast Room and is adjacent to the Laundry Area and Garage entry

■ The Master Bedroom is privately located and has a plush Bath and walk-in closet

■ The two secondary Bedrooms share a full Bath

Main floor – 2,050 sq. ft.
Bonus – 377 sq. ft.
Garage – 503 sq. ft.

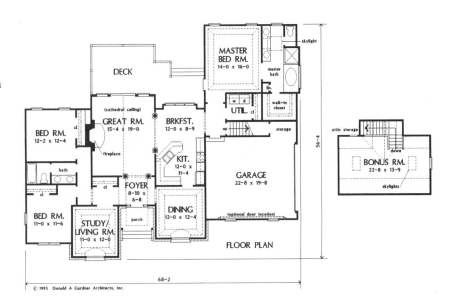

Split Bedroom Plan

Design by Frank Betz Associates, Inc.

Total living area 2,051 sq. ft. ■ *Price Code C* ■

No. 98427 BL ✕

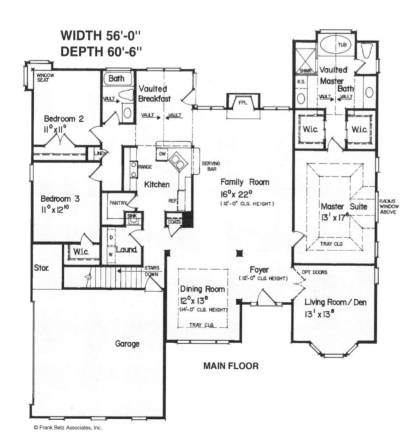

WIDTH 56'-0"
DEPTH 60'-6"

MAIN FLOOR

© Frank Betz Associates, Inc.

This plan features:

— Three bedrooms

— Two full baths

■ The elegant Dining Room features a tray ceiling and a large arched front window

■ The Living Room/Den has optional double doors for privacy and is enhanced by a bay window

■ The Kitchen includes a walk-in Pantry, a corner double sink and adjacent Breakfast Room

■ The spacious Master Bedroom has a tray ceiling, dual walk-in closets and a luxurious Bath

■ An optional basement, slab or crawl space foundation — please specify when ordering

Main floor — 2,051 sq. ft.
Basement — 2,051 sq. ft.
Garage — 441 sq. ft.

Take In the View

Total living area 2,054 sq. ft. ■ Price Code C ■

No. 61005 **BL**

■ This plan features:

— Three bedrooms

— Two full and one half baths

■ The Great Room has a vaulted ceiling, a fireplace and a built-in Media Center

■ The Kitchen is open to the Great Room and includes a peninsula counter/snack bar

■ A vaulted ceiling is featured in the formal Dining Room

■ The front and rear Decks expand living space to the outdoors

■ No materials list is available for this plan

First floor – 1,413 sq. ft.
Second floor – 641 sq. ft.

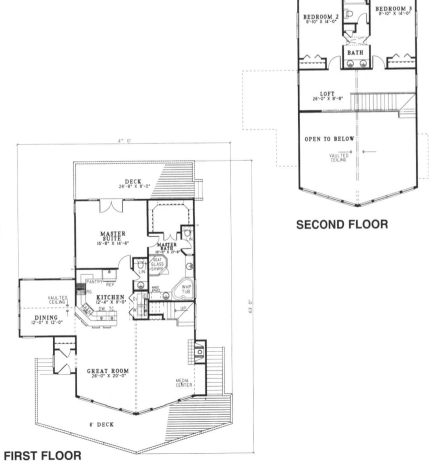

FIRST FLOOR

SECOND FLOOR

Solid Looking

Design by Studer Residential Design, Inc.

■ *Total living area 2,063 sq. ft.* ■ *Price Code C* ■

No. 97723

■ This plan features:

— Three bedrooms

— Two full baths

■ The covered front Porch has decorative columns

■ A beamed ceiling highlights the Great Room

■ The Dining Room has a lovely tray ceiling

■ The Breakfast Nook has access to the wooden Deck

■ One of the secondary Bedrooms could be used as a Study

■ The Master Bedroom features a walk-in closet and private Bath

■ No materials list is available for this plan

Main floor — 2,063 sq. ft.
Basement — 2,063 sq. ft.
Garage — 481 sq. ft.

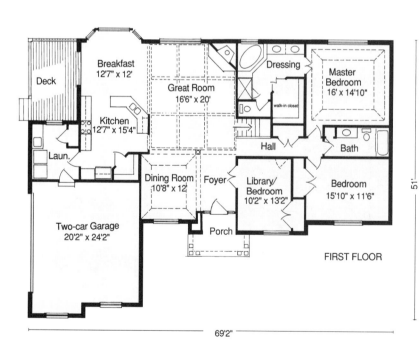

Design by Studer Residential Design, Inc.

Total living area 2,068 sq. ft. ■ Price Code C ■

No. 97726 BL

■ **This plan features:**

- Two bedrooms

- One full and one half baths

■ Decorative ceilings highlight many rooms in this home

■ Windows in the Great Room overlook the rear Deck

■ The Kitchen has ample counter space and a center island

■ The guest Bedroom or Library has a special bay shape

■ The optional lower level has room for more Bedrooms and entertainment space

■ No materials list is available for this plan

First floor – 2,068 sq. ft.
Bonus – 1,552 sq. ft.
Basement – 516 sq. ft.

First Floor Plan

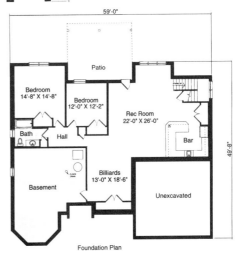

Foundation Plan

Columns and Arches

Design by The Garlinghouse Company

■ *Total living area 2,070 sq. ft.* ■ *Price Code C* ■

No. 24730 **BL**

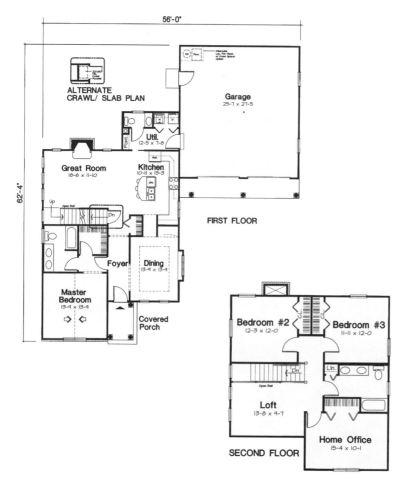

■ This plan features:

— Three bedrooms

— Two full and one half baths

■ The Great Room is open to the Kitchen for a comfortable and relaxed living space

■ The Utility Room and Garage entry are convenient to the Kitchen

■ The Formal Dining Room is enhanced by a decorative ceiling and boxed window

■ The Private Master Suite has a vaulted ceiling, walk-in closet and comfortable Bath

■ No materials list is available for this plan

First floor – 1,194 sq. ft.
Second floor – 876 sq. ft.
Basement – 1,194 sq. ft.
Garage – 736 sq. ft.

Design by Fillmore Design Group

Packed with Options

■ *Total living area 2,081 sq. ft.* ■ *Price Code C* ■

No. 98559

■ This plan features:

— Three bedrooms

— Three full baths

■ This home has a tiled Entry and Gallery that connect the living spaces

■ The Great Room has a rear wall fireplace set between windows

■ Both Dining Areas are convenient to the Kitchen

■ The Study has a sloped ceiling and a front bay window

■ The privately located Master Bedroom has a private Bath and a walk-in closet

■ The two secondary Bedrooms share a full Bath

■ No materials list is available for this plan

Main Floor – 2,081 sq. ft.
Garage – 422 sq. ft.

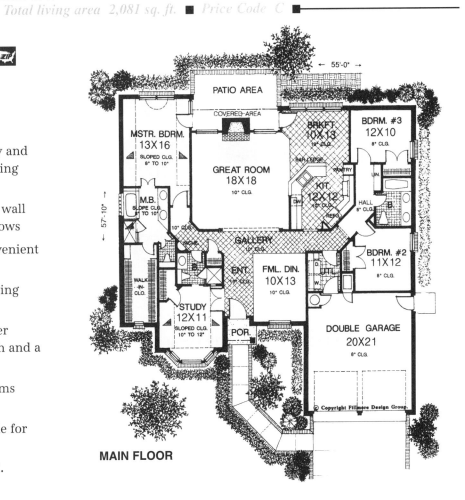

MAIN FLOOR

A Distinct Personality

Design by Design Basics, Inc.

■ *Total living area 2,089 sq. ft.* ■ *Price Code C* ■

FIRST FLOOR

Bfst.
16³ x 11⁹

Grt. rm.
16⁰ x 18⁰
SLOPED CEILING

SLOPED CEILING

TRANSOMS

WHIRLPOOL

10'-0"
CLG.

SNACK BAR

Kit.
11² x 11⁶

DRESSER/
ENT. CENTER

Mbr.
13⁰ x 15⁰
10'-0" CLG.

TRANSOM

DN UP

Din.
11⁰ x 14⁰

Gar.
20⁰ x 25⁸

COVERED
PORCH

TRANSOMS

© Design basics, Inc.

50' - 0"

54' - 0"

SECOND FLOOR

Br. 4
10⁸ x 11⁰

OPEN TO
GREAT ROOM

DN

Br. 2
12⁰ x 11⁰

OPEN
TO
BELOW

Br. 3
11⁰ x 11⁸
10'-0"
CEILING

No. 99433

■ **This plan features:**

– Four bedrooms

– Two full and one half baths

■ The tiled Entry opens to the
Dining Room with a boxed bay
window

■ A see-through fireplace and
multiple windows enhance the
Breakfast Nook and the Great
Room

■ The efficient Kitchen includes a
snack bar and Pantry and is
convenient to the Laundry Area
and Garage entry

■ The Master Bedroom is located on
the first floor for privacy and
includes a boxed window

First floor — 1,510 sq. ft.
Second floor — 579 sq. ft.
Basement — 1,510 sq. ft.

Traditional Country Home

Design by Design Basics, Inc.

■ *Total living area 2,090 sq. ft.* ■ *Price Code C* ■

No. 94931

■ This plan features:

— Four bedrooms

— Two full and one half baths

■ The wrap-around Porch has access to the tiled Entry and Kitchen

■ The expansive Great Room has a triple window and an inviting fireplace

■ The large Kitchen, with a built-in Pantry and a work island, opens to the Breakfast Area with a built-in desk

■ The private Master Bedroom has a decorative ceiling and deluxe Bath

■ The three secondary Bedrooms share a double vanity Bath

First floor — 927 sq. ft.
Second floor — 1,163 sq. ft.
Garage — 463 sq. ft.
Basement — 927 sq. ft.

© design basics, inc.

Kit.
9x14

Bfst.
11x13

Grt. rm.
18x14

DESK

DN UP

SHELVES

Dn.
12x11

38'-0"

WRAP - AROUND PORCH

Gar.
20x22

48'-0"

FIRST FLOOR

Br.
12x10

Mbr.
15x13

DN

Br.
11x11

Br.
11x11

WHIRL POOL

SECOND FLOOR

171

Unique Turret

Design by Studer Residential Design, Inc.

■ *Total living area 2,101 sq. ft.* ■ *Price Code C* ■

WIDTH 59'-0"
DEPTH 60'-8"

Deck

Bath

Walk-in closet

Sunken
Great Room
16-10 x 21

Breakfast
9-2 x 16

Kitchen
8 x 13-4

Master Bedroom
14 x 17-4

Slope ceiling   Slope ceiling

Foyer

Dining Room
16 x 11-8

Bath

Hall

Laundry

Two-car Garage
21 x 20-8

FIRST FLOOR

Great Room
Below

Bedroom
15x 10-8

Bath

Bedroom
14x 10-6

Foyer Below

SECOND FLOOR

No. 92610

■ **This plan features:**

— Three bedrooms

— Two full and one half baths

■ The sunken Great Room has a focal point fireplace and an atrium door to the Deck

■ The efficient U-shaped Kitchen with work island, built-in Pantry, a Breakfast Alcove and adjoins the Dining Room with a bay window

■ A sloped ceiling highlights the window alcove in the Master Bedroom which has a plush Bath and walk-in closet

■ No materials list is available for this plan

First floor — 1,625 sq. ft.
Second floor — 475 sq. ft.
Basement — 1,512 sq. ft.
Garage — 437 sq. ft.

Inviting Country Style

© Design basics, Inc.

■ *Total living area 2,103 sq. ft.* ■ *Price Code C* ■

No. 94942

■ **This plan features:**

– Four bedrooms

– Two full and one half baths

■ Built-in bookcases frame the Fireplace in the Family Room

■ The Kitchen features a work island and a planning desk

■ The Dining Room has a wall of windows overlooking the Porch

■ The Master Bedroom has a decorative ceiling and a walk-in closet

■ The three additional Bedrooms share a full Bath

■ A two-car Garage completes this design

First floor — 1,082 sq. ft.
Second floor — 1,021 sq. ft.
Basement — 1,082 sq. ft.
Garage — 478 sq. ft.

FIRST FLOOR

SECOND FLOOR

173

Decorative Ceilings

Design by Nelson Design Group

■ *Total living area 2,107 sq. ft.* ■ *Price Code C* ■

MAIN FLOOR

No. 82082

■ **This plan features:**

— Four bedrooms

— Two full and one half baths

■ There are decorative ceilings in the Dining Room and Master Suite

■ The Great Room has access to the rear covered Porch

■ The Breakfast Room features a bay window

■ The Kitchen includes a work island with seating

■ There is a Storage Room in the rear of the Garage

■ All of the Bedrooms have large closets

■ No materials list is available for this plan

Main floor — 2,107 sq. ft.

Design by The Garlinghouse Company

Welcoming Porch

■ *Total living area 2,108 sq. ft.* ■ *Price Code C* ■

No. 24257 BL ✗

■ This plan features:

— Three Bedrooms

— Two full baths

■ Vaulted ceilings enhance the Living Room, Dining Room, Family Room and Eating Nook

■ The gourmet Kitchen which has a work island, built-in Pantry and peninsula eating bar is open to the Eating Nook and formal Dining Room

■ The Master Suite with a private Master Bath has direct access to the Patio

■ The two additional Bedrooms share a full hall Bath

Main level — 2,108 sq. ft.
Garage — 462 sq. ft.
Optional den — 121 sq. ft.

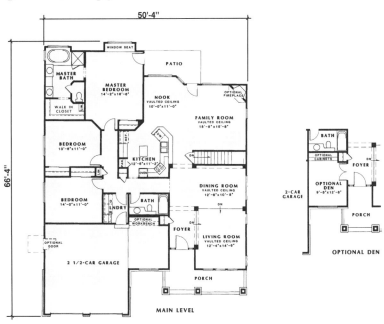

MAIN LEVEL

OPTIONAL DEN

OPTIONAL 3-CAR GARAGE

Dressed to Impress

Design by Donald A. Gardner Architects, Inc.

© 1997 Donald A Gardner Architects, Inc.

Total living area 2,121 sq. ft. ■ Price Code E

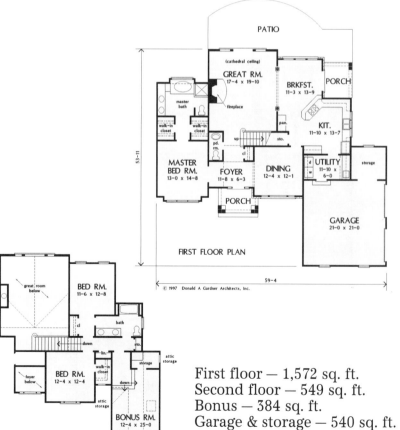

PATIO

(cathedral ceiling)

GREAT RM.
17-4 x 19-10

fireplace

BRKFST.
11-3 x 13-9

PORCH

master bath

KIT.
11-10 x 13-7

walk-in closet

walk-in closet

pan.

pd. rm.

up

sto.

cl

UTILITY
11-10 x 6-0

storage

MASTER BED RM.
13-0 x 14-8

FOYER
11-8 x 6-3

DINING
12-4 x 12-1

53-11

w

PORCH

GARAGE
21-0 x 21-0

FIRST FLOOR PLAN

59-4

© 1997 Donald A Gardner Architects, Inc.

great room below

BED RM.
11-6 x 12-8

cl

bath

down

sto.

lin.

foyer below

BED RM.
12-4 x 12-4

walk-in closet

storage

attic storage

down

attic storage

BONUS RM.
12-4 x 25-0

skylights

SECOND FLOOR PLAN

First floor — 1,572 sq. ft.
Second floor — 549 sq. ft.
Bonus — 384 sq. ft.
Garage & storage — 540 sq. ft.

No. 99824

■ This plan features:

— Three bedrooms

— Two full and one half baths

■ The Great Room has a cathedral ceiling and adjoins the Breakfast Area

■ The Kitchen is enhanced by an angled counter with a cooktop

■ A separate Utility Room with built-in cabinets, counter top space and a Laundry sink adds efficiency

■ Double doors lead into the Master Suite with a boxed bay window, two walk-in closets and a lavish Bath

■ The two additional Bedrooms, a full Bath, a linen closet and skylit Bonus Room are located on the second floor

See Through Fireplace

■ *Total living area 2,132 sq. ft.* ■ *Price Code C* ■

No. 82083 🆅🅻

This plan features:

- Three bedrooms

- Two full baths

- The Foyer opens to the Formal Dining Room and the Great Room

- The Hearth Room and the Great Room share a see-through fireplace

- The Master Suite has a dual vanity Bath

- The privately located secondary Bedrooms share a full Bath

- No materials list is available for this plan

- An optional basement, slab or crawl space foundation — please specify when ordering

Main floor — 2,132 sq. ft.
Bonus — 316 sq. ft.
Garage — 467 sq. ft.

MAIN FLOOR

BONUS

Stunningly Styled

Design by Fillmore Design Group

■ *Total living area 2,132 sq. ft.* ■ *Price Code C* ■

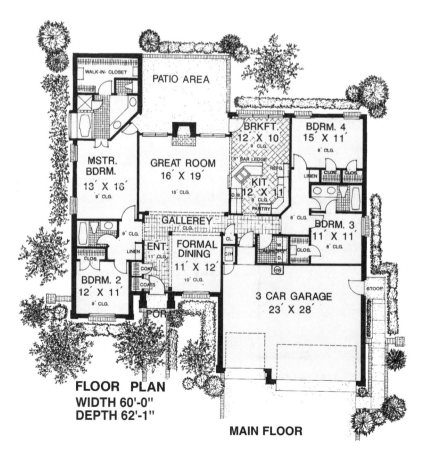

FLOOR PLAN
WIDTH 60'-0"
DEPTH 62'-1"

MAIN FLOOR

No. 92280

■ This plan features:

— Four bedrooms

— Three full baths

■ Decorative columns seperate the formal Dining Room from the tiled Entry

■ A fireplace flanked by windows is the focal point in the Great Room

■ The efficient Kitchen features a built-in Pantry, double sink and an angled peninsula counter

■ The private Master Suite has a lavish Bath and a huge walk-in closet

■ The additional Bedrooms all have ample closet space

■ No materials list is available for this plan

Main floor – 2,132 sq. ft.
Garage – 644 sq. ft.

Design by Design Basics, Inc.

Visually Open Plan

© design basics, Inc.

■ *Total living area 2,133 sq. ft.* ■ *Price Code C* ■

No. 94959

This plan features:

- Three bedrooms

- Two full and one half baths

■ The diagonal design gives this house an expansive look

■ The covered stoop opens into a Y-shaped tiled Foyer with direct access to the Great Room

■ The Great Room has a high ceiling, a fireplace, and louvered openings in the roof

■ The Kitchen features a working island/ snack bar and is open to the Breakfast Room with a bay window

■ The Bedroom wing contains three large Bedrooms and two full Baths

■ A three-car Garage with storage completes this Plan

Main floor – 2,133 sq. ft.
Garage – 656 sq. ft.

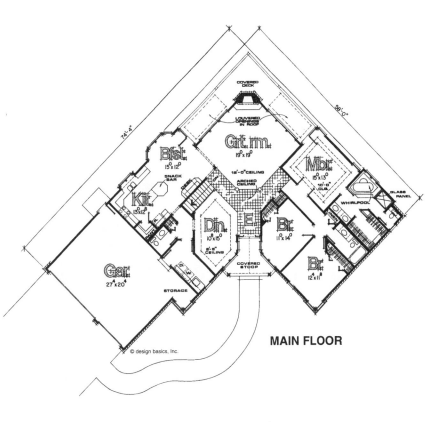

MAIN FLOOR

© design basics, Inc.

Open and Airy

■ *Total living area 2,133 sq. ft.* ■ *Price Code C* ■

MAIN FLOOR

© 1999 NELSON DESIGN GROUP, LLC.

No. 82084

■ **This plan features:**

— Three bedrooms

— Two full baths

■ The Great Room, Dining Room and Foyer are open to each other for a feeling of spaciousness

■ A boxed ceiling decorates the Master Bedroom, Great Room and Hearth Room

■ The Garage opens to the Laundry Room for a Mud Room effect

■ An optional basement, slab or crawl space foundation — please specify when ordering

■ No materials list is available for this plan

Main floor — 2,133 sq. ft.
Garage/Storage — 484 sq. ft.
Porches — 89 sq. ft.

Design by Nelson Design Group

No. 82085 **BL**

This plan features:

- Four bedrooms

- Two full baths

- A convenient Butler's Pantry connects the Kitchen and Dining Room

- French doors add to the beauty of the Dining Room

- A glass block window overlooks the whirlpool tub in the Master Bath

- The Kitchen is a cook's dream

- The Family Room has a rear wall fireplace

- No materials list is available for this plan

Main floor — 2,140 sq. ft.

Butler's Pantry

Total living area 2,140 sq. ft. ■ Price Code C

MAIN FLOOR

Design by Nelson Design Group

No. 82099 **BL**

This plan features:

- Three bedrooms

- Two full and one half baths

- The Study/Office of this home has a private location directly off the Foyer

- The Great Room is enhanced by a focal point fireplace

- The Kitchen is separated from the Breakfast Room by a peninsula counter/snack bar

- The Master Suite has a secluded location and a private Bath

- The two additional Bedrooms are on the second floor and share a full Bath

- No materials list is available for this plan

First floor — 1,690 sq. ft.
Second floor — 450 sq. ft.

Private Study

Total living area 2,140 sq. ft. ■ Price Code C

SECOND FLOOR

FIRST FLOOR

Family Home

Design by The Garlinghouse Company

■ *Total living area 2,149 sq. ft.* ■ *Price Code C* ■

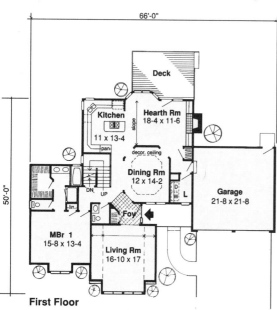

First Floor

66'-0"

50'-0"

Deck

Kitchen
11 x 13-4

Hearth Rm
18-4 x 11-6

pan

decor. ceiling

Dining Rm
12 x 14-2

DN UP

Garage
21-8 x 21-8

Foy

MBr 1
15-8 x 13-4

Living Rm
16-10 x 17

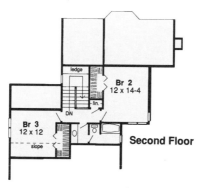

Second Floor

ledge

Br 2
12 x 14-4

DN

Br 3
12 x 12

slope

No. 20178 BL

■ This plan features:

– Three bedrooms

– Two full and one half baths

■ The formal Living Room is enhanced by a large front window

■ The distinctive formal Dining Room has a decorative ceiling

■ A sloped ceiling and a fireplace highlight the Hearth Room

■ The Kitchen features a range-top island, a corner double sink, a built-in Pantry and ample counter space

■ The first floor Master Suite has a luxury Bath with a double vanity and a walk-in closet

■ The two additional Bedrooms share a full Bath

First floor — 1,606 sq. ft.
Second floor — 543 sq. ft.
Basement — 1,606 sq. ft.
Garage — 484 sq. ft.

Four Bedroom Family

■ *Total living area 2,154 sq. ft.* ■ *Price Code C* ■

No. 82086

■ **This plan features:**

– Four bedrooms

– Two full and one half baths

■ A clean burning gas fireplace highlights the Great Room

■ The Master Suite has a boxed ceiling

■ Upstairs, three Bedrooms share a full Bath

■ No materials list is available for this plan

■ An optional basement, slab or crawl space foundation — please specify when ordering

First floor – 1,443 sq. ft.
Second floor – 711 sq. ft.
Garage – 400 sq. ft.

FIRST FLOOR

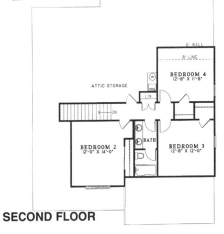

SECOND FLOOR

Details, Details, Details

Design by Frank Betz Associates, Inc.

■ *Total living area 2,155 sq. ft.* ■ *Price Code C* ■

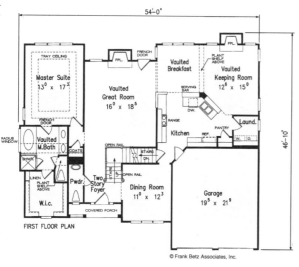

FIRST FLOOR PLAN

© Frank Betz Associates, Inc.

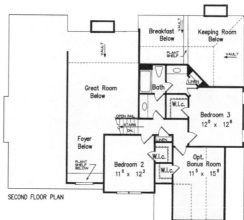

SECOND FLOOR PLAN

No. 98447

■ This plan features:

— Three bedrooms

— Two full and one half baths

■ This elevation is highlighted by stucco, stone and detailing around the arched windows

■ A vaulted ceiling and a fireplace enhance the Great Room

■ The two secondary Bedrooms, with walk-in closets, share a full Bath

■ The Master Suite has a tray ceiling, a huge walk-in closet and a plush Bath

■ An optional basement or crawl space foundation — please specify when ordering

First floor – 1,628 sq. ft.
Second floor – 527 sq. ft.
Bonus – 207 sq. ft.
Basement – 1,628 sq. ft.
Garage – 440 sq. ft.

Attractive Exterior

■ *Total living area 2,167 sq. ft.* ■ *Price Code C* ■

No. 98512   BL

■ This plan features:

— Three bedrooms

— Two full baths

■ Columns separate the Great Room and the Dining Room from the tiled Gallery

■ The Breakfast Nook has a bay window and access to the backyard and covered Patio

■ The large Kitchen is a chef's dream with ample counter space

■ The Master Bedroom is privately located and has a luxurious Bath

■ The two secondary Bedrooms share a full Skylight Bath

■ No materials list is available for this plan

Main floor – 2,167 sq. ft.
Garage – 690 sq. ft.

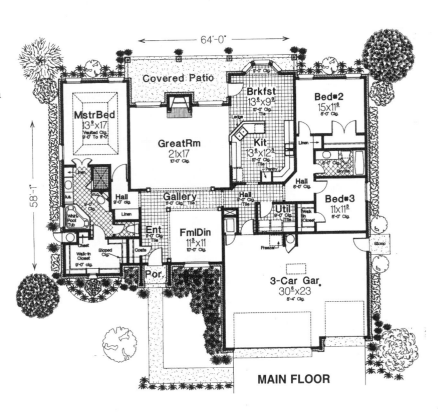

MAIN FLOOR

Appealing Brick Elevation

Design by Design Basics, Inc.

Total living area 2,172 sq. ft. ■ *Price Code C* ■

No. 94971 BL

■ **This plan features:**

— Three bedrooms

— Two full and one three quarter baths

■ The tiled Entry opens to the formal Living and Dining Rooms

■ The Great Room has an eleven foot ceiling, a raised hearth fireplace and decorative windows

■ The Kitchen has a walk-in Pantry, a work island and is open to the Breakfast Area

■ The Master Suite has a private Bath

Main floor — 2,172 sq. ft.
Garage — 680 sq. ft.

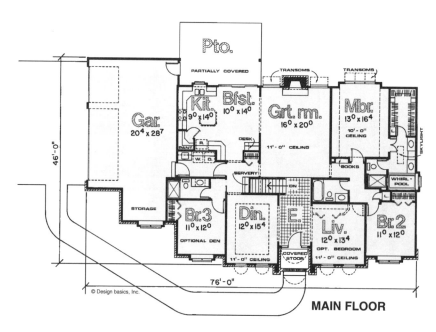

MAIN FLOOR

Vacation Getaway

Total living area 2,143 sq. ft. ■ *Price Code C* ■

No. 61006

■ This plan features:

— Three bedrooms

— Two full baths

■ The Great Room has a large fireplace and is open to the sunken Sun Room

■ The Kitchen includes a work island cooktop and eating bar

■ The upstairs Master Suite includes skylights, a fireplace, a Kitchenette and a Office

■ No materials list is available for this plan

First floor — 1,400 sq. ft.
Second floor — 743 sq. ft.

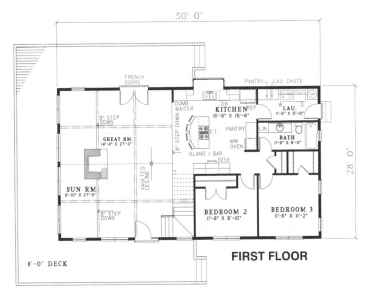

FIRST FLOOR

SECOND FLOOR

187

Homey Covered Porch

Design by Nelson Design Group

■ *Total living area 2,186 sq. ft.* ■ *Price Code C* ■

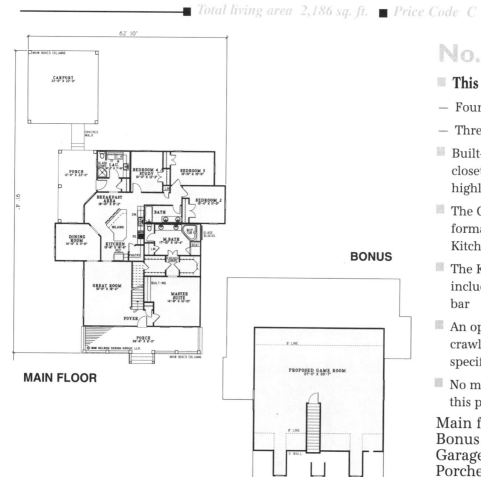

MAIN FLOOR

BONUS

No. 82087

■ **This plan features:**

— Four bedrooms

— Three full baths

■ Built-in cabinets, two walk-in closets and a whirlpool Bath highlight the Master Suite

■ The Great Room has access to the formal Dining Room and the Kitchen/Breakfast Room

■ The Kitchen/Breakfast Area includes a large work island/snack bar

■ An optional basement, slab or crawl space foundation — please specify when ordering

■ No materials list is available for this plan

Main floor – 2,186 sq. ft.
Bonus – 1,283 sq. ft.
Garage/storage – 484 sq. ft.
Porches – 567 sq. ft.

Design by Donald A. Gardner Architects, Inc.

B. NATHAN

© 1996 Donald A. Gardner Architects, Inc.

■ *Total living area 2,190 sq. ft.* ■ *Price Code E* ■

No. 96471 BL ✕ R

This plan features:

- Three bedrooms

- Two full and one half baths

■ A hip roof, gables and brick accent this Traditional home

■ A curved transom window and sidelights illuminate the gracious Foyer

■ A curved balcony overlooks the Great Room which has a cathedral ceiling, fireplace and a triple window overlooking the Patio

■ The private Master Bedroom is enhanced by a tray ceiling, walk-in closet and a deluxe Bath

First floor – 1,577 sq. ft.
Second floor – 613 sq. ft.
Bonus – 390 sq. ft.
Garage & storage – 634 sq. ft.

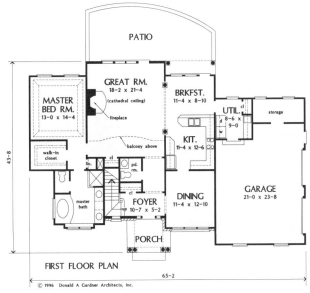

FIRST FLOOR PLAN

© 1996 Donald A Gardner Architects, Inc.

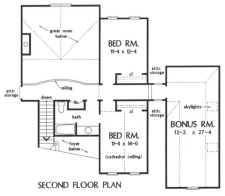

SECOND FLOOR PLAN

Roof Lines Add Interest

Design by Jannis Vann & Associates, Inc.

■ *Total living area 2,192 sq. ft.* ■ *Price Code C* ■

No. 93255

MAIN FLOOR

64-0

■ **This plan features:**

— Three bedrooms

— Two full and one half baths

■ The formal rooms are located at the front of the home

■ A decorative ceiling enhances the Dining Room

■ Columns seperate the Living Room from the Foyer and the Family Room

■ The large Family Room has a cozy fireplace and direct access to the Deck

■ The efficient Kitchen is located between the Dining Room and the Breakfast Room

■ The private Master Suite includes a Master Bath and walk-in closet

Main floor — 2,192 sq. ft.
Basement — 2,192 sq. ft.
Garage — 564 sq. ft.

Design by Ahmann Design, Inc.

Luxury on One Level

■ *Total living area 2,196 sq. ft.* ■ *Price Code C* ■

No. 93190

■ **This plan features:**

— Three bedrooms

— Two full and one half baths

■ The covered front Porch leads into the tiled Entry

■ The huge Great Room is perfect for entertaining and has a cozy fireplace and a vaulted ceiling

■ The large Kitchen has a Pantry, a work island, and a bright Eating Nook with access to the screened Porch beyond

■ The Master Bedroom features a large walk-in closet and a luxurious Bath

■ The two additional Bedrooms, with over-sized closets, share a full Bath

Main floor — 2,196 sq. ft.
Basement — 2,196 sq. ft.

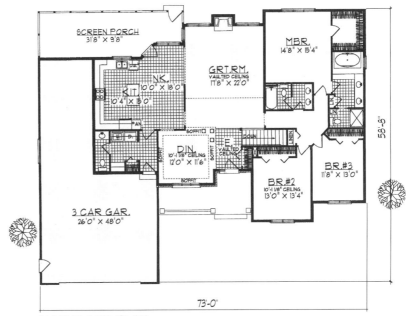

MAIN FLOOR PLAN

Style and Versatility

Design by Donald A. Gardner Architects, Inc.

©1997 Donald A. Gardner Architects, Inc.

■ *Total living area 2,201 sq. ft.* ■ *Price Code E* ■

FIRST FLOOR PLAN

© 1997 Donald A Gardner Architects, Inc.

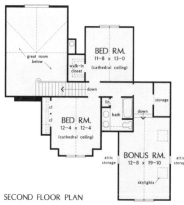

SECOND FLOOR PLAN

No. 96494

■ This plan features:

— Four bedrooms

— Three full baths

■ The stunning Great Room has a magnificent cathedral ceiling, a fireplace and French doors to the Deck

■ The Kitchen has a cooktop island and is open to the Breakfast Room

■ The secluded Master Suite has dual walk-in closets, a stately tray ceiling and a luxurious Bath

■ Cathedral ceilings enhance both Bedrooms on the second floor

■ The flexible first floor Study/Bedroom is near a full Bath

First floor — 1,687 sq. ft.
Second floor — 514 sq. ft.
Bonus — 336 sq. ft.
Garage — 489 sq. ft.

Sun Room with Vaulted Ceiling

■ *Total living area 2,201 sq. ft.* ■ *Price Code D* ■

No. 93710

This plan features:

- Four bedrooms

- Two full baths

■ The Sun Room has a vaulted ceiling

■ The expansive Great Room has an eleven-foot ceiling, a fireplace and built-in shelves

■ The efficient Kitchen open to the Breakfast Room with access to the Patio

■ The privately located Master Bedroom features a walk-in closet and dual vanity Bath

■ The Sun Room has a vaulted ceiling and is open to the Great Room and the Breakfast Room

■ An optional slab or crawl space foundation — please specify when ordering

■ No materials list is available for this plan

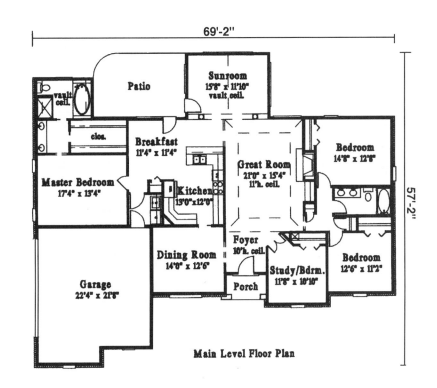

Main Level Floor Plan

Main floor — 2,201 sq. ft.
Garage — 532 sq. ft.

Brick and Fieldstone Facade

Design by Studer Residential Design, Inc.

Total living area 2,205 sq. ft. ■ *Price Code D* ■

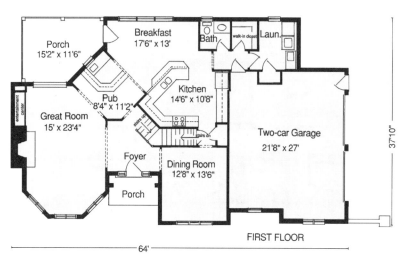

FIRST FLOOR

Porch 15'2" x 11'6"

Breakfast 17'6" x 13'

Bath

walk-in closet

Laun.

Great Room 15' x 23'4"

Pub 8'4" x 11'2"

Kitchen 14'6" x 10'8"

Two-car Garage 21'8" x 27'

Foyer

Dining Room 12'8" x 13'6"

Porch

entertainment center

37'10"

64'

SECOND FLOOR

Bedroom 11' x 13'2"

Master Bedroom 12'6" x 16'

Bath

walk-in closet

Hall

Bath

Bedroom 12'8" x 11'1"

No. 92675

■ This plan features:

— Three bedrooms

— Two full and one half baths

■ The open Foyer is enhanced by a graceful staircase

■ The Great Room has a twelve-foot ceiling, an alcove of windows, fireplace, built-in entertainment center and Porch access

■ The spacious Kitchen and Breakfast Area has a extended counter/snack bar and is near a walk-in closet, Laundry Area and Garage Entry

■ The comfortable Master Bedroom has a large walk-in closet and double vanity Bath

■ No materials list is available for this plan

First floor — 1,192 sq. ft.
Second floor — 1,013 sq. ft.
Basement — 1,157 sq. ft.

Design by Studer Residential Design, Inc.

Arched Accents Give Impact

■ *Total living area 2,209 sq. ft.* ■ *Price Code D* ■

No. 92643

This plan features:

- Three bedrooms
- Two full and one half baths
- The Great Room is enhanced by an entertainment center, hearth fireplace and a wall of windows
- The angled Kitchen features a work island/snack bar and a Breakfast Area
- The second floor has two Bedrooms with walk-in closets, skylit Study, a double vanity Bath and a Bonus Room
- The first floor Master Bedroom has a deluxe Bath and a large walk-in closet
- No materials list is available for this plan

First floor — 1,542 sq. ft.
Second floor — 667 sq. ft.
Bonus — 236 sq. ft.
Basement — 1,470 sq. ft.
Garage — 420 sq. ft.

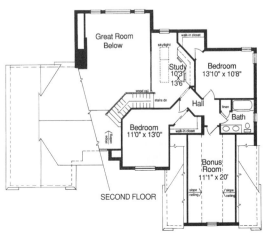

Charming and Convenient

Design by Alan Mascord Design Associates

■ *Total living area 2,209 sq. ft.* ■ *Price Code D* ■

No. 91534 BL X

■ This plan features:

— Three bedrooms

— Two full and one half baths

■ The center Foyer opens to the formal Dining and Living Areas

■ The spacious Family Room has an inviting fireplace and backyard view

■ The convenient Kitchen has a peninsula counter/snack bar, a Pantry, a built-in Desk, a large Eating Nook and is near the Laundry/ Garage entry

■ The Master Suite features an arched window, a vaulted ceiling and a plush Bath with a walk-in closet and Spa tub

■ The additional Bedrooms, with ample closets, share a double vanity Bath

First floor — 1,214 sq. ft.
Second floor — 995 sq. ft.
Bonus Room — 261 sq. ft.

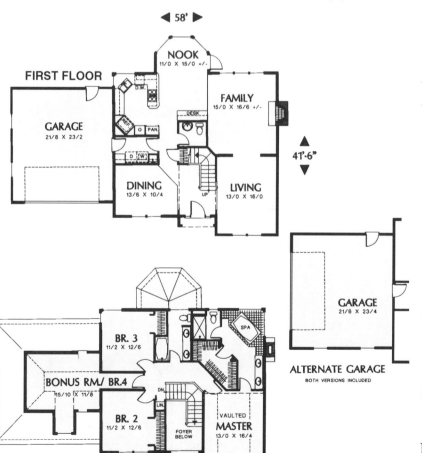

Design by Frank Betz Associates, Inc.

■ *Total living area 2,212 sq. ft.* ■ *Price Code D* ■

No. 98450 BL X

This plan features:

- Three bedrooms

- Two full and one half baths

- The two story Foyer opens to the formal Living and Dining Rooms

- A vaulted ceiling and a boxed window highlight the Living Room

- The Kitchen has ample counter space, an angled sink and a Pantry

- The Family Room features a fireplace and a vaulted ceiling

- The Master Suite has a tray ceiling, Sitting Room and private Bath

- An optional basement or crawl space foundation — please specify when ordering

First floor — 1,135 sq. ft.
Second floor — 1,077 sq. ft.
Basement — 1,135 sq. ft.
Garage — 452 sq. ft.

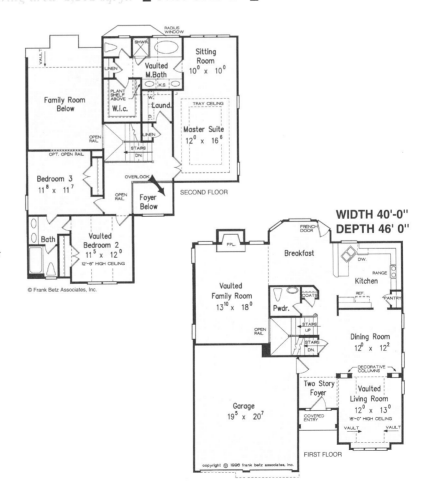

Expansive Master Suite

Design by Fillmore Design Group

■ *Total living area 2,214 sq. ft.* ■ *Price Code D* ■

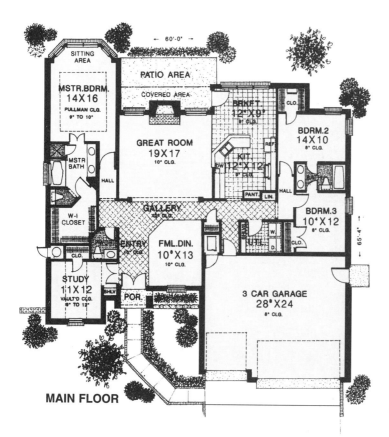

MAIN FLOOR

No. 98579

■ This plan features:

— Three bedrooms

— Two full and one half baths

■ The tiled Entry/ Gallery Hall is open to the formal Dining Room and Great Room

■ The privately located Study has a vaulted ceiling and French doors

■ The Kitchen has a peninsula counter and is open to the Breakfast Room and the Great Room

■ The large Master Bedroom features a Sitting Area with a bay window, a full private Bath, and a walk-in closet

■ The two secondary Bedrooms share a full Bath

■ No materials list is available for this plan

Main floor — 2,214 sq. ft.
Garage — 687 sq. ft.

Design by Nelson Design Group

Total living area 2,217 sq. ft. ■ *Price Code D* ■

No. 61000 [BL]

■ This plan features:

— Three bedrooms

— Two full and one half baths

■ The Great Room has a fireplace and built-in Media Center

■ The efficient Kitchen has an eating bar, opens to the Breakfast Room and the formal Dining Room

■ The private Master Suite has a full Bath and a large walk-in closet

■ The two additional Bedrooms have walk-in closets and share a full Bath and a Computer Center

■ An optional basement, slab, or crawl space foundation — please specify when ordering

■ No materials list is available for this plan

First floor — 1,644 sq. ft.
Second floor — 573 sq. ft.
Garage — 465 sq. ft.

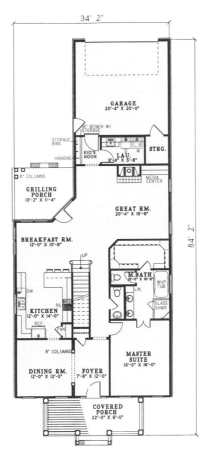

FIRST FLOOR

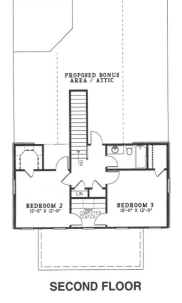

SECOND FLOOR

Kid's Nook

Design by Nelson Design Group

■ *Total living area 2,231 sq. ft.* ■ *Price Code D* ■

FIRST FLOOR

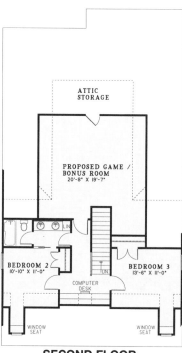

SECOND FLOOR

No. 61013

■ This plan features:

— Three bedrooms

— Two full and one half baths

■ The large Great Room, with a fireplace and wetbar, is perfect for entertaining

■ The Kitchen has an eating bar and opens to the Breakfast Room and formal Dining Room

■ The Master Suite has a deluxe Bath and walk-in closet

■ The second floor Bedrooms share a Computer Center and a full Bath

■ The Garage Entry open to the Laundry Area and a convenient Kid's Nook

■ No materials list is available for this plan

First floor — 1,698 sq. ft.
Second floor — 533 sq. ft.
Bonus — 394 sq. ft.

Optional Sun Room

■ Total living area 2,235 sq. ft. ■ Price Code D ■

No. 82094 BL

This plan features:

- Four bedrooms
- Two full baths
- Columns separate the Dining Room and the Great Room from the Foyer
- There are Sun Room and Bonus Room options for expanded living space
- The spacious Laundry Room has counter space, a hanging rod and a sink
- There is a vaulted ceiling in the Great Room
- The private Master Bedroom has two walk-in closets
- No materials list is available for this plan

Main floor — 2,235 sq. ft.
Bonus — 399 sq. ft.
Sun Room — 250 sq. ft.

FIRST FLOOR

SECOND FLOOR

Stately Entrance

Design by The Garlinghouse Company

■ *Total living area 2,244 sq. ft.* ■ *Price Code D* ■

FIRST FLOOR

SECOND FLOOR

No. 24268

■ This plan features:

– Three or four bedrooms

– Two full and one half baths

■ A vaulted ceiling highlights the Living Room adding to its spaciousness

■ The formal Dining Room has easy access to both the Living Room and the Kitchen

■ The efficient Kitchen has ample storage and counter space, and is open to an informal Eating Nook with a built-in Pantry

■ The large Family Room has a fireplace and access to the Patio

■ The plush Master Suite features a vaulted ceiling, a luxurious Master Bath and two walk-in closets

First floor — 1,115 sq. ft.
Second floor — 1,129 sq. ft.
Basement — 1,096 sq. ft.
Garage — 415 sq. ft.

Traditional Two-Story

© 1997 Donald A. Gardner Architects, Inc.

Total living area 2,250 sq. ft. ■ Price Code E

No. 96491

■ This plan features:

— Three bedrooms

— Two full and two half baths

■ This handsome design features multiple gables, keystone arches, transom windows and a covered Porch

■ An arched clerestory window lights the dramatic two-story Foyer

■ The two-story Great Room has an inviting fireplace, a wall of windows and back Porch access

■ The open Kitchen has access to the Breakfast Room and Dining Room

■ The private Master Bedroom Suite features two walk-in closets and a deluxe Bath

First floor — 1,644 sq. ft.
Second floor — 606 sq. ft.
Bonus — 548 sq. ft.
Garage & storage — 657 sq. ft.

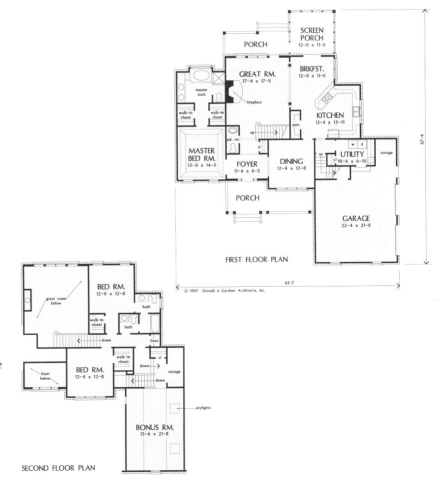

203

Design by Nelson Design Group

■ Total living area 2,252 sq. ft. ■ Price Code D ■

FIRST FLOOR

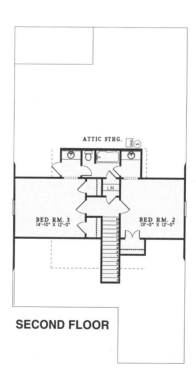

SECOND FLOOR

No. 61012 BL

■ **This plan features:**

— Three bedrooms

— Three full baths

■ From the Garage enter the home into the kid's Nook

■ A Computer Desk is located centrally on the main floor

■ The Great Room includes a built-in Media Center and a fireplace

■ The Kitchen is convenient to both Dining Areas

■ The Laundry Area and convenient Kid's Nook are adjacent to the Kitchen and the Garage

■ The large Master Suite has a private Bath

■ Upstairs are two Bedrooms, a full Bath and Attic Storage

■ No materials list is available for this plan

First floor — 1,694 sq. ft.
Second floor — 558 sq. ft.

Design by Studer Residential Design, Inc.

Friendly Front Porch

■ *Total living area 2,259 sq. ft.* ■ *Price Code D* ■

No. 92638

■ This plan features:

— Four bedrooms

— Two full and one half baths

■ Soft arches and keystones accent this delightful home

■ An inviting fireplace and windows on two walls highlight the Great Room

■ The L-shaped Kitchen has a work island/snackbar, a Butler's Pantry and is open to the Breakfast Room

■ The Garage entry opens to a spacious Laundry Room and a walk-in closet

■ The Master Bedroom is accented by a sloped ceiling, deluxe Bath and walk-in closet

■ No materials list is available for this plan

First floor — 1,199 sq. ft.
Second floor — 1,060 sq. ft.

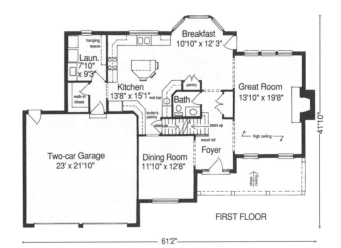

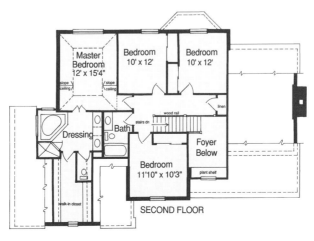

Traditional Treasure

Design by Nelson Design Group

Total living area 2,260 sq. ft. ■ Price Code D

No. 61001 BL

■ This plan features:

— Four bedrooms

— Two full and one half baths

■ The covered front Porch has decorative columns

■ Built-in shelves and a media center flank the fireplace in the Great Room

■ The Kitchen includes a convenient serving bar open to the Breakfast Room

■ The private Master Suite has a walk-in closet and plush Bath

■ The second floor Bedrooms have walk-in closets

■ An optional basement, slab, or crawl space foundation — please specify when ordering

■ No materials list is available for this plan

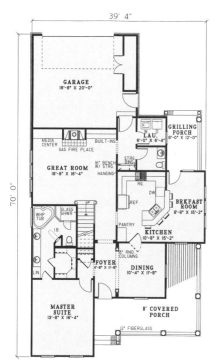

FIRST FLOOR

SECOND FLOOR

First floor — 1,419 sq. ft.
Second floor — 841 sq. ft.
Garage — 469 sq. ft.

Design by Design Basics, Inc.

Expansive Covered Porch

■ *Total living area 2,270 sq. ft.* ■ *Price Code D* ■

No. 99457

■ This plan features:

- Four bedrooms

- Two full and one half baths

■ The spacious two-story Entry opens to the formal Dining Room which is enhanced by a built-in hutch

■ A built-in entertainment center, a see-through fireplace and an elegant bay window highlight the Great Room

■ The Kitchen is open to the Breakfast/Hearth Room

■ The luxurious Master Suite has a decorative ceiling and a lavish Bath with a whirlpool tub and two vanities

First floor — 1,150 sq. ft.
Second floor — 1,120 sq. ft.
Basement — 1,150 sq. ft.
Garage — 457 sq. ft.

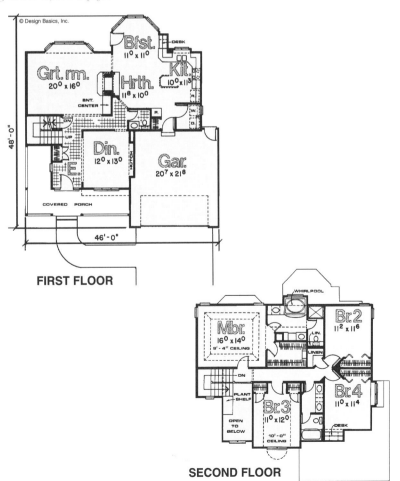

FIRST FLOOR

SECOND FLOOR

Brick and Stone

Design by Studer Residential Design, Inc.

■ *Total living area 2,278 sq. ft.* ■ *Price Code E* ■

No. 97737 ■BL

■ This plan features:

— Three bedrooms

— One full and one three quarter Bath

■ A covered front Porch shelters the Entry

■ Columns separate the Dining Room and the Great Room from the Foyer

■ All of the Bedrooms are in one wing of the home

■ A fireplace warms the Great Room

■ The Kitchen has a work island with a seating space

■ The Laundry Room has a convenient built-in seat

■ No materials list is available for this plan

Main floor — 2,278 sq. ft.
Basement — 2,278 sq. ft.
Garage — 540 sq. ft.

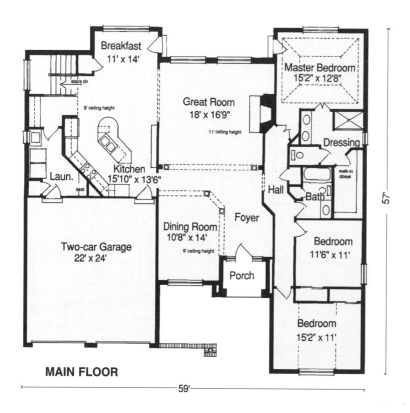

MAIN FLOOR

Bonus Room

■ *Total living area 2,279 sq. ft.* ■ *Price Code D* ■

No. 61002 BL

This plan features:

- Three bedrooms

- Two full and one half baths

- The Garage is in the rear of the home

- A clean-burning gas fireplace adds ambiance to the Great Room

- The U-shaped Kitchen shares an eating bar with the Breakfast Room

- A Bonus Room provides expansion possibilities

- An optional basement, slab, or crawl space foundation — please specify when ordering

- No materials list is available for this plan

First floor — 1,675 sq. ft.
Second floor — 604 sq. ft.
Bonus — 285 sq. ft.
Garage — 465 sq. ft.

FIRST FLOOR

SECOND FLOOR

209

Comfortable Atmosphere

Design by Design Basics, Inc.

■ *Total living area 2,282 sq. ft.* ■ *Price Code D* ■

© Design Basics, Inc.

FIRST FLOOR

TRANSOMS

Kit.
10⁰ x 13⁰

Bfst.
14⁸ x 14⁴

Grt. rm.
16⁰ x 20⁰

13'-0" CEILING

Mbr.
13⁰ x 16⁰

10'-0" CEILING

PANT.

W. D.

DN

UP

LIN.

SEAT

Din.
12⁰ x 14⁰

HUTCH

Gar.
31⁴ x 22⁴

COVERED PORCH

WHIRLPOOL

48' - 8"

65' - 4"

SECOND FLOOR

Br. 4
10⁸ x 13⁰

Br. 3
11⁰ x 13⁰

DN

UNFINISHED BONUS ROOM
20⁸ x 20⁸

Br. 2
11⁰ x 13⁶

10'-0" CLG.

No. 99406

■ This plan features:

— Four bedrooms

— Two full and one half baths

■ The Entry leads into the formal Dining Room which has a hutch space

■ The Kitchen has a central island and a Pantry

■ The Breakfast Area and the Great Room share a see-through fireplace

■ Prominent windows and a thirteen-foot ceiling enhance the Great Room

■ The Master Bedroom features a vaulted ceiling and a large walk-in closet

■ The Bonus Room is available for storage or expansion

First floor — 1,597 sq. ft.
Second floor — 685 sq. ft.
Basement — 1,597 sq. ft.

Guest Room

■ *Total living area 2,286 sq. ft.* ■ *Price Code E* ■

No. 61003 **BL**

This plan features:

— Four bedrooms

— Three full baths

— The Guest Room has a walk-in closet and is near a full Bath

— The Butler's Pantry opens into a food Pantry

— The Great Room has a fireplace between built-in shelves and a media center

— The Breakfast Room overlooks the side yard

— The Master Suite includes dual walk-in closets

— An optional basement, slab, or crawl space foundation — please specify when ordering

— No materials list is available for this plan

First floor — 1,831 sq. ft.
Second floor — 455 sq. ft.
Garage — 429 sq. ft.

FIRST FLOOR

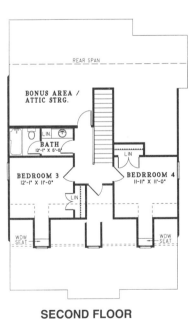

SECOND FLOOR

Garage to the Rear

Design by Nelson Design Group

■ *Total living area 2,323 sq. ft.* ■ *Price Code D* ■

No. 61011 BL

■ This plan features:

- Three bedrooms
- Three full baths

■ The first floor Master Suite has a ten-foot boxed ceiling and a private whirlpool Bath

■ The U-shaped Kitchen includes a snack bar and a built-in Pantry

■ There is a built-in Computer Center in the Breakfast Room

■ The Great Room is highlighted by a fireplace and a built-in Media Center

■ The front covered Porch and the grilling Porch expand living space outdoors

■ No materials list is available for this plan

First floor — 1,713 sq. ft.
Second floor — 610 sq. ft.
Bonus — 384 sq. ft.

FIRST FLOOR

37' 0"

73' 0"

GARAGE
19'-4" X 20'-0"

GRILLING
PORCH
16'-8" X 8'-0"

MEDIA
CENTER

GREAT RM.
10' BOXED CEILING
16'-8" X 14'-8"

LAU.

M. BATH
9'-6" X 14'-8"

WHP
TUB

8' COLUMNS

BREAKFAST
AREA
16'-8" X 10'-0"

COMPUTER
DESK

MASTER SUITE
10' BOXED CEILING
14'-7" X 19'-0"

PANTRY

REF.

DW

KITCHEN

BATH

RG

GUEST RM. /
STUDY
12'-3" X 10'-0"

FOYER
7'-6" X 11'-0"

DINING RM.
13'-3" X 11'-0"

8' COLUMNS

COVERED
PORCH
37'-0" X 8'-0"

SECOND FLOOR

ATTIC STORAGE

LIN

BED RM. 2
15'-6" X 10'-6"

GAME RM. /
BONUS
12'-10" X 27'-7"

BED RM. 3
15'-6" X 11'-0"

8' LINE

6' WALL

Design by Andy McDonald Design Group

European Flavor

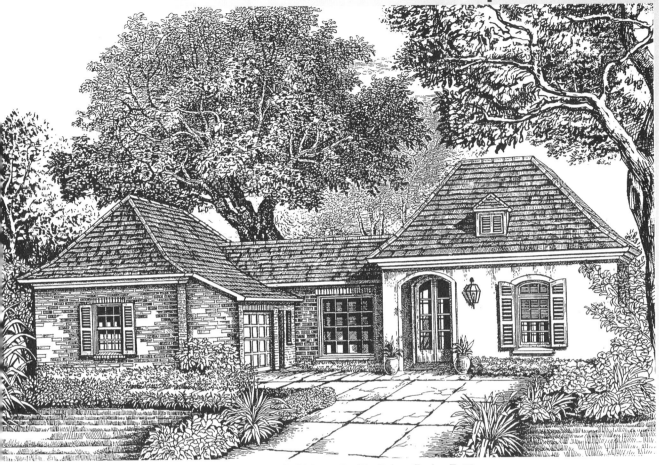

Total living area 2,364 sq. ft. ■ Price Code D

No. 97530 BL

This plan features:

– Four bedrooms

– Three full baths

- The two-car Garage has a storage space
- The Dining Room has a large front window
- The Kitchen has a cooktop island
- The Family Room has a warming fireplace
- The rear Patio has a place for a soothing fountain
- No materials list is available for this plan

Main floor – 2,364 sq. ft.
Garage – 494 sq. ft.

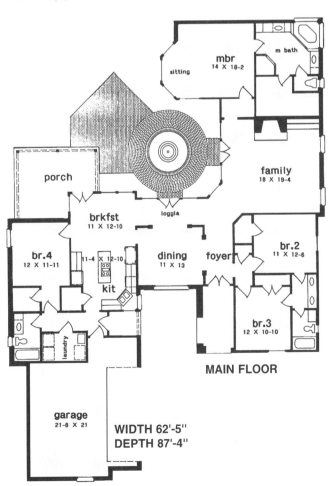

mbr
14 X 18-2
sitting
m bath
porch
family
18 X 19-4
loggia
brkfst
11 X 12-10
br.4
12 X 11-11
11-4 X 12-10
kit
dining
11 X 13
foyer
br.2
11 X 12-6
br.3
12 X 10-10
laundry
garage
21-8 X 21
WIDTH 62'-5"
DEPTH 87'-4"
MAIN FLOOR

Easy Street

Design by Fillmore Design Group

■ *Total living area 2,370 sq. ft.* ■ *Price Code D* ■

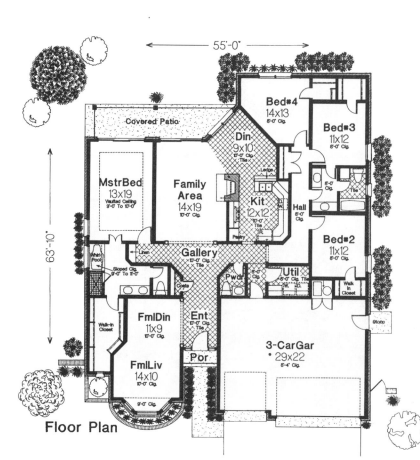

Floor Plan

No. 98572

■ This plan features:

— Four bedrooms

— Two full and one half baths

■ The private Master Suite features a whirlpool Bath and a vaulted ceiling

■ The three secondary Bedrooms have walk-in closets and share a Full Bath

■ The adjoining formal Dining and Living Rooms are enhanced by the bay window

■ The Family Room has a fireplace and opens to the informal Dining Room

■ The Garage Entry is convenient to the Laundry Room and the Kitchen

■ No materials list is available for this plan

Main floor — 2,370 sq. ft.
Garage — 638 sq. ft.

Windows Brighten Rooms

Total living area 2,392 sq. ft. ■ Price Code D

No. 82088

■ This plan features:

– Four bedrooms

– Two full and one half baths

■ Columns separate the Foyer and the Dining Room

■ The Great Room has a fireplace

■ The Kitchen has an eating bar/island

■ The Master Suite has two walk-in closets and a deluxe Bath

■ There is a large storage space in the Garage

■ An optional slab or crawl space foundation — please specify when ordering

■ No materials list is available for this plan

Main floor — 2,392 sq. ft.
Garage — 427 sq. ft.

MAIN FLOOR

Charming Home

Design by Studer Residential Design, Inc.

■ *Total living area 2,396 sq. ft.* ■ *Price Code D* ■

FIRST FLOOR

53'4"

37'8"

Deck

Breakfast
12'2" x 11'

Laun.

Family Room
18'3" x 15'4"

Kitchen
12' x 10'6"

Two-car Garage
21' x 20'5"

stairs up

Hall

Dining Room
12'2" x 13'2"

Living Room
11'4" x 15'6"

Foyer

Porch

No. 97739

■ **This plan features:**

— Four bedrooms

— Two full and one half baths

■ The covered Porch adds charm to the exterior

■ The Living Room has a lovely boxed window

■ The Kitchen is convenient to both Dining Areas

■ The Family Room has a fireplace and access to the rear Deck

■ There is storage space in the rear of the Garage

■ The Master Bedroom has a decorative ceiling and a private Bath

■ No materials list is available for this plan

First floor — 1,244 sq. ft.
Second floor — 1,152 sq. ft.
Basement — 1,244 sq. ft.
Garage — 484 sq. ft.

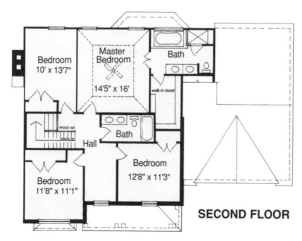

SECOND FLOOR

Bedroom
10' x 13'7"

Master
Bedroom
14'5" x 16'

Bath

walk-in closet

wood rail

Bath

Hall

Bedroom
12'8" x 11'3"

Bedroom
11'8" x 11'1"

216

Design by Studer Residential Design, Inc.

Beautiful Brick

Total living area   2,397 sq. ft.   ■   Price Code D

No. 97725

■ **This plan features:**

— Three bedrooms

— Two full and one half baths

■ Sidelights and an arched window frame the elegant entrance to this home

■ The Great Room has a fireplace and wall of windows

■ The Kitchen has a work island and is conveniently located between both Dining Areas

■ The Master Bedroom is privately located

■ The Loft upstairs is a perfect place for a computer

■ No materials list is available for this plan

First floor — 1,730 sq. ft.
Second floor — 667 sq. ft.
Bonus — 237 sq. ft.
Basement — 1,730 sq. ft.
Garage — 420 sq. ft.

FIRST FLOOR

SECOND FLOOR

217

Elegant Brick Two-Story

Design by Corley Plan Service

■ *Total living area 2,398 sq. ft.* ■ *Price Code D* ■

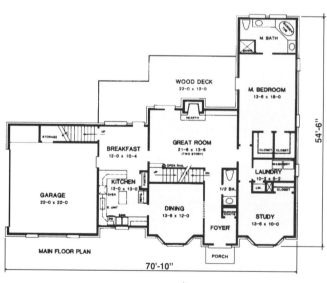

No. 90450

■ This plan features:

- Four bedrooms
- Two full and one half baths
- ■ The large two-story Great Room has a fireplace and access to a Deck
- ■ The secluded Master Suite has two walk-in closets and a lavish Bath
- ■ The large Kitchen has a center island and opens to the formal Dining Room and the Breakfast Nook
- ■ The optional Bonus Room has a private staircase
- ■ An optional basement or crawl space foundation — please specify when ordering

Main floor — 1,637 sq. ft.
Second floor — 761 sq. ft.
Bonus — 453 sq. ft.

Eye-Catching Turret

■ *Total living area 2,403 sq. ft.* ■ *Price Code D* ■

No. 9265 I

■ This plan features:

- Four bedrooms

- Three full and one half baths

- The Foyer opens to the Great Room with a high ceiling, hearth fireplace and atrium door to the backyard

- Columns frame the entrance to the Dining Room

- The Kitchen features a Pantry, a work island and the Breakfast Area, and is near the Laundry Room and Garage entry

- The private Master Bedroom has a Sitting Area, a walk-in closet, and a deluxe Bath

- No materials list is available for this plan

First floor — 1,710 sq. ft.
Second floor — 693 sq. ft.
Basement — 1,620 sq. ft.
Garage — 467 sq. ft.

FIRST FLOOR

SECOND FLOOR

Hip and Valley Style Roof

Design by The Garlinghouse Company

Total living area 2,411 sq. ft. ■ Price Code D

No. 24262

This plan features:

— Four bedrooms

— Two full and one half baths

■ A see-through fireplace is between the Living Room and the Family Room

■ The gourmet Kitchen has a center island, built-in Pantry, double sink and is open to the Eating Nook

■ The Master Bedroom has a vaulted ceiling and a deluxe Bath

■ The three additional Bedrooms share a double vanity Bath

First floor — 1,241 sq. ft.
Second floor — 1,170 sq. ft.
Garage — 500 sq. ft.

Design by Fillmore Design Group

One Level Luxury

Total living area 2,416 sq. ft. ■ Price Code D

No. 98566 BL

This plan features:

– Four bedrooms

– Three full baths

■ The spacious Master Suite is privately located and has a plush Spa Bath, an enormous walk-in closet, a Dressing Area and direct access to the Patio

■ The Kitchen has a center work island and is convenient to both Dining Areas

■ The Family Room is highlighted by a cathedral ceiling and a fireplace

■ An optional slab or crawl space foundation — please specify when ordering

■ No materials list is available for this plan

Main floor – 2,416 sq. ft.
Garage – 432 sq. ft.
Porch – 425 sq. ft.

Main Floor

Sunken Great Room

Design by Nelson Design Group

© Michael E. Nelson

■ Total living area 2,422 sq. ft. ■ Price Code D ■

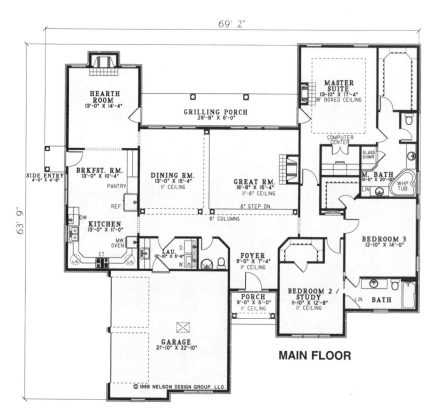

MAIN FLOOR

© 1998 NELSON DESIGN GROUP, LLC.

No. 82089

■ **This plan features:**

— Three bedrooms

— Two full and one half baths

■ Columns separate the Great Room and the formal Dining Room from the Foyer

■ The Kitchen opens to the Breakfast Room and the Hearth Room for a spacious informal Living Area

■ A Computer Center has been placed in the Master Suite

■ The two additional Bedrooms have large walk-in closets and share a full Bath

■ An optional basement, slab, or crawl space foundation — please specify when ordering

■ No materials list is available for this plan

Main floor — 2,422 sq. ft.
Garage — 499 sq. ft.

Design by Nelson Design Group

Walk-In Pantry

Total living area 2,425 sq. ft. ■ Price Code

No. 82090 BL

This plan features:

- Four bedrooms

- Two full baths

- The Living and Dining Rooms are traditionally located

- The Great Room includes a built-in media center

- The Kitchen shares an eating bar with the Breakfast Area

- The Master Suite a huge walk-in closet

- The rear secondary Bedroom would make a great Office

- An optional basement, slab, or crawl space foundation — please specify when ordering

- No materials list is available for this plan

Main floor — 2,425 sq. ft.
Garage — 441 sq. ft.

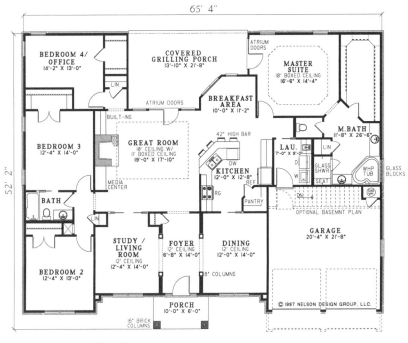

MAIN FLOOR

223

Stucco & Stone

Design by Frank Betz Associates, Inc.

■ *Total living area 2,425 sq. ft.* ■ *Price Code E* ■

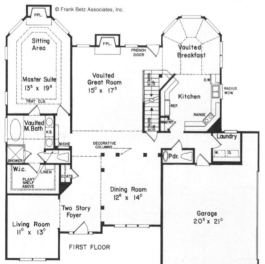

© Frank Betz Associates, Inc.

WIDTH 54'-0"
DEPTH 53'-10"

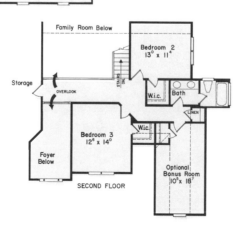

No. 98419

■ **This plan features:**

— Three bedrooms

— Two full and one half baths

■ The Great Room is highlighted by a fireplace, a vaulted ceiling and French doors to the rear yard

■ The Breakfast Area is crowned by a vaulted ceiling

■ A tray ceiling tops the Master Bedroom and Sitting Area and a vaulted ceiling crowns the Master Bath

■ Please specify a basement, crawl space or slab foundation when ordering

■ No material list is available for this plan

First floor — 1,796 sq. ft.
Second floor — 629 sq. ft.
Bonus — 208 sq. ft.
Basement — 1,796 sq. ft.
Garage — 588 sq. ft.

Design by Nelson Design Group

Modern Floor Plan

■ *Total living area 2,439 sq. ft.* ■ *Price Code D* ■

No. 82091 **BL**

■ This plan features:

- Four bedrooms

- Three full baths

- The Foyer and the Gallery area are enhanced by columns defining the Dining Room and the entrance to the Great Room

- French doors provide access to the Study which has lovely decorative window

- A double-sided fireplace and an open layout highlight the Family Room, the breakfast Room and the Kitchen

- The private Master Suite features a deluxe Bath

- Two secondary Bedrooms have private access to a full Bath

- No materials list is available for this plan

Main floor — 2,439 sq. ft.

MAIN FLOOR

225

Stylish Two-Story

Design by Living Concepts

■ *Total living area 2,443 sq. ft.* ■ *Price Code D* ■

PATIO

MASTER SUITE
14'-6" x 14'-0"

BREAKFAST
11'-8" x 9'-4"

FAMILY ROOM
20'-6" x 15'-4"

KITCHEN
13'-0" x 15'-2"

W.I.C

W.I.C

UP

P.

MASTER BATH

FOYER

DINING ROOM
12'-6" x 12'-6"

PDR.

LAUNDRY

**WIDTH 55'-10"
DEPTH 63'-6"**

FIRST FLOOR

GARAGE
20'-10" x 22'-6"

SUITE 2
11'-8" x 14'-8"

OPEN TO BELOW

LIN.

BATH

LOFT

DN

UNFIN. STOR.
9'-6" x 10'-6"

SUITE 3
10'-10" x 12'-6"

W.I.C

BATH

DN

SECOND FLOOR

BONUS ROOM
11'-0" x 17'-8"

No. 96919

■ **This plan features:**

— Three bedrooms

— Three full and one half baths

■ An arched, covered entry leads through double doors into the Foyer

■ The Dining Room is highlighted by a triple window

■ The Master Suite features two walk-in closets, two vanities and patio access

■ The large Family Room opens to the Kitchen and the Patio

■ The Breakfast Area overlooks the rear yard

■ No materials list is available for this plan

First floor — 1,758 sq. ft.
Second floor — 685 sq. ft.
Bonus — 260 sq. ft.
Garage — 515 sq. ft.

Design by Nelson Design Group

Built In's

Total living area 2,444 sq. ft. ■ Price Code D ■

No. 82092 BL

This plan features:

- Three bedrooms

- Two full and one half baths

- A bay window fronts the study

- Built-ins flank the fireplace in the Great Room

- A walk-in Pantry is located next to the Kitchen

- There are two walk-in closets and a whirlpool tub in the Master Suite

- A built-in desk is set between closets in Bedroom one

- No materials list is available for this plan

Main floor — 2,444 sq. ft.

MAIN FLOOR

Efficient Floor Plan

Design by Studer Residential Design, Inc.

Total living area 2,453 sq. ft. ■ *Price Code D* ■

53'-0"

Deck

Breakfast
13'-6" X 10'-2"

Great Room
16'-2" X 19'-3"

Kitchen
16'-2" X 11'-6"

Bath Laun.

Hall

42'-0"

Library
11'-0" X 12'-8"

Foyer

STAIR UP   STAIR DN.

Dining
Room
11'-8" X 15'-6"

Garage
20'-8" X 28'-4"

Porch

First Floor Plan

Master
Bedroom
14'-0" X 15'-10"

Bedroom
11'-3" X 13'-4"

Bath

Bath

Balcony

Bedroom /
Bonus Rm.
18'-0" X 15'-0"

Foyer
Below

STAIR DN.

Bedroom
11'-8" X 13'-2"

Second Floor Plan

No. 97728

■ This plan features:

— Three bedrooms

— Two full and one half baths

■ The Library is located in a quiet corner of the home

■ Triple arched windows brighten the Dining Room

■ Only columns separate the main living areas

■ The Kitchen has an island serving bar and Deck access

■ The Master Bath has a whirlpool tub and a large walk-in closet

■ There is a Bonus Room over the Garage

■ No materials list is available for this plan

First floor — 1,411 sq. ft.
Second floor — 1,042 sq. ft.
Bonus — 331 sq. ft.
Basement — 1,411 sq. ft.
Garage — 473 sq. ft.

Design by Patrick Morabito A.I.A.

■ *Total living area 2,457 sq. ft.* ■ *Price Code D* ■

No. 93341

■ This plan features:

– Three bedrooms

– Two full and one half baths

■ The Living Room is accented by a tray ceiling, a boxed window and pocket doors to the Family Room

■ The comfortable Family Room has a cozy fireplace and Deck access

■ The open Kitchen has a cooktop island, a peninsula counter/snack bar, a bright Dinette Area, and is near the Dining Room

■ The Master Bedroom has a plush Bath and a roomy, walk-in closet

■ No materials list is available for this plan

First floor — 1,430 sq. ft.
Second floor — 1,027 sq. ft.
Garage — 528 sq. ft.
Basement — 1,430 sq. ft.

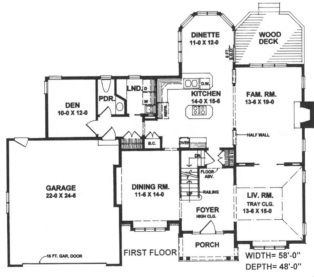

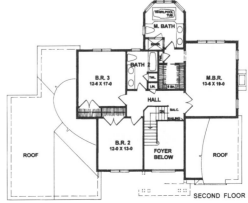

Luxurious Living

Design by Living Concepts

No. 96918 BL

■ **This plan features:**

— Four bedrooms

— Two full and one half baths

■ The Dining Room is separated from the Foyer and the Living Room by columns

■ The Living Room has a rear wall fireplace

■ The Kitchen has an island with a cooktop and a peninsula serving counter

■ The Master Bedroom has a tray ceiling, a plush bath and a walk-in closet

■ The Bonus Room upstairs would make a great playroom

■ No materials list is available for this plan

■ An optional basement, or crawl space foundation — please specify when ordering

First floor — 1,737 sq. ft.
Second floor — 727 sq. ft.
Bonus — 376 sq. ft.
Garage — 534 sq. ft.
Basement — 1,737 sq. ft.

Total living area 2,464 sq. ft. ■ Price Code D

FIRST FLOOR

SECOND FLOOR

WIDTH 65'-6"
DEPTH 53'-0"

Attention to Details

Design by Frank Betz Associates, Inc.

No. 97230 BL

■ **This plan features:**

— Four bedrooms

— Two full and one half baths

■ Exquisite attention to detail is evident on the front elevation

■ The Foyer leads into the open layout of the Dining and Living Rooms

■ French doors lead into the vaulted Sitting Room and the Master Suite beyond

■ The Family Room has a rear wall fireplace set between windows

■ The Kitchen shares a serving bar with the Breakfast Area

■ Upstairs are three Bedrooms, all with walk-in closets

■ No materials list is available for this plan

■ An optional basement, slab or crawl space foundation — please specify when ordering

First floor — 1,750 sq. ft.
Second floor — 718 sq. ft.
Bonus — 294 sq. ft.
Basement — 1,750 sq. ft.
Garage — 440 sq. ft.

Total living area 2,468 sq. ft. ■ Price Code D

FIRST FLOOR

SECOND FLOOR

Design by Ahmann Design

No. 97132 BL

This plan features:

- Three bedrooms

- Two full and one half baths

- The Great Room is accented by a fireplace

- The screened Porch off the Nook creates a private area for relaxing

- The Master Suite is your private retreat with two generous walk-in closets, a Spa tub, and a dual vanity

- The spacious Kitchen with a peninsula counter/serving bar makes meal prep a breeze

- Two additional Bedrooms, one with a walk-in closet, the other with a cathedral ceiling, share a full Bath with a linen closet

- Other amenities include a Powder Room, main floor Laundry Room and an attached three-car Garage with steps leading to the Basement

- No materials list is available for this plan

First floor – 2,469 sq. ft.

Perfect for Family Gatherings

■ Total living area 2,469 sq. ft. ■ Price Code D ■

MAIN FLOOR

Design by Design Basics, Inc.

No. 94940 BL

This plan features:

– Four bedrooms

– Two full and one half baths

- This impressive elevation masterfully combines brick and wood

- The highlight of the sixteen-foot high Entry is an angled staircase

- The formal Living and Dining Rooms are ideal for entertaining with tapered columns and decorative windows

- The ideal Kitchen has a work island, adjoins the Breakfast Area and the Family Room beyond

- The double door entrance into the Master Bedroom Suite creates an elegant feeling that continues into the plush Bath

First floor — 1,369 sq. ft.
Second floor — 1,111 sq. ft.
Basement — 1,369 sq. ft.
Garage — 716 sq. ft.

Magnificent Elevation

■ Total living area 2,480 sq. ft. ■ Price Code D ■

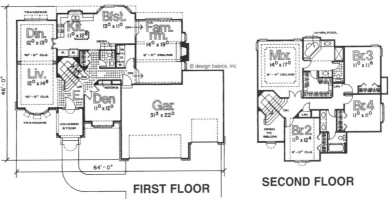

FIRST FLOOR   **SECOND FLOOR**

Grand Styling

Design by Frank Betz Associates, Inc.

No. 97255 BL

This plan features:

— Four bedrooms

— Two full and one half baths

■ The formal Dining and Living Room are located to either side of the Foyer

■ The Family Room, Breakfast Room, and Kitchen are laid out to create an open feeling

■ There is a fireplace in the Family Room and a serving bar between the Kitchen and the Breakfast Room

■ The Master Suite includes a walk-in closet, a vaulted ceiling over the plush bath, and a cozy Sitting Room

■ The three additional Bedrooms are roomy and share the full Bath in the hall

■ An optional basement or crawl space foundation — please specify when ordering

■ No materials list is available for this plan

First floor — 1,205 sq. ft.
Second floor — 1,277 sq. ft.
Basement — 1,128 sq. ft.
Garage — 528 sq. ft.

Total living area 2,482 sq. ft. ■ Price Code D

FIRST FLOOR PLAN

SECOND FLOOR

A Bold Statement

Design by Frank Betz Associates, Inc.

No. 97223 BL

This plan features:

— Four bedrooms

— Two full and one half baths

■ The dramatic exterior creates a bold architectural statement

■ The Living Room and the Entry are separated by columns with a plant shelf above

■ The Dining Room has a bright front window

■ A fireplace warms the large Family Room

■ The Kitchen is separated from the Nook by a serving counter

■ The expansive Master Suite is comprised of a Bedroom, a Sitting Room, and a vaulted Master Bath

■ Three additional large Bedrooms, on the second floor, share a full bath with three vanities

■ No materials list is available for this plan

First floor — 1,192 sq. ft.
Second floor — 1,301 sq. ft.
Basement — 1,192 sq. ft.
Garage — 487 sq. ft.

Total living area 2,493 sq. ft. ■ Price Code D

SECOND FLOOR

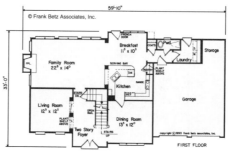

FIRST FLOOR

Design by Nelson Design Group

No. 82095

This plan features:

— One bedroom

— One full and two half baths

- There is plenty of living space outdoors on the covered Porches

- The Living and Dining Rooms have fireplaces

- There is a conveniently planned Kitchen

- The Breakfast Room has a wall of windows

- The upstairs may be used for many purposes

- The Master Suite has two walk in closets

- No materials list is available for this plan

First floor — 1,786 sq. ft.
Second floor — 715 sq. ft.

Tin Roof

Total living area 2,501 sq. ft. ■ Price Code D

SECOND FLOOR

FIRST FLOOR

Design by Nelson Design Group

No. 82096

This plan features:

— Four bedrooms

— Two full baths

- This home has three separate covered Porches

- The Kitchen has plenty of work space

- Optional French doors turn a Bedroom into the Study

- The other secondary Bedrooms have walk-in closets

- The Garage has plenty of Storage Space

- The Master Bedroom has a plush Bath

- No materials list is available for this plan

Main floor — 2,502 sq. ft.

Covered Porches

Total living area 2,502 sq. ft. ■ Price Code D

MAIN FLOOR

One-Level Living

■ *Total living area 2,504 sq. ft.* ■ *Price Code D* ■

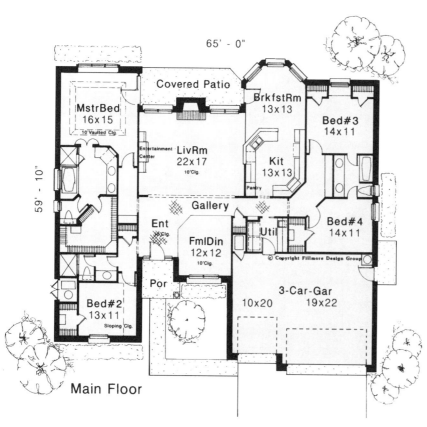

Main Floor

No. 98558 BL

■ This plan features:

— Four bedrooms

— Two full and one three-quarter baths

■ This home has a three-car Garage

■ The formal Dining Room is located off the Entry

■ The Living Room has a built-in entertainment center

■ The Breakfast Room has access to the covered Patio

■ Bedroom two could be a great Guest Room

■ The Master Bedroom has plenty of privacy and room

■ No materials list is available for this plan

Main floor — 2,504 sq. ft.
Garage — 622 sq. ft.

Design by Larry E. Belk

Open Concept Floor Plan

■ *Total living area 2,511 sq. ft.* ■ *Price Code D* ■

No. 93050 **BL**

■ This plan features:

— Four bedrooms

— Two full and one half baths

■ The Kitchen, Breakfast Room and the Family Room are open to one another

■ The well-appointed Kitchen includes ample cabinet space and a serving counter

■ The expansive Living Room has backyard views and opens to the Dining Room

■ Two additional Bedrooms with walk-in closets, share a full Bath in the hall

■ The private Master Bedroom Suite has a whirlpool tub

■ No materials list is available for this plan

Main floor — 2,511 sq. ft.
Garage — 469 sq. ft.

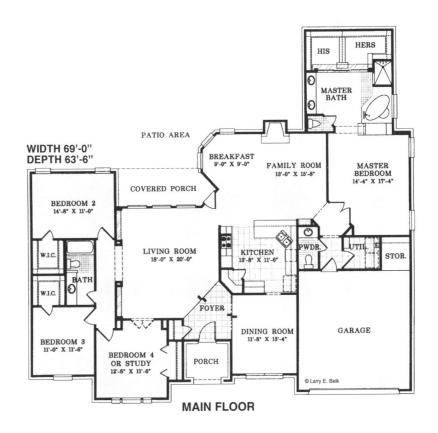

WIDTH 69'-0"
DEPTH 63'-6"

PATIO AREA

BREAKFAST 9'-0" X 9'-0"

FAMILY ROOM 13'-0" X 15'-8"

MASTER BEDROOM 14'-4" X 17'-4"

HIS   HERS

MASTER BATH

COVERED PORCH

BEDROOM 2 14'-8" X 11'-0"

W.I.C.

BATH

W.I.C.

LIVING ROOM 18'-0" X 20'-0"

KITCHEN 13'-8" X 11'-6"

PWDR.

UTIL.

STOR.

FOYER

BEDROOM 3 11'-0" X 11'-6"

BEDROOM 4 OR STUDY 12'-6" X 11'-6"

PORCH

DINING ROOM 11'-8" X 13'-4"

GARAGE

© Larry E. Belk

MAIN FLOOR

Sunroom in the Rear

Design by Nelson Design Group

© Michael E. Nelson
NELSON DESIGN GROUP, LLC

■ Total living area 2,525 sq. ft. ■ Price Code D ■

No. 82097 BL

■ This plan features:

— Three bedrooms

— Two full and one half baths

■ Columns separate the Foyer and the gallery from the formal spaces

■ The Great Room has a fireplace set between built-ins

■ French doors open from the Sun Room to the Grilling Porch

■ The Laundry Room has an area for sewing

■ The ideal Kitchen includes a work island, a serving bar and the Breakfast/Hearth Room

■ No materials list is available for this plan

■ An optional basement, slab or crawl space foundation — please specify when ordering

Main floor — 2,525 sq. ft.
Garage — 537 sq. ft.

MAIN FLOOR

Cozy Yet Spacious

Total living area 2,526 sq. ft. ■ *Price Code D* ■

No. 98576 **BL**

This plan features:

- Four bedrooms

- Three full baths

■ An easy care brick floor starts in the Entry and continues in the Gallery area, the Laundry, the Kitchen and the Dining Room

■ The formal Dining and Living Rooms are open to each other for easy traffic flow

■ The Master Bedroom is topped by a vaulted ceiling and has access to a Covered Patio

■ The Master Bath features a whirlpool tub and a large walk-in closet

■ No materials list is available for this plan

Main floor — 2,526 sq. ft.
Garage — 720 sq. ft.

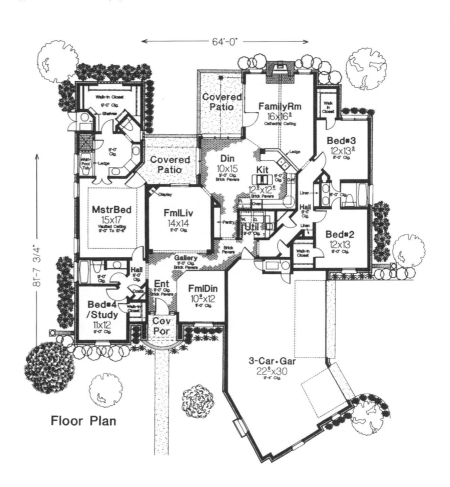

Floor Plan

Unique Texture

Design by Fillmore Design Group

Total living area 2,538 sq. ft. ■ Price Code E

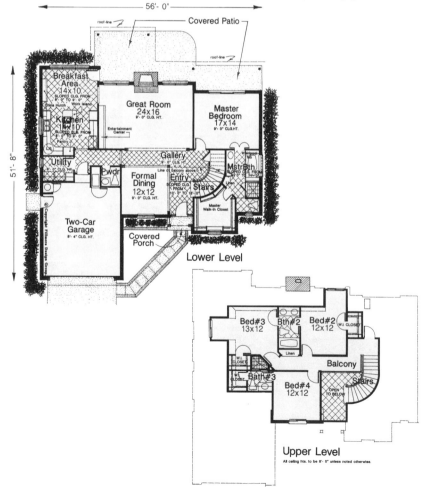

Lower Level

Upper Level

All ceiling hts. to be 8'- 0" unless noted otherwise.

No. 97803

■ This plan features:

— Four bedrooms

— Two full, one three quarter and one half baths

■ Varying exterior materials add a unique texture to the home

■ Columns separate the Dining Room from the Entry and the Gallery

■ The Great Room has a built-in entertainment center

■ The Kitchen has many built-in conveniences

■ The Master Bedroom has a room-sized walk-in closet

■ The secondary Bedrooms are located upstairs

■ No materials list is available for this plan

Lower level — 1,719 sq. ft.
Upper level — 819 sq. ft.
Garage — 470 sq. ft.

Narrow Lot Home

■ Total living area 2,561 sq. ft. ■ Price Code D ■

No. 97729 BL

■ This plan features:

— Four bedrooms

— Two full and one half baths

■ The Garage is located in the rear

■ A Porch wraps around the home in the front

■ The Parlor features a wonderful alcove

■ The Kitchen is convenient to all the Dining Areas

■ The Great Room has a corner fireplace

■ The sleeping quarters are all upstairs

■ No materials list is available for this plan

Main floor — 1,331 sq. ft.
Upper floor — 1,230 sq. ft.
Garage — 514 sq. ft.

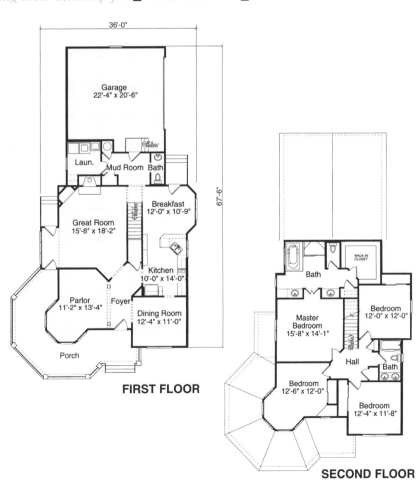

FIRST FLOOR

SECOND FLOOR

239

Dignified Family Home

Design by The Garlinghouse Company

■ *Total living area 2,578 sq. ft.* ■ *Price Code D* ■

No. 24653 **BL**

■ This plan features:

— Three bedrooms

— Two full and one half baths

■ This beautiful elevation has multi-paned windows and an arched entrance

■ The formal Living Room adjoins the formal Dining Room

■ The U-shaped Kitchen is equipped with a built-in Pantry, a built-in planning desk and work island

■ Two additional Bedrooms share a full Bath

■ A Bonus Room is available for future needs

■ No materials list is available for this plan

First floor — 1,245 sq. ft.
Second floor — 1,333 sq. ft.
Bonus room — 192 sq. ft.
Garage — 650 sq. ft.
Basement — 1,245 sq. ft.

Crawl Space/
Slab Option

First Floor

Second Floor

A View to the Side

Total living area 2,579 sq. ft. ■ *Price Code D* ■

No. 93708

This plan features:

- Three/Four bedrooms
- Three full and one half baths
- This design is for a homesite with a view to the side, and perfect for entertaining as well as everyday living
- The domed Foyer has French doors leading to the private Study or guest Bedroom which has a vaulted ceiling and built-ins
- The sunken Great Room has a tray ceiling punctuated by arches and columns, and an inviting fireplace
- The Breakfast Room, with an optional planning desk, opens to the Kitchen via a serving bar
- No materials list is available for this plan

Main floor — 2,579 sq. ft.
Garage — 536 sq. ft.

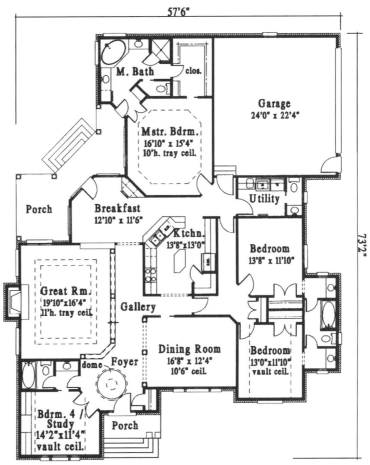

Main Level Floor Plan

With Room for All

■ *Total living area 2,606 sq. ft.* ■ *Price Code E* ■

MAIN FLOOR

BONUS

No. 61015

■ This plan features:

— Four bedrooms

— Two full and one half baths

■ Two large walk-in closets and a lavish Bath highlight the Master Suite

■ High ceilings add volume to the Great Room, the Dining Room, the Foyer and the Study

■ Columns define the Dining Room from the Foyer and the Great Room

■ A corner fireplace and French doors accent the Great Room

■ An optional basement, slab or crawl space foundation — please specify when ordering

■ No materials list is available for this plan

Main floor — 2,606 sq. ft.
Bonus — 751 sq. ft.
Garage/storage — 534 sq. ft.

Design by Larry E. Belk

The English Countryside

■ *Total living area 2,611 sq. ft.* ■ *Price Code D* ■

No. 93099

■ This plan features:

- Four bedrooms

- Three full baths

■ This beautiful manor house looks to be straight from the English Countryside

■ From the Foyer there are arched entrances into the Dining Room and the Great Room

■ The secluded Master Suite offers a plush Bath and a large walk-in closet

■ The Breakfast Room shares a see-through fireplace with the Great Room

■ Upstairs are two Bedrooms, a Bath, and a large Bonus Space

■ No materials list is available for this plan

First floor — 2,050 sq. ft.
Second floor — 561 sq. ft.
Bonus — 272 sq. ft.
Garage — 599 sq. ft.

WIDTH 64-10

MASTER BEDRM
13-4 X 16-4
10 FT TRAY CLG

BRKFST RM
11-4 X 13-0
10 FT TRAY CLG

PORCH

KITCHEN
16-6 X 13-4
9 FT CLG

GREAT ROOM
17-4 X 20-4
10 FT TRAY CLG

MASTER BATH

LIN

DESK

LIN

PAN

BATH 2

STORAGE

UTIL
11-4 X 6-0
9 FT CLG

ARCH

BEDROOM 2
12-6 X 13-6
9 FT CLG

GARAGE

DINING ROOM
12-6 X 15-4
10 FT CLG

FOYER
2 STORY CLG

ARCH

DEPTH 64-0

COPYRIGHT LARRY E. BELK

PORCH

FIRST FLOOR

BEDROOM 4
13-4 X 10-4

EXPANDABLE
17-4 X 18-0

LIN

BATH 3

UP

BEDROOM 3
13-0 X 11-6

OPEN TO FOYER BELOW

PLANT LEDGE

SECOND FLOOR

243

Vintage America

Design by Larry E. Belk

Total living area 2,615 sq. ft. ■ Price Code E ■

No. 93092

■ This plan features:

— Four bedrooms

— Two full and one half baths

■ The wide front Porch and triple dormers frame the front of the home

■ The huge Great Room opens through classic arches to the Kitchen and the Breakfast Room

■ The Kitchen has all the amenities, including a work island with a cooktop and an eating bar

■ All the upstairs Bedrooms feature picturesque dormer windows, perfect for a window seat or toy box

■ No materials list is available for this plan

First floor — 1,785 sq. ft.
Second floor — 830 sq. ft.
Bonus room — 280 sq. ft.
Garage — 583 sq. ft.

Design by Donald A. Gardner Architects, Inc.

Dynamic Floor Plan

© 1994 Donald A. Gardner Architects, Inc.
B. NATHAN

Total living area 2,625 sq. ft. ■ Price Code F

No. 99839

This plan features:

— Four bedrooms

— Two full and one half baths

■ Elegant columns separate the Great Room from the spacious, angled Kitchen

■ The Great Room accesses the covered Porch and the Deck beyond

■ The Master Suite features a well-appointed Bath with a skylit whirlpool tub

■ The front Bedroom may be used as a Study

■ The Bonus Room over the Garage adds more flexibility

Main floor — 2,625 sq. ft.
Bonus room — 447 sq. ft.
Garage — 753 sq. ft.

FIRST FLOOR PLAN

© Donald A. Gardner Architects, Inc.

245

Colonial Styling

Design by Design Basics, Inc.

■ *Total living area 2,639 sq. ft.* ■ *Price Code C* ■

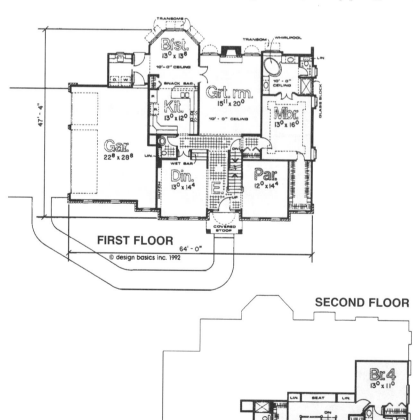

FIRST FLOOR
© design basics inc. 1992

SECOND FLOOR

No. 97412

■ This plan features:

— Four bedrooms

— Two full, one three-quarter and one half baths

■ Colonial styling on the outside contrasts with the thoroughly modern conveniences on the inside

■ The Dining Room has a hutch space and a wetbar

■ The Parlor may be used for formal entertaining or quiet time

■ The Kitchen has a smart arrangement and shares a snack bar with the Breakfast Area

■ The Master Bath has a whirlpool tub, and a large walk-in closet

■ All the upstairs Bedrooms have private access to a Bath

First floor — 1,865 sq. ft.
Second floor — 774 sq. ft.

Stately Elevation

© design basics inc.

■ *Total living area 2,655 sq. ft.* ■ *Price Code L* ■

No. 99448 BL X

■ This plan features:

— Four bedrooms

— Three full and one half baths

■ The tiled Entry provides access to the Dining Room, which features a decorative ceiling

■ The Great Room is the center of the home and has a fireplace nestled between decorative windows

■ The bright Breakfast Bay is a great place to start your day

■ The secluded Master Bedroom has a tray ceiling, a walk-in closet, a private covered Porch, and a whirlpool Bath

Main floor — 2,655 sq. ft.
Basement — 2,655 sq. ft.
Garage — 695 sq. ft.

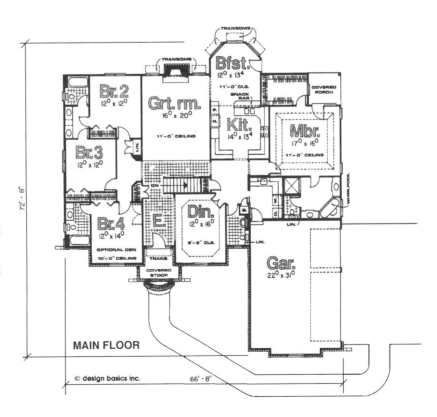

MAIN FLOOR

© design basics inc.   66' - 8"

Outstanding Elevation

Design by Living Concepts Home Planning

■ *Total living area 2,677 sq. ft.* ■ *Price Code E* ■

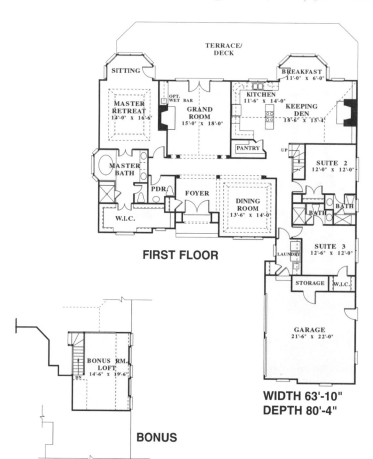

FIRST FLOOR

- TERRACE/DECK
- SITTING
- MASTER RETREAT 14'-0" x 16'-6"
- OPT. WET BAR
- GRAND ROOM 15'-0" x 18'-0"
- BREAKFAST 11'-0" x 6'-0"
- KITCHEN 11'-6" x 14'-0"
- KEEPING DEN 18'-6" x 15'-3"
- PANTRY
- MASTER BATH
- PDR.
- FOYER
- DINING ROOM 13'-6" x 14'-0"
- W.I.C.
- UP
- SUITE 2 12'-0" x 12'-0"
- BATH
- BATH
- SUITE 3 12'-6" x 12'-0"
- LAUNDRY
- STORAGE
- W.I.C.
- GARAGE 21'-6" x 22'-0"

BONUS

- BONUS RM. LOFT 14'-6" x 19'-6"
- DN

WIDTH 63'-10"
DEPTH 80'-4"

No. 96913

■ **This plan features:**

— Three bedrooms

— One full, two three quarter and one half baths

■ The open floor plan between the Keeping Room, the Breakfast Area and the Kitchen provides convenience

■ The large Terrace/Deck at the rear of the home expands living space outdoors

■ The Bonus Room loft stands ready for future needs

■ The Master Suite has outdoor access, tray ceiling, a plush Bath and a walk-in closet

■ No materials list is available for this plan

First floor — 2,677 sq. ft.
Bonus — 319 sq. ft.
Garage — 543 sq. ft.
Deck — 676 sq. ft.

Design by Larry E. Belk

A Classic Design

Total living area 2,678 sq. ft. ■ *Price Code E* ■

No. 96600

This plan features:

— Four bedrooms

— Two full and one half baths

■ An elegant, arched opening graces
the entrance of this classic design

■ The Kitchen, the Breakfast Room
and the Family Room open to one
another for easy living

■ The Kitchen includes a walk in
Pantry, double ovens and a
peninsula counter/serving bar

■ The Master Suite is set apart from
the other Bedrooms for privacy

■ Three additional Bedrooms share
a Bath and have walk-in closets

■ No materials list is available for
this plan

Main floor — 2,678 sq. ft
Garage — 474 sq. ft.

Fashionable Country Style

Design by Design Basics, Inc.

■ *Total living area 2,695 sq. ft.* ■ *Price Code E* ■

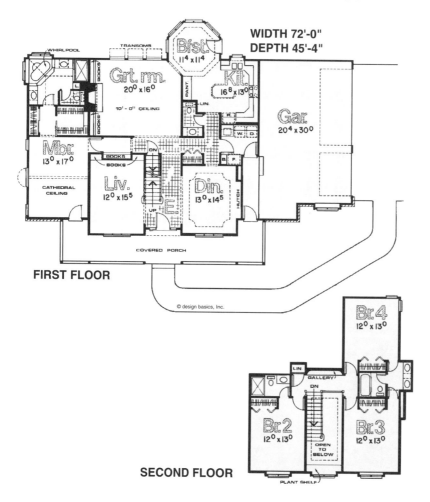

WIDTH 72'-0"
DEPTH 45'-4"

FIRST FLOOR

© design basics, inc.

SECOND FLOOR

No. 99450

■ **This plan features:**

— Four bedrooms

— Two full, one three quarter and one half baths

■ The Dining Room features a decorative ceiling and a built in Hutch

■ The Kitchen has a center island and a Breakfast Area

■ The Master Bedroom has a cathedral ceiling, a door to the front Porch, and a Bath with a whirlpool tub

■ Upstairs there are three additional Bedrooms and two Baths

■ An optional basement or slab foundation — please specify when ordering

First floor — 1,881 sq. ft.
Second floor — 814 sq. ft.
Garage — 534 sq. ft.
Basement — 1,020 sq. ft.

Design by Nelson Design Group

Island Kitchen

■ *Total living area 2,698 sq. ft.* ■ *Price Code E* ■

No. 61017 **BL**

■ **This plan features:**

– Four bedrooms

– Two full and one half baths

 The Kitchen has a walk in Pantry

■ A Storage Room is located off the Garage

■ The Breakfast Room overlooks the rear yard

■ The Master Bedroom has dual walk-in closets

■ Three secondary Bedrooms are located upstairs

■ No materials list is available for this plan

First floor — 1,813 sq. ft.
Second floor — 885 sq. ft.

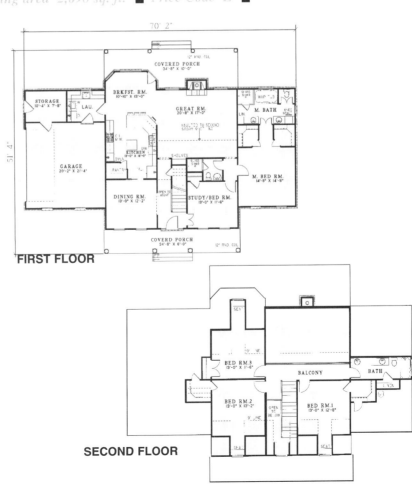

FIRST FLOOR

SECOND FLOOR

Covered Porch

Design by Ahmann Design, Inc.

■ *Total living area 2,717 sq. ft.* ■ *Price Code E* ■

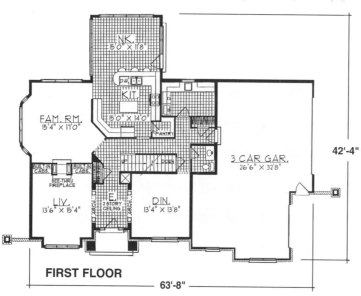

FIRST FLOOR

63'-8"

42'-4"

SECOND FLOOR

No. 97129 **BL**

■ **This plan features:**

— Three bedrooms

— Two full baths

■ The Family Room, with a see-through fireplace, provides a comfortable place for everyday activities

■ The Kitchen, with wrap-around counters and a work island, makes meal prep easy

■ The formal Living and Dining Rooms have graceful arches from the Entry

■ Upstairs, the Master Bedroom is your private retreat with two ample closets and a luxurious Spa tub

■ No materials list is available for this plan

First floor – 1,614 sq. ft.
Second floor – 1,103 sq. ft.

See Through Fireplace

© design basics, Inc.

■ *Total living area 2,727 sq. ft.* ■ *Price Code E* ■

No. 99435

This plan features:

- Four bedrooms

- Two full and one half baths

- The formal rooms have beautiful bay windows and flank the two-story Entry

- The Family Room has a wetbar and shares a see-through fireplace with the Kitchen/Breakfast Area

- The corner Master Bedroom has a large walk-in closet and a skylit Bath

- Upstairs, three secondary Bedrooms share a double vanity Bath and two linen closets

First floor — 1,392 sq. ft.
Second floor — 1,335 sq. ft.
Basement — 1,392 sq. ft.
Garage — 545 sq. ft.

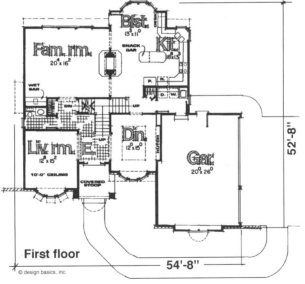

First floor

© design basics, inc.

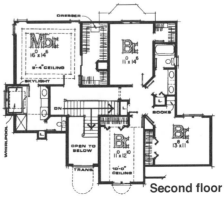

Second floor

Modern Elegance

Design by Frank Betz Associates, Inc

■ *Total living area 2,731 sq. ft.* ■ *Price Code E* ■

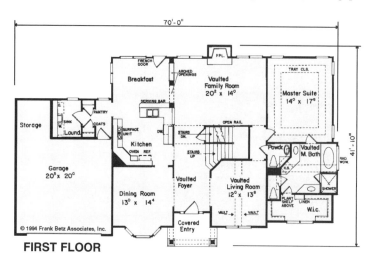

FIRST FLOOR

© 1994 Frank Betz Associates, Inc.

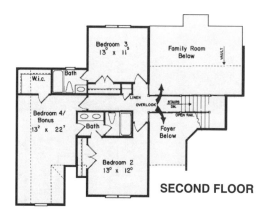

SECOND FLOOR

No. 97257

■ This plan features:

— Four bedrooms

— Three full and one half baths

■ The vaulted Family Room is highlighted by a fireplace with windows to either side

■ The Kitchen opens into the Breakfast Area with a serving bar

■ The Master Suite is topped by a tray ceiling in the Bedroom and a vaulted ceiling in the Bath

■ Two additional Bedrooms and the Bonus Room/Bedroom have private access to full Baths

■ An optional basement or crawl space foundation — please specify when ordering

■ No materials list is available for this plan

First floor — 1,809 sq. ft.
Second floor — 922 sq. ft.
Basement — 1,809 sq. ft.
Garage — 483 sq. ft.

Design by Living Concepts Home Planning

Traditional Style

■ *Total living area 2,741 sq. ft.* ■ *Price Code D* ■

No. 96912

This plan features:

- Four bedrooms

- Two full and one half baths

- The front Portico shelters the entry to the traditional Foyer

- The Dining Room opens into the Living Room

- The Library is in a quiet location

- Two separate staircases access the second floor and all the bedrooms

- The Laundry and the Bonus Room are located on the second floor

- No materials list is available for this plan

First floor — 1,426 sq. ft.
Second floor — 1,315 sq. ft.
Bonus — 200 sq. ft.
Garage — 508 sq. ft.

DECK

KITCHEN
13'-0" x 17'-6"

BREAKFAST
10'-0" x 13'-0"

FAMILY
ROOM
18'-0" x 14'-6"

DINING
ROOM
12'-0" x 14'-

PDR.

STOR.

LIVING
ROOM
12'-8" x 14'-0"

LIBRARY
11'-4" x 10'-2"

GARAGE
20'-6" x 20'-8"

FOYER

PORITICO

FIRST FLOOR

SUITE 2
12'-6" x 12'-0

BATH

W.I.C.

MASTER
BATH

MASTER
SUITE
19'-0" x 14'-6"

LIN.

SUITE 3
12'-8" x 11'-6

SUITE 4
11'-4" x 13'-4"

LAUN.

BONUS
ROOM
12'-2" x 14'-

OPEN
TO
BELOW

WIDTH 57'-8"
DEPTH 44'-10"

SECOND FLOOR

255

Enhanced by a Fireplace

Design by Design Basics, Inc.

■ *Total living area 2,741 sq. ft.* ■ *Price Code E* ■

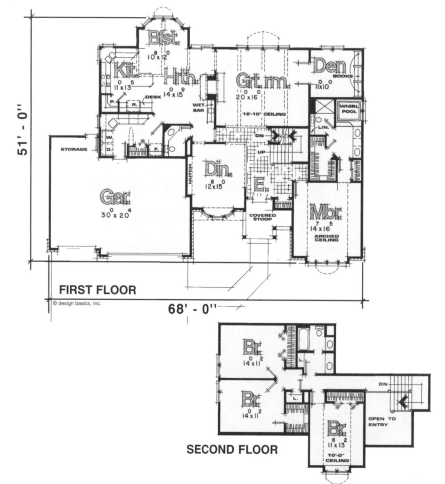

FIRST FLOOR

© design basics, Inc.

68' - 0"

51' - 0"

SECOND FLOOR

No. 94988

■ **This plan features:**

— Four bedrooms

— Two full and one half baths

■ A shared fireplace enhances the Great Room and the Hearth Room

■ A bow window and a hutch space distinguish the Dining Room

■ The Kitchen has plenty of counter space, a Breakfast and Hearth area, and an adjacent Laundry

■ The secluded Den has built-in bookcases

■ The large Master Bedroom is a luxurious retreat

■ Upstairs, find three additional large Bedrooms and a full Bath

First floor — 1,963 sq. ft.
Second floor — 778 sq. ft.
Basement — 1,963 sq. ft.
Garage — 658 sq. ft.

Breakfast Bar

Total living area 2,744 sq. ft. ■ *Price Code E*

No. 82093

This plan features:

- Four bedrooms

- Two full and one half baths

- Graceful French doors lead into the formal Living and dining Rooms from the Foyer

- A rear wall fireplace and covered Porch access accent the Great Room

- A long Breakfast Bar in the kitchen is terrific for quick meals

- The Laundry Room is in a great location

- The private Master Suite has a huge closet and a plush Master Bath

- No materials list is available for this plan

Main floor — 2,744 sq. ft.

MAIN FLOOR

European Influence

Design by Larry E. Belk

■ Total living area 2,745 sq. ft. ■ Price Code E ■

WIDTH 69-6

COVERED PORCH

FAMILY ROOM
15-4 X 16-0
12 FT VAULTED CLG

LIVING ROOM
17-0 X 16-0
12 FT CLG

BEDRM 4/STUDY
13-4 X 14-8
10 FT CLG

MASTER BEDROOM
15-4 X 15-4
12 FT TRAY CLG

MASTER BATH

BRKFST RM
15-4 X.7-6
12 FT VAULTED CLG

UP

DOWN

KITCHEN
15-4 X 16-4
10 FT CLG

DINING ROOM
12-8 X 14-4
12 FT CLG

FOYER
12 FT CLG

PWDR

BATH 2

DEPTH 76-6

UTIL

PAN

PORCH

BEDROOM 3
12-4 X 13-6
10 FT CLG

BEDROOM 2
12-8 X 12-6
10 FT CLG

COPYRIGHT LARRY E. BELK

GARAGE

MAIN FLOOR

No. 96602

■ **This plan features:**

— Four bedrooms

— Two full and one half baths

■ The old world Country French influence evident in this home

■ The Foyer opens to the well-proportioned Dining Room

■ Double French doors with transoms lead off the Living Room to the Covered Porch

■ The spacious Kitchen is adjacent to the Breakfast and Family Room

■ A see-thru fireplace is shared by the living Room and the Family Room

■ An optional basement, slab or crawl space foundation — please specify when ordering

■ No materials list is available for this plan

Main floor — 2,745 sq. ft.
Garage — 525 sq. ft.

Especially Unique

■ *Total living area 2,748 sq. ft.* ■ *Price Code E*

No. 98528

■ **This plan features:**

– Four bedrooms

– Three full and one half baths

■ The Study/Media Room just off the front Entry offers many options

■ The formal Dining Room is open to the Gallery, and the Living Room for ease in entertaining

■ The Family Room has a built-in entertainment center, a fireplace, and access to the rear Patio

■ The Master Bedroom is secluded, and has it's own fireplace, Bath, and walk-in closet

■ No materials list is available for this plan

Main floor — 2,748 sq. ft.
Garage — 660 sq. ft.

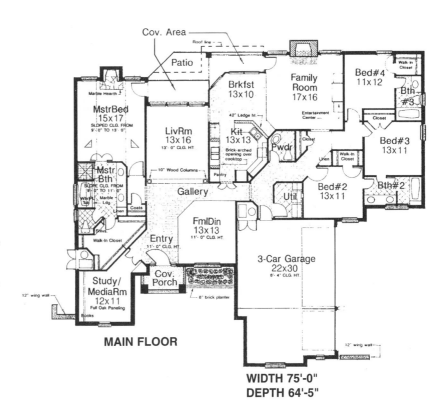

MAIN FLOOR

WIDTH 75'-0"
DEPTH 64'-5"

Past the Garden Gate

Design by Larry E. Belk

■ *Total living area 2,757 sq. ft.* ■ *Price Code E* ■

MAIN FLOOR

GARAGE

COPYRIGHT LARRY E. BELK

UTIL

PAN

KITCHEN
15-4 X 13-8
10 FT CLG

PORCH

MASTER
BATH
10 FT
CLG

K.S.

LIVING ROOM
17-0 X 16-4
12 FT CLG

BEDRM 4/STUDY
13-4 X 15-0
10 FT CLG

MASTER BEDROOM
15-6 X 15-0
12 FT TRAY CLG

DEPTH 68-8

42" LEDGE

BRKFST ROOM
15-4 X 9-4
14 FT CLG

UP→

←DOWN

BATH 2

SLOPE→

←SLOPE

DINING ROOM
12-4 X 14-4
12 FT CLG

FOYER
10 FT CLG

PWDR

FAMILY ROOM
15-4 X 14-0
14 FT CLG

PORCH

BEDROOM 3
12-4 X 12-8
10 FT CLG

BEDROOM 2
12-6 X 12-8
10 FT CLG

FP

WIDTH 69-6

No. 93097

■ **This plan features:**

— Four bedrooms

— Two full and one half baths

■ From the covered front Porch step through double doors into the Foyer

■ The Family Room and Breakfast Room are warmed by a fireplace and share a sloped ceiling

■ The Living Room has double French doors that open to the rear Porch

■ The Kitchen has a cooktop island, a serving bar and a built-in Pantry

■ No materials list is available for this plan

■ The pampering Master Bedroom has a huge Master Bath

Main floor — 2,757 sq. ft.
Garage — 484 sq. ft.

Definite Presence

■ *Total living area 2,764 sq. ft.* ■ *Price Code E* ■

No. 96911

■ This plan features:

— Four bedrooms

— Three full and one half baths

■ The pleasing exterior combines brick and various window styles

■ The Dining Room and Living Room are at the front of the home

■ The Master Suite offers a decorative ceiling, deck access and luxurious Master Bath

■ A fireplace is set between built-in bookcases in the Grand Room

■ The Kitchen has an angled serving bar

■ The second floor has three Bedrooms, all with walk-in closets

■ No materials list is available for this plan

First floor — 1,878 sq. ft.
Second floor — 886 sq. ft.
Basement — 942 sq. ft.
Garage — 593 sq. ft.

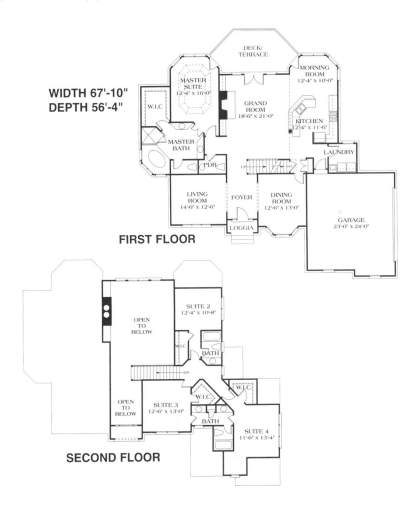

WIDTH 67'-10"
DEPTH 56'-4"

FIRST FLOOR

SECOND FLOOR

Impressive Presence

Design by Frank Betz Associates, Inc.

■ *Total living area 2,764 sq. ft.* ■ *Price Code E* ■

FIRST FLOOR

SECOND FLOOR

No. 97239

■ **This plan features:**

— Four bedrooms

— Three full and one half baths

■ The Living Room has a vaulted ceiling and a beautiful arched window

■ The Kitchen is open to the Breakfast Area and has loads of counter and storage space

■ The Master Suite is secluded behind the Garage on the first floor

■ An optional Bonus Room is located over the Garage

■ No materials list is available for this plan

■ An optional basement or crawlspace foundation — please specify when ordering

First floor — 1,904 sq. ft.
Second floor — 860 sq. ft.
Bonus — 388 sq. ft.

Ideal Family Home

■ *Total living area 2,771 sq. ft.* ■ *Price Code C*

No. 93609 **BL**

This plan features:

— Four bedrooms

— Two full and one half baths

■ From the two-story Foyer enter either the Living Room or the Dining Room

■ In the rear of the home there is the Grand Room and the Keeping Room both with fireplaces

■ The L-shaped Kitchen has a center work island and a walk-in Pantry

■ The second floor master bedroom has a spacious Sitting Area

■ No materials list is available for this plan

■ An optional basement or slab foundation — please specify when ordering

First floor — 1,534 sq. ft.
Second floor — 1,236 sq. ft.
Garage — 418 sq. ft.

© design basics inc.

■ *Total living area 2,775 sq. ft.* ■ *Price Code E* ■

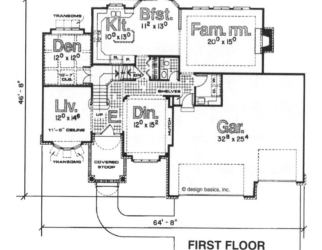

FIRST FLOOR

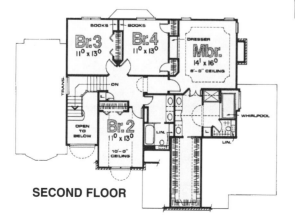

SECOND FLOOR

No. 99446

■ This plan features:

— Four bedrooms

— Two full and one half baths

■ The volume Living Room and formal Dining Room provide elegance with a large decorative window

■ The sensible and spacious Kitchen has a large Pantry, a work island and a Breakfast Area

■ The distinctive Master Suite is highlighted by a built-in dresser and a luxurious Bath with an arched opening to the whirlpool and shower area

First floor — 1,469 sq. ft.
Second floor — 1,306 sq. ft.
Basement — 1,469 sq. ft.
Garage — 814 sq. ft.

Adding Ease

■ *Total living area 2,788 sq. ft.* ■ *Price Code E* ■

No. 97130

■ This plan features:

— Three bedrooms

— Two full and one half baths

■ The Family Room has built-in cabinets next to the cozy fireplace

■ The den, with a built-in desk, is off the Family Room

■ The open Kitchen has ample counter space, a walk-in Pantry, an island Breakfast Bar, and a bright Nook for family meals

■ The formal Dining and Living Rooms provide an elegant atmosphere for entertaining

■ Three Bedrooms, one for the master and two Baths occupy the second floor

■ No materials list is available for this plan

First floor — 1,533 sq. ft.
Second floor — 1,255 sq. ft.
Basement — 1,533 sq. ft.

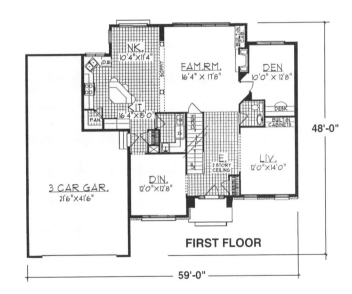

FIRST FLOOR

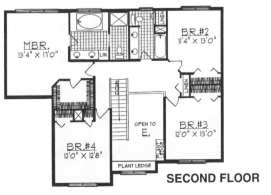

SECOND FLOOR

Streetside Charmer

Design by Fillmore Design Group

■ *Total living area 2,789 sq. ft.* ■ *Price Code E* ■

MAIN FLOOR

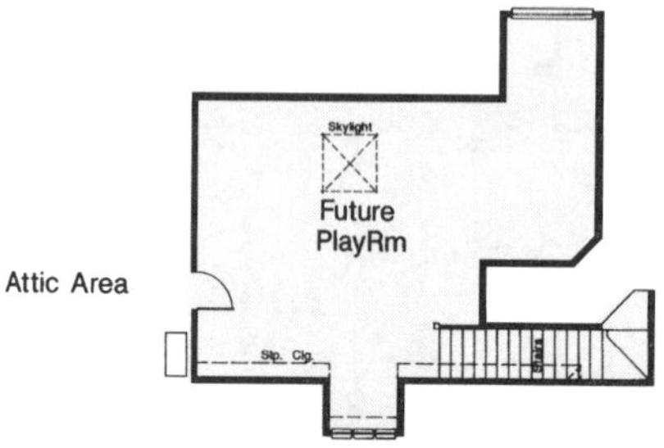

OPTIONAL PLAYROOM

No. 97804 BL

■ **This plan features:**

— Three bedrooms

— Three full baths

■ Gables, brick and fieldstone accent the exterior of this home

■ The open Dining Room is outlined by elegant columns

■ The open, angular Kitchen has a handy serving bar

■ The Study could also serve as a Guest Room

■ The Master Bedroom accesses the covered Patio

■ A Bonus Room is located on the second floor

■ No materials list is available for this plan

Main floor — 2,789 sq. ft.
Bonus — 637 sq. ft.
Garage — 632 sq. ft.

Design by Ahmann Design, Inc.

Family Togetherness

Total living area 2,798 sq. ft. ■ Price Code E ■

No. 97128 BL

This plan features:

- Four bedrooms

- Three full and one half baths

■ The airy Family Room has a cozy fireplace to gather around

■ The Kitchen has a center work island and a walk-in Pantry

■ The formal Dining and Living Rooms provide an elegant atmosphere for formal entertaining

■ Upstairs, the Master Bedroom has a generous walk-in closet and a Spa tub

■ Three additional Bedrooms have private access to a full Bath

■ No materials list is available for this plan

First floor — 1,492 sq. ft.
Second floor — 1,306 sq. ft.

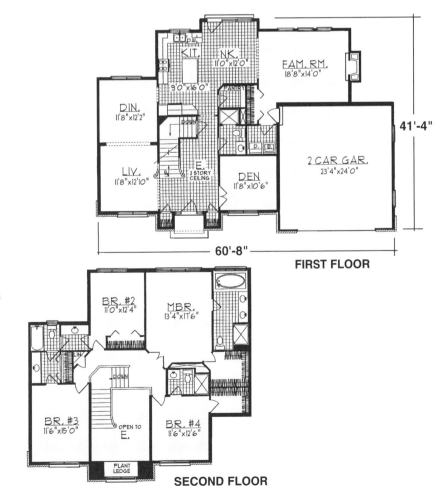

KIT.
NK.
11'0"x12'0"
FAM. RM.
18'8"x14'0"
9'0"x16'0"
DIN.
11'8"x12'2"
PANTRY
LIV.
11'8"x12'10"
2 STORY CEILING
DEN
11'8"x10'6"
2 CAR GAR.
23'4"x24'0"

41'-4"

60'-8"

FIRST FLOOR

BR. #2
11'0"x12'4"
MBR.
13'4"x17'6"

BR. #3
11'6"x15'0"
DOWN
OPEN TO
E.
BR. #4
11'6"x12'6"

PLANT LEDGE

SECOND FLOOR

For a Growing Family

Design by Ahmann Design, Inc.

■ *Total living area 2,800 sq. ft.* ■ *Price Code E* ■

FIRST FLOOR

SECOND FLOOR

No. 97127 BL

■ **This plan features:**

— Three bedrooms

— Two full and one half baths

■ Inside the two-story Entry find a lovely staircase and a plant ledge

■ Step through an arched opening into the formal Dining Room

■ The Great Room has a fireplace set between built-in cabinets

■ The three-season Porch has access to the Deck and covered Patio

■ The Kitchen is open to the Nook and features a work island/snackbar

■ There is a Bonus Room located over the three-car Garage

■ No materials list is available for this plan

First floor — 1,481 sq. ft.
Second floor — 1,319 sq. ft.
Bonus — 487 sq. ft.

Four Dramatic Gables

B. NATHAN

© 1994 Donald A. Gardner Architects, Inc.

■ *Total living area 2,833 sq. ft.* ■ *Price Code F* ■

No. 99841

This plan features:

— Three bedrooms

— Two full and one half baths

■ Four dramatic gables create curb appeal for this home

■ Two fireplaces add warmth to the Study/Living Room and The Family Room

■ Vaulted and nine-foot ceilings create a feeling of spaciousness

■ The first floor Master Suite has a Sitting Area, a walk-in closet and a deluxe Bath

■ Extra room is provided on the second floor by a skylight Bonus Room and attic storage

First floor — 2,162 sq. ft.
Second floor — 671 sq. ft.
Bonus — 345 sq. ft.
Garage — 587 sq. ft.

Classic Front Porch

Design by The Garlinghouse Company

■ *Total living area 2,861 sq. ft.* ■ *Price Code E* ■

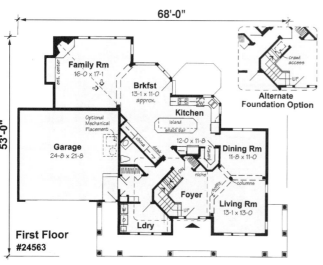

First Floor
#24563

68'-0"

53'-0"

Family Rm
16-0 x 17-1

Brkfst
13-1 x 11-0
approx.

Kitchen

island
snack bar

12-0 x 11-8

Dining Rm
11-8 x 11-0

Garage
24-8 x 21-8

Optional
Mechanical
Placement

china   desk

pantry

niche

columns

Foyer

Living Rm
13-1 x 13-0

Ldry

ent. center

UP
DN

crawl
access

UP

**Alternate
Foundation Option**

Second Floor

Master Suite
14-3 x 12-6
approx.

Br 2
11-8 x 12-0

Br 4
13-0 x 10-0
approx.

Br 3
13-0 x 11-9

open to below

ledge

railing   railing

whirlpool

decor clg

window seat   window seat

No. 24563

■ **This plan features:**

— Four bedrooms

— Two full and one half baths

■ The formal Living and Dining Rooms are accented with columns

■ The open Kitchen has a work island/snackbar, plenty of cabinet and counter space, and a walk-in Pantry

■ The Breakfast Room connects the Family Room and the Kitchen

■ A corner fireplace and a built-in entertainment center enhance the Family Room

■ The lavish Master Suite is topped by a decorative ceiling and has an ultra Bath

First floor — 1,584 sq. ft.
Second floor — 1,277 sq. ft.
Basement — 1,584 sq. ft.
Garage — 550 sq. ft.

Charming Two-Story

■ Total living area 2,862 sq. ft. ■ Price Code E

No. 97126

■ This plan features:

– Three bedrooms

– Two full and one half baths

– The two-story Entryway leads to an airy Great Room

– A cathedral ceiling, built-in cabinets and a fireplace accent the Great Room

– The Kitchen has ample counter space and an eat-in island

– The formal Dining/Living Rooms offer quiet elegance when entertaining

– An optional room upstairs can serve as a fourth Bedroom or a Game Room

– No materials list is available for this plan

First floor — 2,172 sq. ft.
Second floor — 690 sq. ft.
Bonus — 450 sq. ft.

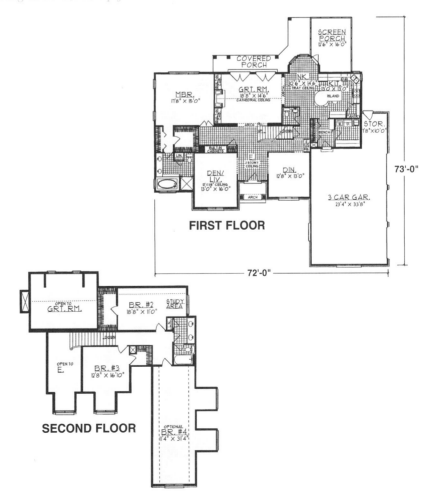

FIRST FLOOR

73'-0"

72'-0"

SECOND FLOOR

Old World Styling

Design by Garrell Associates, Inc.

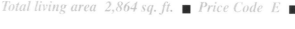

■ *Total living area 2,864 sq. ft.* ■ *Price Code E* ■

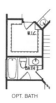

OPT. BATH

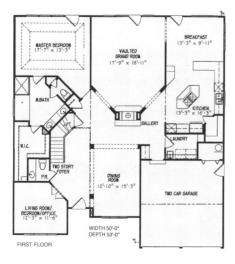

FIRST FLOOR

WIDTH 50'-0"
DEPTH 53'-0"

MASTER BEDROOM
17'-7" × 13'-3"

VAULTED
GRAND ROOM
17'-9" × 18'-11"

BREAKFAST
13'-3" × 9'-11"

M.BATH

KITCHEN
13'-3" × 16'-3"

GALLERY

LAUNDRY

W.I.C.

TWO STORY
FOYER

P.R.

DINING
ROOM
10'-10" × 15'-3"

TWO CAR GARAGE

LIVING ROOM/
BEDROOM/OFFICE
12'-3" × 11'-6"

SECOND FLOOR

TWO STORY
GRAND ROOM

LOFT

B½

W.I.C.

BEDROOM 3
11'-7" × 14'-5"

BEDROOM 2
13'-3" × 13'-7"

W.I.C.

OPT. SITTING
8'-4" × 9'-7"

No. 93612

■ This plan features:

— Four bedrooms

— Two full and one half baths

■ Gables and arched windows accent the facade of this home

■ The two-story Foyer is accented by a lonely, angled staircase

■ Columns and a decorative window highlight the Dining Room

■ A two-sided fireplace warms the Gallery and the Grand Room

■ A uniquely shaped cooktop island and a walk-in Pantry provide efficient in the Kitchen

■ Upstairs, a Loft overlooks the Grand Room below

■ No materials list is available for this plan

First floor — 2,062 sq. ft.
Second floor — 802 sq. ft.
Garage — 400 sq. ft.

Magnificent Grandeur

■ *Total living area 2,865 sq. ft.* ■ *Price Code E* ■

No. 99461

This plan features:

- Four bedrooms

- Two full, one three quarter and one half baths

■ Decorative ceilings and built-ins enhance the Living Room and the Dining Room

■ The Kitchen with a cooktop island serves the Dining Room and the Breakfast Area with equal ease

■ The Great Room is topped by a valley cathedral ceiling over a fireplace

■ The Master Suite includes a decorative ceiling, a whirlpool tub and a walk-in closet

First floor — 1,972 sq. ft.
Second floor — 893 sq. ft.
Garage — 658 sq. ft.

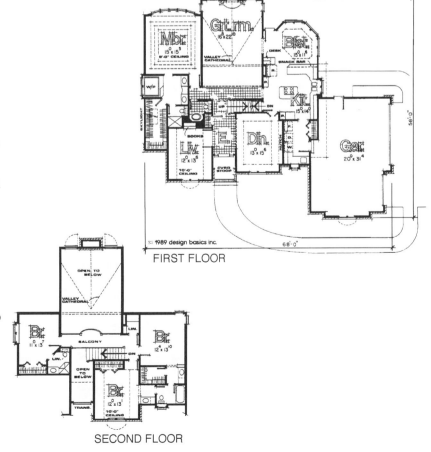

FIRST FLOOR

SECOND FLOOR

Luxury Found Within

Design by Design Basics, Inc.

■ *Total living area 2,870 sq. ft.* ■ *Price Code E* ■

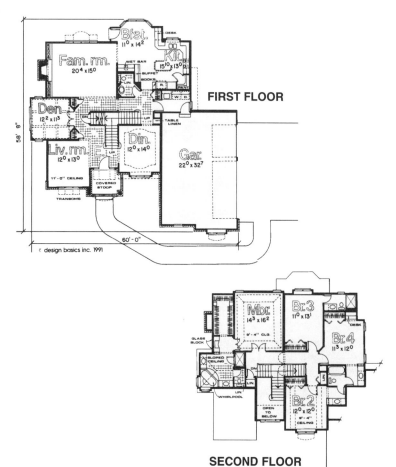

FIRST FLOOR

© design basics inc. 1991

SECOND FLOOR

No. 97402

■ **This plan features:**

— Four bedrooms

— Three full and one half baths

■ The covered stoop leads into the tiled entry and the formal living and Dining Rooms

■ The Dining Room has a boxed bay window and a decorative ceiling

■ The Kitchen is equipped with a wetbar, a buffet counter and a center work island

■ The Family Room has a fireplace set between bookshelves

■ Upstairs, find the Master Bedroom, which has a decorative ceiling and a luxurious Bath

First floor — 1,575 sq. ft.
Second floor — 1,295 sq. ft.
Garage — 724 sq. ft.

With Room for All

■ *Total living area 2,886 sq. ft.* ■ *Price Code E* ■

No. 93249 **BL**

■ This plan features:

- Four bedrooms

- Three full and one half baths

■ The expansive Living Area has a fireplace, built-in shelves, and double doors to the rear Porch

■ The U-shaped Kitchen includes a double sink, a peninsula counter and a work island

■ The sunny Breakfast Room and the formal Dining Room are adjacent to the Kitchen

■ The main floor Master Suite has double doors to the covered Porch and a luxurious private Bath

■ No materials list is available for this plan

Main level — 1,871 sq. ft.
Lower level — 1,015 sq. ft.
Basement — 826 sq. ft.
Garage — 558 sq. ft.

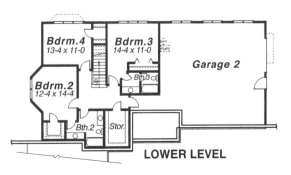

Visually Dramatic Exterior

Design by Design Basics, Inc.

■ *Total living area 2,888 sq. ft.* ■ *Price Code E* ■

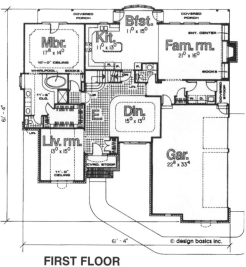

FIRST FLOOR

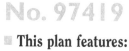

SECOND FLOOR

No. 97419

■ **This plan features:**

— Four bedrooms

— Two full, one three quarter and one half baths

■ The Living Room has a high ceiling and a decorative front window

■ The Dining Room is open to the Entry and is convenient to the Kitchen

■ The U-shaped Kitchen has a center work island and a Breakfast Area

■ The Family Room has a fireplace set between built-in cabinets

■ The first floor Master Bedroom has a decorative ceiling and a private Bath

First floor — 2,098 sq. ft.
Second floor — 790 sq. ft.
Garage — 739 sq. ft.

Design by Fillmore Design Group

Essence of Style & Grace

■ *Total living area 2,902 sq. ft.* ■ *Price Code E* ■

No. 98524

■ This plan features:

– Four bedrooms

– Three full and one half baths

■ Columns enhance the Gallery and formal areas

■ The expansive Family Room has an inviting fireplace and a cathedral ceiling

■ The Kitchen features a cooktop island, a Butler's Pantry, a Breakfast Area and Patio access

■ The first floor Master Bedroom private Patio access and two walk-in closets

■ No materials list is available for this plan

■ An optional basement or slab foundation – please specify when ordering this plan

First floor — 2,036 sq. ft.
Second floor — 866 sq. ft.
Garage — 720 sq. ft.

FIRST FLOOR

SECOND FLOOR

Executive Digs

Design by Design Basics, Inc.

© 1990 design basics inc.

Total living area 2,914 sq. ft. ■ Price Code E

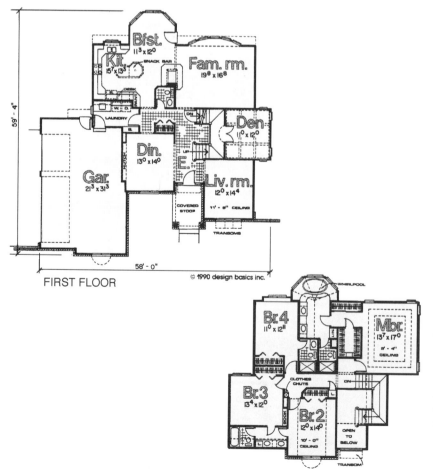

FIRST FLOOR

© 1990 design basics inc.

SECOND FLOOR

No. 99463

■ **This plan features:**

— Four bedrooms

— Three full and one half baths

■ The Family Room features an elegant bow window and shares a cozy three-sided fireplace with the Breakfast Room and the Kitchen

■ An work island/snack bar, a built-in desk and a Pantry highlight the Kitchen

■ The Master Suite features a tiered ceiling and an irresistible whirlpool tub in the luxurious Bath

■ All the secondary Bedrooms have private access to a private full Bath

First floor — 1,583 sq. ft.
Second floor — 1,331 sq. ft.
Garage — 676 sq. ft.

Design by Design Basics, Inc.

Total living area 2,932 sq. ft. ■ Price Code E ■

No. 99400

This plan features:

— Four bedrooms

— Three full and one half baths

■ The expansive Great Room shares a see-through fireplace with the Hearth Room, and French doors to the Covered Veranda

■ The lovely Hearth Room enhanced by three skylights above triple windows and an entertainment center

■ The hub Kitchen has a work island/snack bar, a Pantry, and a bright Breakfast Bay

■ The Master Bedroom with corner windows, has two closets and two vanities

First floor — 2,084 sq. ft.
Second floor — 848 sq. ft.
Garage — 682 sq. ft.
Basement — 2,084 sq. ft.

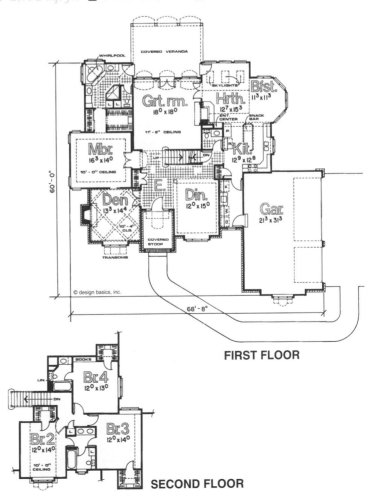

279

Timeless Beauty

Design by Design Basics, Inc.

■ Total living area 2,957 sq. ft. ■ Price Code E ■

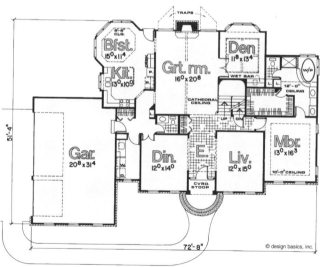

FIRST FLOOR

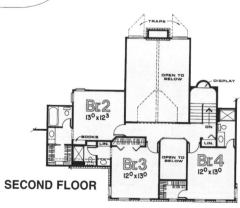

SECOND FLOOR

No. 94994

■ **This plan features:**

— Four bedrooms

— Two full, two three-quarter and one half baths

■ The two-story Entry hall leads to the formal Dining and Living Rooms

■ The spacious Great Room has a cathedral ceiling and a fireplace

■ The ideal Kitchen has a built-in desk and Pantry, a work island, a glass Breakfast Area, and nearby, a Laundry and a Garage entry

■ The Master Bedroom wing offers a decorative ceiling, and the luxurious Dressing/Bath Area with a large walk-in closet and a whirlpool tub

First floor — 2,063 sq. ft.
Second floor — 894 sq. ft.
Garage — 666 sq. ft.
Basement — 2,063 sq. ft.

Allude to Elegance

© 1987 design basics inc.

■ *Total living area 2,967 sq. ft.* ■ *Price Code E* ■

No. 99460

■ This plan features:

– Four bedrooms

– Two full and one half baths

■ The dynamic Entry views the Den, the formal Dining Room and a curved stairway

■ The first floor Master Bedroom has outdoor access and a whirlpool Bath

■ A unique ceiling and outdoor access highlight the bayed Dinette

■ The Kitchen features a work island, a walk-in Pantry and abundance of counter space

■ The Great Room has a see-through fireplace, and multiple arched windows

First floor — 2,040 sq. ft.
Second floor — 927 sq. ft.

© 1987 design basics inc.

FIRST FLOOR

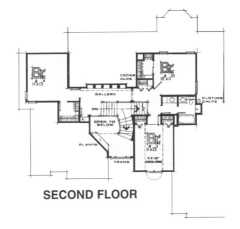

SECOND FLOOR

Traditional Home

Design by Design Basics, Inc.

© design basics inc.

■ *Total living area 2,979 sq. ft.* ■ *Price Code E* ■

FIRST FLOOR

SECOND FLOOR

No. 99452

■ This plan features:

— Four bedrooms

— Three full and one half baths

■ The Entry provides access to the Dining Room which has a built-in hutch and a bay window

■ The cozy Den and the Great Room both have high ceilings and transom windows

■ The Kitchen is conveniently arranged and opens to Breakfast Nook

■ The warm Gathering Room features a fireplace and a cathedral ceiling

■ The secluded Master Bedroom offers a large walk-in closet and an inviting whirlpool Bath

First floor — 2,158 sq. ft.
Second floor — 821 sq. ft.
Basement — 2,158 sq. ft.
Garage — 692 sq. ft.

Design by Fillmore Design Group

No. 98568

■ **This plan features:**

- Four bedrooms

- Three full and one half baths

- This four Bedroom home has a first floor Master Suite

- The Master Bath includes a whirlpool tub and a divided walk-in closet

- French doors open into the Study/Living Room, which has a bay window

- A vaulted ceiling and a decorative window highlight the formal Dining Room

- The gourmet Kitchen includes a Pantry, a double oven and a serving bar

- The Great Room overlooks the rear Patio and is warmed by a fireplace

- The huge three-car Garage is set at an angle and adds flair and storage space to the elevation

- No materials list is available for this plan

First floor — 2,039 sq. ft.
Second floor — 978 sq. ft.
Bonus — 234 sq. ft.
Garage — 738 sq. ft.

■ Total living area 3,017 sq. ft. ■ Price Code E

Main Floor

Upper Floor

Design by Frank Betz Associates, Inc.

No. 98402

Stately Stone and Stucco

■ **This plan features:**

- Four bedrooms

- Three full and one half baths

- The two-story Foyer, with an angled staircase, welcomes all with elegance

- The expansive two-story Great Room is enhanced by a fireplace, a wetbar, and French doors to rear yard

- The convenient Kitchen has a cooktop island, a Pantry, a Breakfast Alcove, and nearby a Laundry/Garage entry

- The open Keeping Room is accented by a wall of windows and backyard access

- The Master Suite wing offers a tray ceiling, a plush Bath with a roomy walk-in closet, and access to a Study/Sitting Room with a fireplace

- An optional basement, slab or crawl space foundation — please specify when ordering

First floor — 2,130 sq. ft.
Second floor — 897 sq. ft.
Garage — 494 sq. ft.
Basement — 2,130 sq. ft.

■ Total living area 3,027 sq. ft. ■ Price Code F

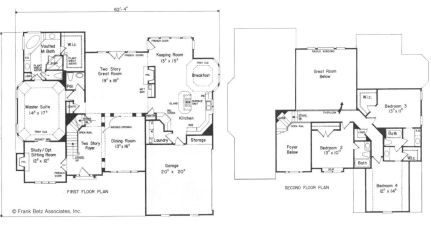

FIRST FLOOR PLAN

© Frank Betz Associates, Inc.

SECOND FLOOR PLAN

Front Terrace

Design by Andy McDonald Design Group

■ *Total living area 3,029 sq. ft.* ■ *Price Code E* ■

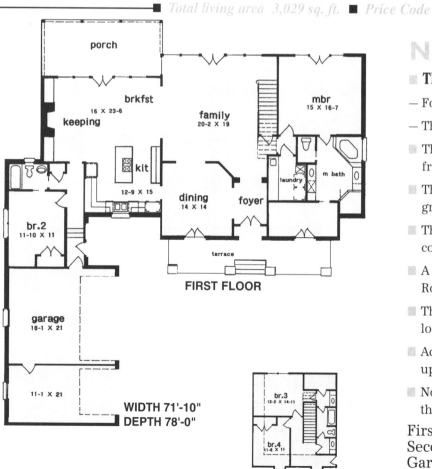

porch

brkfst
16 X 23-6

keeping

family
20-2 X 19

mbr
15 X 16-7

kit
12-9 X 15

dining
14 X 14

laundry

m bath

foyer

br.2
11-10 X 11

terrace

FIRST FLOOR

garage
18-1 X 21

11-1 X 21

WIDTH 71'-10"
DEPTH 78'-0"

br.3
12-2 X 14-11

br.4
11-6 X 11

SECOND FLOOR

No. 97525

■ This plan features:

— Four bedrooms

— Three full baths

■ The Dining Room overlooks the front terrace

■ The Bedroom off the Garage is great for guests

■ The Kitchen has an island with a cooktop

■ A fireplace warms the Keeping Room

■ The Master Bedroom is privately located

■ Additional Bedrooms are located upstairs

■ No materials list is available for this plan

First floor — 2,298 sq. ft.
Second floor — 731 sq. ft.
Garage — 685 sq. ft.

Columns and Keystones

■ *Total living area 3,029 sq. ft.* ■ *Price Code E* ■

No. 93603

This plan features:

- Four bedrooms

- Three full and one half baths

- The gracious two-story Foyer opens to the vaulted Living Room and the formal Dining Room

- The expansive two-story Grand Room has an impressive fireplace between outdoor views

- The spacious and efficient Kitchen has a work island, a Breakfast Area and nearby a Laundry/Garage entry

- The private Master Bedroom offers a decorative ceiling, two walk-in closets and vanities, and a garden window tub

- No materials list is available for this plan

First floor — 2,115 sq. ft.
Second floor — 914 sq. ft.
Garage — 448 sq. ft.
Basement — 2,115 sq. ft.

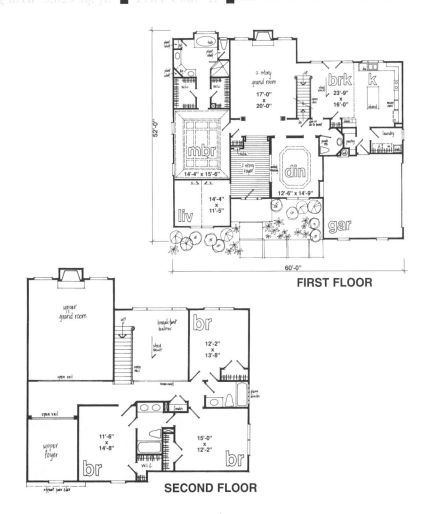

FIRST FLOOR

SECOND FLOOR

Arched Top Windows

Design by Jannis Vann & Associates, Inc.

■ *Total living area 2,946 sq. ft.* ■ *Price Code E* ■

FIRST FLOOR

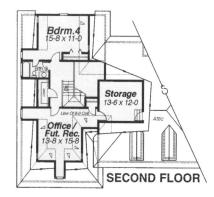

SECOND FLOOR

No. 98941 BL

■ **This plan features:**

— Four bedrooms

— Three full and one half baths

■ The formal Dining Room has focal point fireplace and Sun Deck access built-in niche

■ The Family Room has a stunning paneled ceiling

■ The open Kitchen with a walk-in Pantry, easily accesses the Breakfast Area

■ The split Bedroom design allows for privacy

■ Upstairs find Storage and Bonus Space

■ No materials list is available for this plan

First floor — 2,311 sq. ft.
Second floor — 635 sq. ft.
Bonus — 635 sq. ft.
Basement — 2,284 sq. ft.
Garage — 531 sq. ft.

Stucco Accents

© design basics inc.

■ *Total living area 3,057 sq. ft.* ■ *Price Code E* ■

No. 99456

■ This plan features:

– Four bedrooms

– Two full, one three-quarter and one half baths

■ The open Living Room and handsome curved staircase add drama to the Entry Area

■ French doors open to a large screened in Veranda ideal for outdoor entertaining

■ The open Living Room and handsome curved staircase add drama to the Entry Area

■ The gourmet Kitchen, the Breakfast Bay and the Family Room combine with each other

First floor — 1,631 sq. ft.
Second floor — 1,426 sq. ft.
Basement — 1,631 sq. ft.
Garage — 681 sq. ft.

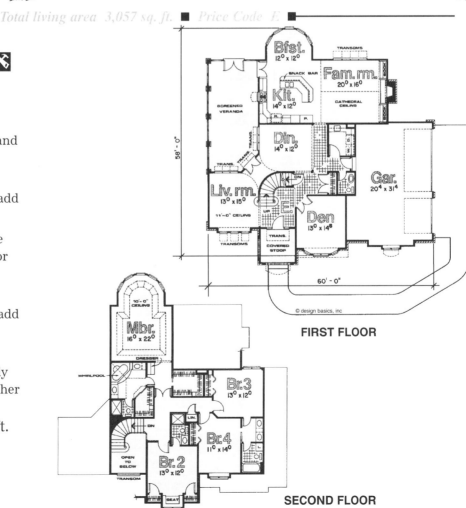

FIRST FLOOR

SECOND FLOOR

Fabulous Living Room

Design by Fillmore Design Group

Total living area 3,115 sq. ft. ■ Price Code C

MAIN LEVEL

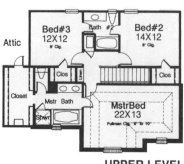

UPPER LEVEL

No. 98570 BL

This plan features:

- Three bedrooms

- Two full and one half baths

- The Living Room has a beautiful hip ceiling adorning it as well as a fireplace

- It is your choice to create either a Study or a formal Dining Room

- A center work island complements the L-shaped Kitchen

- The Breakfast Nook is open to the Kitchen for convenient everyday meals

- The large Master Bedroom includes a Pullman ceiling, a double vanity Bath, and a walk-in closet

- No materials list is available for this plan

Main level — 2,132 sq. ft.
Upper level — 983 sq. ft.
Garage — 660 sq. ft.

Design by Studer Residential Design, Inc.

Splendid Two-Story

Total living area 3,127 sq. ft. ■ Price Code D

No. 92689 **BL**

This plan features:

- Four bedrooms
- Two full and one half baths
- High ceilings in the Foyer and the Great Room create a grand feeling of spaciousness
- The gourmet Kitchen has a cooktop island and a large Breakfast Room adjoining the cozy Hearth Room
- The Master Suite has a exciting ceiling treatment and a luxurious, private Bath
- The roomy second floor Bedrooms share a full Bath
- No materials list is available for this plan

First floor — 2,297 sq. ft.
Second floor — 830 sq. ft.
Basement — 2,171 sq. ft.
Garage — 462 sq. ft.

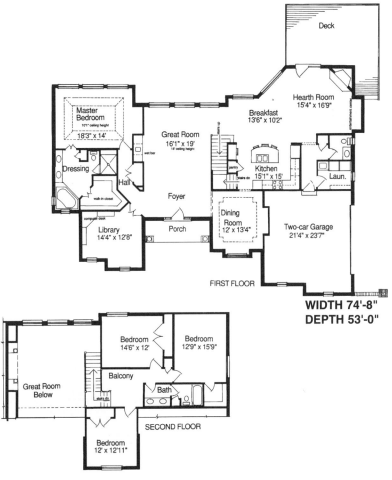

WIDTH 74'-8"
DEPTH 53'-0"

French Country

Total living area 3,202 sq. ft. ■ *Price Code F*

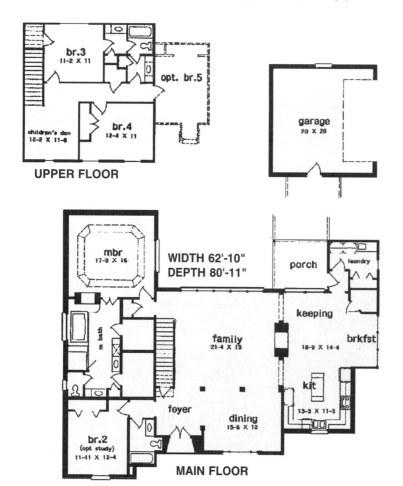

UPPER FLOOR

br.3
11-2 X 11

opt. br.5

children's den
18-2 X 11-6

br.4
12-4 X 11

garage
20 X 20

WIDTH 62'-10"
DEPTH 80'-11"

mbr
17-3 X 16

porch

laundry

keeping

m bath

family
21-4 X 19

18-9 X 14-4

brkfst

kit

13-3 X 11-9

foyer

dining
15-6 X 12

br.2
(opt study)
11-11 X 12-4

MAIN FLOOR

No. 97522

■ **This plan features:**

— Four bedrooms

— Three full baths

■ An arched Entry leads into the Foyer and the open Family and Dining Areas divided by columns

■ A fireplace is shared by the Family and Keeping Rooms

■ The U-shaped Kitchen has a work island and a nearby Laundry Room

■ The additional Bedroom on the main floor can be for guests

■ The Master Bedroom has a tray ceiling and see - thru fireplace

■ No materials list is available for this plan

Main floor — 2,345 sq. ft.
Upper floor — 857 sq. ft.
Garage — 462 sq. ft.

Design by Design Basics, Inc.

Expand Your Options

■ *Total living area 3,225 sq. ft.* ■ *Price Code F* ■

No. 97410 BL

This plan features:

- Three Bedroom
- Two full and one half baths
- On the lower level, find a Family Room with a fireplace and a bar
- The Great Room has a rear bow window with transoms
- The Kitchen the Breakfast Room and the Great Room form a wonderful gathering place
- Two additional Bedrooms with ample closets share a full Bath and outdoor access
- The large walk-in closet in the Master Bedroom contains a built-in cedar chest

Main Level — 1,887 sq. ft.
Lower Level — 1,388 sq. ft.
Garage — 738 sq. ft.
Basement — 549 sq. ft.

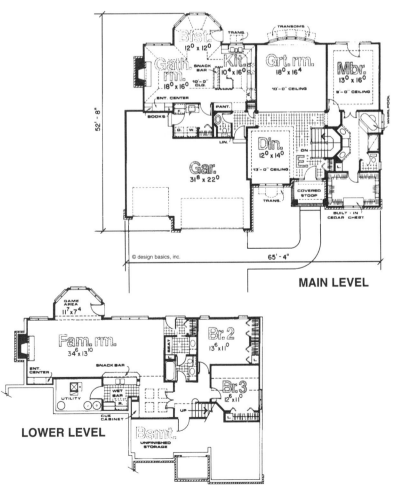

MAIN LEVEL

LOWER LEVEL

Three-Car Garage

■ *Total living area 3,253 sq. ft.* ■ *Price Code F* ■

FIRST FLOOR

SECOND FLOOR

No. 97742 **BL**

■ This plan features:

— Four bedrooms

— Two full and one half baths

■ A covered entry Porch reveals sidelights around the door

■ The Dining Room has a boxed window and a decorative ceiling

■ The Great Room has a sloped ceiling and an inviting fireplace

■ A work island makes the Kitchen more efficient

■ The screened Porch in the rear offers outdoor relaxation

■ The Master Bedroom has a tray ceiling and a whirlpool Bath

■ No materials list is available for this plan

First floor — 2,181 sq. ft.
Second floor — 1,072 sq. ft.
Basement — 2,181 sq. ft.
Garage , 915 sq. ft.

Design by Fillmore Design Group

Luxurious One-Floor Living

■ Total living area 3,254 sq. ft. ■ Price Code F ■

No. 92273

■ This plan features:

– Four bedrooms

– Two full and one three quarter baths

■ The formal Living Room is accented by a fireplace

■ The formal Dining Room is highlighted by a decorative window

■ A serving bar and a work island are featured in the Kitchen

■ A bright alcove provides for informal dining

■ The spacious Master Bedroom has a huge walk-in closet and access to the covered Patio

■ No materials list is available for this plan

■ Three additional Bedrooms have private Bath access

Main floor — 3,254 sq. ft.
Garage — 588 sq. ft.

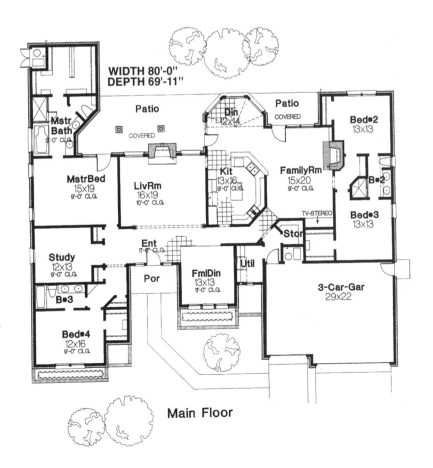

WIDTH 80'-0"
DEPTH 69'-11"

Patio

Patio COVERED

Din 12x14

Mstr Bath 2'-0" CLG

Bed#2 13x13

MstrBed 15x19 9'-0" CLG

LivRm 16x19 10'-0" CLG

Kit 13x16 9'-0" CLG

FamilyRm 15x20 9'-0" CLG

B#2

TV-STEREO

Bed#3 13x13

Stor

Study 12x13 9'-0" CLG

Ent 11'-0" CLG

Util

B#3

Por

FmlDin 13x13 11'-0" CLG

3-Car-Gar 29x22

Bed#4 12x16 9'-0" CLG

Main Floor

Vaulted Great Room

Design by Nelson Design Group

■ *Total living area 3,267 sq. ft.* ■ *Price Code F* ■

FIRST FLOOR

SECOND FLOOR

No. 82098 BL

■ **This plan features:**

— Four bedrooms

— Three full baths

■ There is a Screened Porch in the rear

■ Built-in cabinets flank the fireplace in the Great Room

■ The Master Suite contains a luxurious Bath

■ Columns accent the Dining Room

■ The Kitchen has a walk-in Pantry

■ No materials list is available for this plan

■ An optional basement, slab, or crawl space foundation — please specify when ordering

First floor — 2,213 sq. ft.
Second floor — 1,054 sq. ft.
Garage — 441 sq. ft.

Glorious Gables

■ *Total living area 3,306 sq. ft.* ■ *Price Code F* ■

No. 94933

◄ This plan features:

- Four bedrooms

- Two full, one three-quarter and one half baths

■ Arched windows graciously greet one and all into the tiled Entry with a cascading staircase

■ An arched ceiling and decorative windows highlight the Living and Dining Rooms

■ Double doors lead into the quiet Library which has built-in bookshelves

■ The Kitchen has an angled, work island/snack bar and a built-in Pantry

■ The comfortable Family Room has a hearth fireplace and a wet/bar

First floor — 1,709 sq. ft.
Second floor — 1,597 sq. ft.
Garage — 721 sq. ft.
Basement — 1,709 sq. ft.

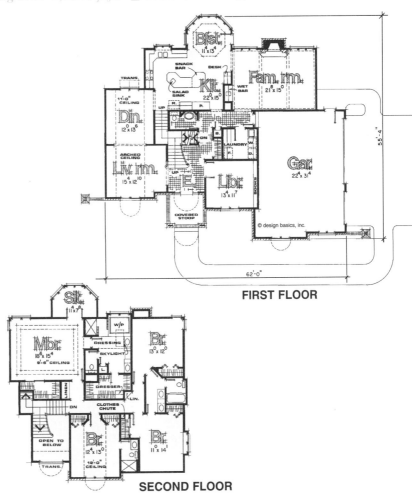

FIRST FLOOR

SECOND FLOOR

A Streamlined Design

Design by Design Basics, Inc

■ *Total living area 3,312 sq. ft.* ■ *Price Code F* ■

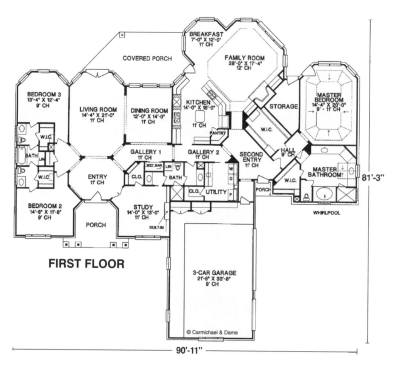

FIRST FLOOR

BASEMENT OPTION

No. 94975 [BL]

■ This plan features:

- Three bedrooms

- Two full and one half baths

■ The recessed, glass-arched entrance leads into a unique Entry

■ The formal Dining Room has a triple - arch window

■ The ideal Kitchen has a walk-in Pantry, a work island and a extended serving bar

■ The open Family Room has a cozy fireplace and lots of windows

■ The Master Bedroom wing offers an alcove of windows, two walk-in closets and a luxurious Bath

■ No materials list is available for this plan

Main floor — 3,312 sq. ft.
Garage — 752 sq. ft.

Design by Andy McDonald Design Group

Entry Courtyard

■ *Total living area 3,327 sq. ft.* ■ *Price Code E* ■

No. 97523 **BL**

■ This plan features:

– Four bedrooms

– Two full and one half baths

■ The Entry Courtyard is perfect for a garden

■ It is your choice to create a Living Room or a Study

■ A cooktop island and a walk-in Pantry enhance the spacious Kitchen, Breakfast/Keeping Area

■ The Family Room has an inviting fireplace with built-ins, and backyard access

■ The Master Bedroom has a huge walk-in closet and a deluxe bath

■ The secondary Bedrooms are spacious and share a double vanity

■ No materials list is available for this plan

Main floor — 3,327 sq. ft.
Garage — 818 sq. ft.

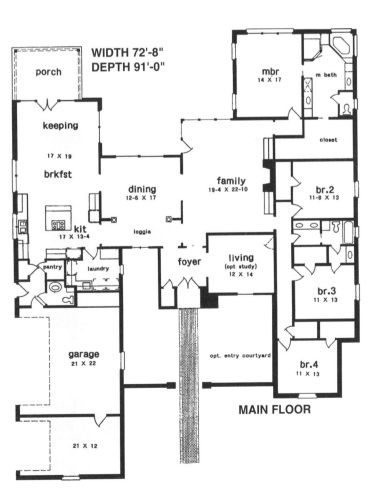

MAIN FLOOR

Outstanding Family Home

Design by Patrick Morobito A.I.A.

■ *Total living area 3,358 sq. ft.* ■ *Price Code F* ■

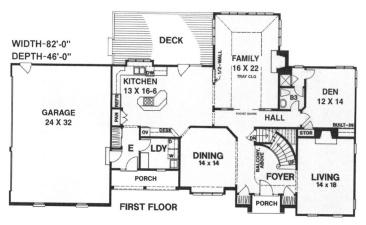

WIDTH-82'-0"
DEPTH-46'-0"

DECK

KITCHEN
13 X 16-6

GARAGE
24 X 32

FAMILY
16 X 22
TRAY CLG

DEN
12 X 14

B3

HALL

BUILT-IN

STOR

POCKET DOORS

1/2-WALL

REFR

PAN

OV

DESK

E

LDY

DINING
14 x 14

DN

UP

BALCONY
ABOVE

FOYER

LIVING
14 x 18

PORCH

PORCH

FIRST FLOOR

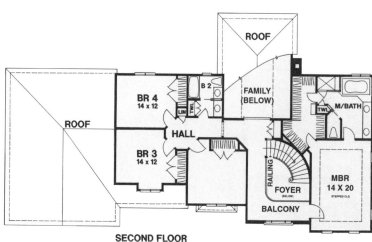

ROOF

BR 4
14 x 12

B 2

FAMILY
(BELOW)

M/BATH

ROOF

LIN
TWL

TWL

TWL

HALL

BR 3
14 x 12

RAILING

FOYER
(BELOW)

MBR
14 X 20
STEPPED CLG

BALCONY

SECOND FLOOR

No. 93367

■ This plan features:

— Four bedrooms

— Two full and one three quarter baths

■ Pocket doors open to the expansive Family Room which has a hearth fireplace and windows on three sides

■ The spacious Kitchen/Dinette area has a cooktop/snack bar and is near the Laundry and Garage entry

■ The private Master Bedroom features a decorative ceiling, a large walk-in closet and a plush Master Bath

■ No materials list is available for this plan

First floor — 1,895 sq. ft.
Second floor — 1,463 sq. ft.
Garage — 768 sq. ft.
Basement — 1,895 sq. ft.

Very Victorian

■ *Total living area 3,390 sq. ft.* ■ *Price Code F* ■

No. 97520   BL

■ **This plan features:**

— Four bedrooms

— Three full baths

■ Columns support the Front Porch and Upper Terrace

■ Inside, the Foyer reveals a curved staircase

■ The Dining Room is an extension of the bay shaped Parlor

■ An optional Bedroom or Study has private access to a full bath

■ The Family Room has a fireplace and French doors to the rear Porch

■ The comfortable Master Bedroom has a bay - shaped Sitting Area

■ No materials list is available for this plan

First floor — 1,844 sq. ft.
Second floor — 1,546 sq. ft.
Garage — 702 sq. ft.

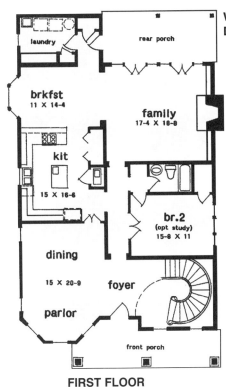

WIDTH 39'-7"
DEPTH 61'-10"

laundry

rear porch

brkfst
11 X 14-4

family
17-4 X 18-8

kit

15 X 16-6

br.2
(opt study)
15-8 X 11

dining

15 X 20-9

foyer

parlor

front porch

FIRST FLOOR

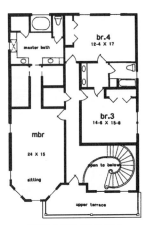

master bath

br.4
12-4 X 17

br.3
14-6 X 15-8

mbr

24 X 15

open to below

sitting

upper terrace

SECOND FLOOR

Smartly Arranged

Design by Nelson Design Group

Total living area 3,472 sq. ft. ■ *Price Code F*

MAIN FLOOR

UPPER FLOOR

No. 61016 BL

This plan features:

— Four bedrooms

— Two full baths

■ There are two fireplaces in the home

■ The Kitchen has options such as a work island and a desk

■ The Breakfast Room features a bay window and extends to the Hearth Room and the Grilling Porch beyond

■ A Computer Center is located upstairs near the kids' Bedrooms

■ No materials list is available for this plan

■ An optional basement, slab, or crawl space foundation — please specify when ordering

Main floor — 2,777 sq. ft.
Upper floor — 695 sq. ft.
Bonus — 310 sq. ft.
Garage — 529 sq. ft.

Luxurious Yet Cozy

Design by Frank Betz Associates, Inc.

Total living area 3,395 sq. ft. ■ *Price Code F*

FIRST FLOOR

SECOND FLOOR

No. 98403 BL

This plan features:

— Four bedrooms

— Three full and one half baths

■ The covered Porch offers a warm welcome and entry into the two-story Foyer

■ Decorative columns define the Dining Room and the Great Room

■ An inviting fireplace between windows, and a vaulted ceiling enhance the Great Room

■ The open and convenient Kitchen has a work island and an open serving counter

■ The corner Master Suite includes a cozy fireplace and a vaulted Sitting Room

■ An optional basement, slab or crawl space foundation — please specify when ordering

First floor — 2,467 sq. ft.
Second floor — 928 sq. ft.
Garage — 566 sq. ft.
Bonus — 296 sq. ft.
Basement — 2,467 sq. ft.

Unusual and Dramatic

Total living area 3,500 sq. ft. ■ ■ Price Code 1

No. 92048

This plan features:

- Four bedrooms

- Three full and one half baths

- The elegant Entry has decorative windows, arched openings and a double-curved staircase

- Cathedral ceilings crown arched windows in the Den and the Living Room

- The spacious Family Room has a vaulted ceiling and a large fireplace between glass doors to the Deck

- The hub Kitchen has a work island/serving counter and a Breakfast Alcove and is near the Deck, the Laundry and the Garage

- The secluded Master Suite has a lovely bay window, two walk-in closets and a plush Bath

First floor — 2,646 sq. ft.
Second floor — 854 sq. ft.
Basement — 2,656 sq. ft.

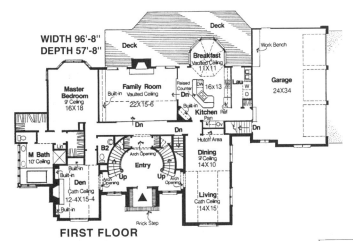

WIDTH 96'-8"
DEPTH 57'-8"

FIRST FLOOR

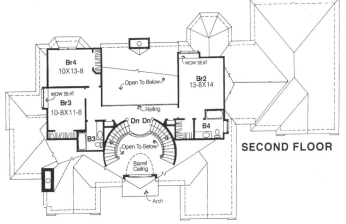

SECOND FLOOR

Arched Covered Entry

Design by Fillmore Design Group

■ *Total living area 3,670 sq. ft.* ■ *Price Code F* ■

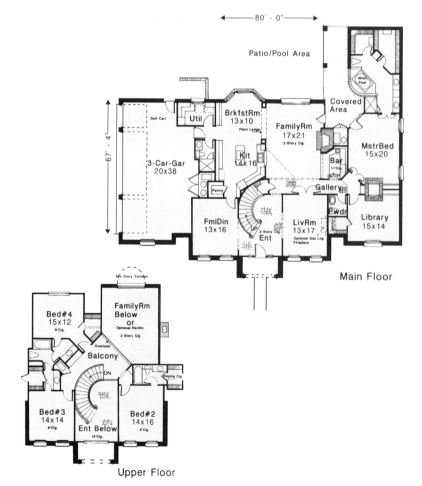

Main Floor

Upper Floor

No. 97802

■ This plan features:

- Four bedrooms

- Three and one Three quarter baths

■ Brick and arched-topped windows highlight the exterior

■ A magnificent staircase accents in the two-story Entry

■ The Living and Dining Rooms are set in traditional locations

■ The Master Bedroom and the Library share a fireplace

■ The three-car Garage has space to store a golf cart

■ No materials list is available for this plan

■ An optional basement, slab, or crawl space foundation — please specify when ordering

Main floor — 2,658 sq. ft.
Upper floor — 1,012 sq. ft.
Garage — 640 sq. ft.

Quoins and Keystones

■ *Total living area 3,840 sq. ft.* ■ *Price Code F* ■

No. 93247

■ This plan features:

— Three bedrooms

— Two full and four half baths

■ The two-story Foyer has a large arched window, a curved staircase and a Balcony

■ The spacious Living Room has a vaulted ceiling

■ The elegant Dining Room has a decorative ceiling and corner built-ins

■ The ideal Kitchen has an extended cooktop, a serving counter, and an octagonal Breakfast Area

■ The palatial Master Bedroom Suite has another fireplace and a luxurious Bath

■ No materials list is available for this plan

First floor — 2,656 sq. ft.
Second floor — 1,184 sq. ft.
Garage — 528 sq. ft.
Bonus — 508 sq. ft.
Basement — 2,642 sq. ft.

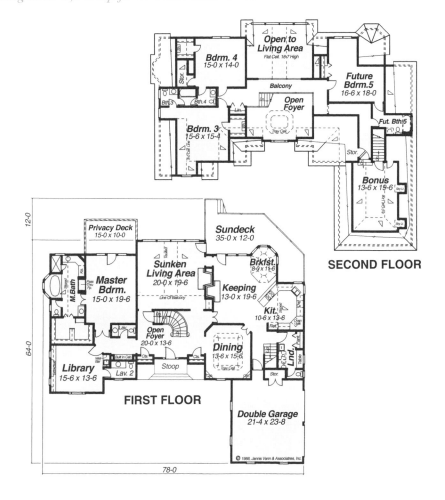

SECOND FLOOR

FIRST FLOOR

"English Manor" House

Design by Design Basics, Inc.

Total living area 3,904 sq. ft. ■ Price Code F

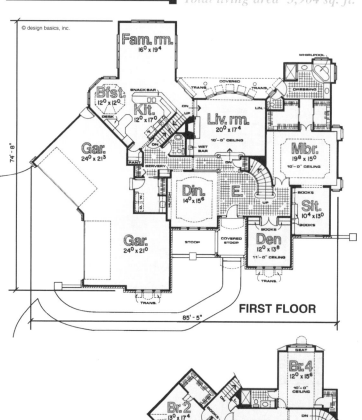

FIRST FLOOR

SECOND FLOOR

No. 99402

This plan features:

— Four bedrooms

— Two full, one three quarter and one half baths

The impressive Entry has columns and a curved staircase

Double doors open to the private Den which has built-in bookshelves

A spectacular bow window highlights the Living Room

The ideal Kitchen has a walk-in Pantry, an angled serving counter/snack bar and a bright Breakfast Alcove

The private Master Bedroom includes a charming Sitting Area

First floor — 2,813 sq. ft.
Second floor — 1,091 sq. ft.
Garage — 1,028 sq. ft.
Basement — 2,813 sq. ft.

Design by Fillmore Design Group

Curved Staircase

■ *Total living area 4,004 sq. ft.* ■ *Price Code F* ■

No. 97805

■ **This plan features:**

- Four bedrooms

- Two full and two three quarter and one half baths

■ Fieldstone and brick accentuate the exterior of this home

■ The front Study has a built-in bookcase and a lovely bay window

■ Columns delineate the Dining Room

■ There is a beamed cathedral ceiling in the huge Family Room

■ The Master Bedroom is on the main floor

■ Upstairs there are three more Bedrooms and a Bonus Room

■ No materials list is available for this plan

Main floor — 2,856 sq. ft.
Upper floor — 1,148 sq. ft.
Bonus — 561 sq. ft.
Garage — 650 sq. ft.

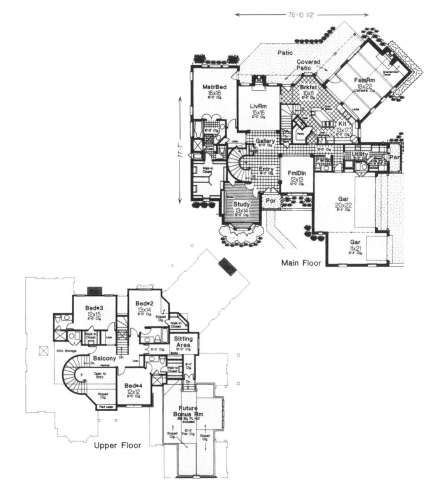

Hillside Home

Design by Jannis Vann & Associates, Inc.

■ Total living area 4,007 sq. ft. ■ Price Code F ■

MAIN LEVEL

LOWER LEVEL

GROUND LEVEL

No. 98940

■ This plan features:

— Three bedrooms

— Two full and two half baths

■ The Master Bedroom has a tray ceiling and Sun Deck access

■ The convenient Kitchen has a cooktop island, Breakfast Area, Family Room and Sun Deck access

■ The lower level has a Media Room close to the Bedrooms

■ Two sections of Decking and a ground level Patio are in the rear

■ The ground level Recreation Room has a convenient wetbar

■ No materials list is available for this plan

Main level — 2,103 sq. ft.
Lower level — 1,130 sq. ft.
Ground level — 774 sq. ft.
Garage — 510 sq. ft.
Deck — 962 sq. ft.

Design by Jannis Vann & Associates, Inc.

Multi-level Living

■ *Total living area 4,511 sq. ft.* ■ *Price Code F* ■

No. 98942

■ This plan features:

- Five bedrooms

- Four full and one half baths

■ The Master Bedroom has a tray ceiling

■ The L-shaped Kitchen has a cooktop island and walk-in Pantry

■ The lower level includes the secondary Bedrooms, the Home office and plenty of storage

■ The ground level has a Rec Room and another Bedroom

■ No materials list is available for this plan

Main level — 2,153 sq. ft.
Lower level — 1,564 sq. ft.
Ground level — 794 sq. ft.
Garage — 462 sq. ft.
Basement — 283 sq. ft.

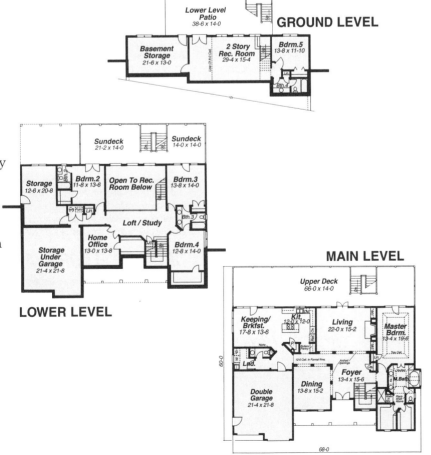

Everything You Need...
...to Make Your Dream Come True!

You pay only a fraction of the original cost for home designs by respected professionals.

You've Picked Your Dream Home!

You can imagine your new home situated on your lot in the morning sunlight. You can visualize living there, enjoying your family, entertaining friends and celebrating holidays. All that remains are the details. That's where we can help. Whether you plan to build it yourself, act as your own general contractor or hire a professional builder, your Garlinghouse Co. home plans will provide the perfect design and specifications to help make your dream home a reality.

We can offer you an array of additional products and services to help you with your planning needs. We can supply materials lists, construction cost estimates based on your local material and labor costs and modifications to your selected plan if you would like.

For over 90 years, homeowners and builders have relied on us for accurate, complete, professional blueprints. Our plans help you get results fast... and save money, too! These pages will give you all the information you need to order. So get started now... We know you'll love your new Garlinghouse home!

Sincerely,

President   Chief Executive Officer

EXTERIOR ELEVATIONS

Elevations are scaled drawings of the front, rear, left, and right sides of a home. All of the necessary information pertaining to the exterior finish materials, roof pitches, and exterior height dimensions of your home are defined.

CABINET PLANS

These plans, or in some cases elevations, will detail the layout of the kitchen and bathroom cabinets at a larger scale. This gives you an accurate layout for your cabinets or an ideal starting point for a modified custom cabinet design. Available for most plans. You may also show the floor plan without a cabinet layout. This will allow you to start from scratch and design your own dream kitchen.

TYPICAL WALL SECTION

This section is provided to help your builder understand the structural components and materials used to construct the exterior walls of your home. This section will address insulation, roof components, and interior and exterior wall finishes. Your plans will be designed with either 2x4 or 2x6 exterior walls, but most professional contractors can easily adapt the plans to the wall thickness you require.

FIREPLACE DETAILS

If the home you have chosen includes a fireplace, the fireplace detail will show typical methods to construct the firebox, hearth and flue chase for masonry units, or a wood frame chase for a zero-clearance unit. Available for most plans.

FOUNDATION PLAN

These plans will accurately dimension the footprint of your home including load bearing points and beam placement if applicable. The foundation style will vary from plan to plan. Your local climatic conditions will dictate whether a basement, slab or crawlspace is best suited for your area. In most cases, if your plan comes with one foundation style, a professional contractor can easily adapt the foundation plan to an alternate style.

ROOF PLAN

The information necessary to construct the roof will be included with your home plans. Some plans will reference roof trusses, while many others contain schematic framing plans. These framing plans will indicate the lumber sizes necessary for the rafters and ridgeboards based on the designated roof loads.

TYPICAL CROSS SECTION

A cut-away cross-section through the entire home shows your building contractor the exact correlation of construction components at all levels of the house. It will help to clarify the load bearing points from the roof all the way down to the basement. Available for most plans.

DETAILED FLOOR PLANS

The floor plans of your home accurately dimension the positioning of all walls, doors, windows, stairs and permanent fixtures. They will show you the relationship and dimensions of rooms, closets and traffic patterns. The schematic of the electrical layout may be included in the plan. This layout is clearly represented and does not hinder the clarity of other pertinent information shown. All these details will help your builder properly construct your new home.

STAIR DETAILS

If stairs are an element of the design you have chosen, the plans will show the necessary information to build these, either through a stair cross section, or on the floor plans. Either way, the information provides your builders the essential reference points that they need to build the stairs.

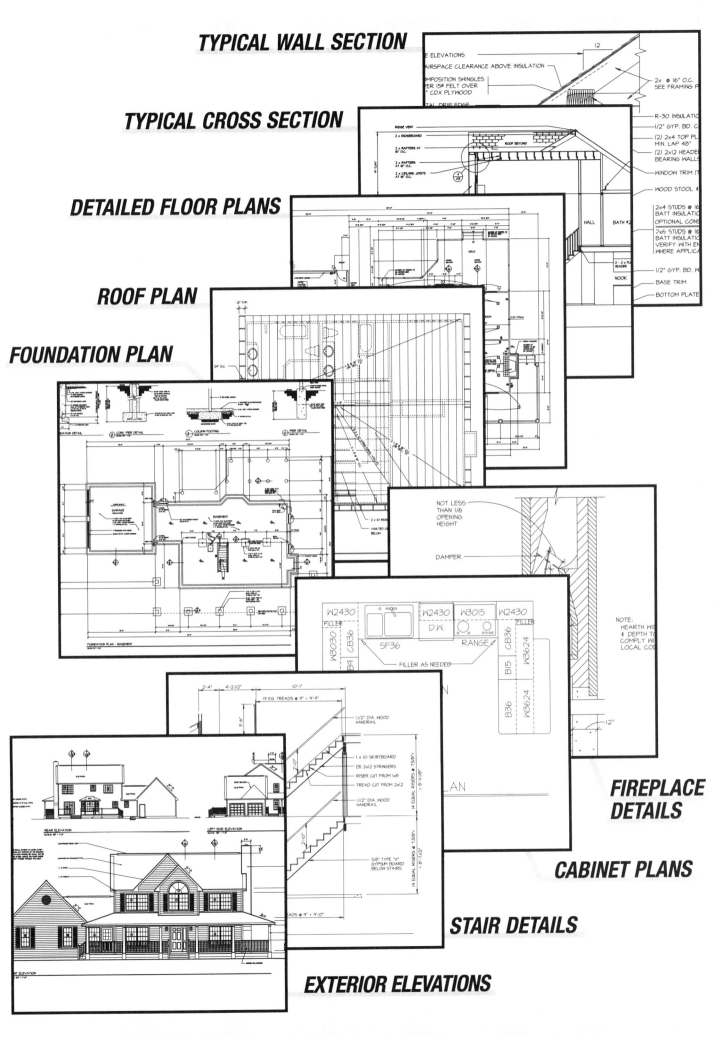

TYPICAL WALL SECTION

TYPICAL CROSS SECTION

DETAILED FLOOR PLANS

ROOF PLAN

FOUNDATION PLAN

FIREPLACE DETAILS

CABINET PLANS

STAIR DETAILS

EXTERIOR ELEVATIONS

Garlinghouse Options & Extras ...Make Your Dream A Home

Reversed Plans Can Make Your Dream Home Just Right!

"That's our dream home...if only the garage were on the other side!"

You could have exactly the home you want by flipping it end-for-end. Check it out by holding your dream home page of this book up to a mirror. Then simply order your plans "reversed." We'll send you one full set of mirror-image plans (with the writing backwards) as a master guide for you and your builder.

The remaining sets of your order will come as shown in this book so the dimensions and specifications are easily read on the job site...but most plans in our collection come stamped "REVERSED" so there is no construction confusion.

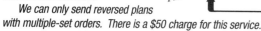

As Shown   Reversed

We can only send reversed plans with multiple-set orders. There is a $50 charge for this service.

Some plans in our collection are available in Right Reading Reverse. Right Reading Reverse plans will show your home in reverse, with the writing on the plan being readable. This easy-to-read format will save you valuable time and money. Please contact our Customer Service Department at (860) 343-5977 to check for Right Reading Reverse availability. (There is a $150 charge for plan series 964, 980, 981 & 998. $125 for all other plans.)

Specifications & Contract Form

We send this form to you free of charge with your home plan order. The form is designed to be filled in by you or your contractor with the exact materials to use in the construction of your new home. Once signed by you and your contractor it will provide you with peace of mind throughout the construction process.

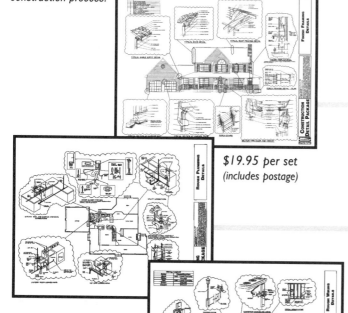

$19.95 per set
(includes postage)

Remember To Order Your Materials List

It'll help you save money. Available at a modest additional charge, the Materials List gives the quantity, dimensions, and specifications for the major materials needed to build your home. You will get faster, more accurate bids from your contractors and building suppliers — and avoid paying for unused materials and waste. Materials Lists are available for all home plans except as otherwise indicated, but can only be ordered with a set of home plans. Due to differences in regional requirements and homeowner or builder preferences... electrical, plumbing and heating/air conditioning equipment specifications are not designed specifically for each plan. However, non-plan specific detailed typical prints of residential electrical, plumbing and construction guidelines can be provided. Please see below for additional information.

Detail Plans Provide Valuable Information About Construction Techniques

Because local codes and requirements vary greatly, we recommend that you obtain drawings and bids from licensed contractors to do your mechanical plans. However, if you want to know more about techniques — and deal more confidently with subcontractors — we offer these remarkably useful detail sheets. These detail sheets will aid in your understanding of these technical subjects. **The detail sheets are not specific to any one home plan and should be used only as a general reference guide.**

RESIDENTIAL CONSTRUCTION DETAILS

Ten sheets that cover the essentials of stick-built residential home construction. Details foundation options — poured concrete basement, concrete block, or monolithic concrete slab. Shows all aspects of floor, wall and roof framing. Provides details for roof dormers, overhangs, chimneys and skylights. Conforms to requirements of Uniform Building code or BOCA code. Includes a quick index and a glossary of terms.

RESIDENTIAL PLUMBING DETAILS

Eight sheets packed with information detailing pipe installation methods, fittings, and sizes. Details plumbing hook-ups for toilets, sinks, washers, sump pumps, and septic system construction. Conforms to requirements of National Plumbing code. Color coded with a glossary of terms and quick index.

RESIDENTIAL ELECTRICAL DETAILS

Eight sheets that cover all aspects of residential wiring, from simple switch wiring to service entrance connections. Details distribution panel layout with outlet and switch schematics, circuit breaker and wiring installation methods, and ground fault interrupter specifications. Conforms to requirements of National Electrical Code. Color coded with a glossary of terms.

Modifying Your Favorite Design, Made *EASY!*

OPTION #1

Modifying Your Garlinghouse Home Plan

Simple modifications to your dream home, including minor non-structural changes and material substitutions, can be made between you and your builder by marking the changes directly on your blueprints. However, if you are considering making significant changes to your chosen design, we recommend that you use the services of The Garlinghouse Design Staff. We will help take your ideas and turn them into a reality, just the way you want. Here's our procedure!

When you place your Vellum order, you may also request a free Garlinghouse Modification Kit. In this kit, you will receive a red marking pencil, furniture cut-out sheet, ruler, a self addressed mailing label and a form for specifying any additional notes or drawings that will help us understand your design ideas. Mark your desired changes directly on the Vellum drawings. NOTE: Please use only a **red pencil** to mark your desired changes on the Vellum. Then, return the redlined Vellum set in the original box to us. **IMPORTANT**: Please **roll** the Vellums for shipping, **do not fold** the Vellums for shipping.

We also offer modification estimates. We will provide you with an estimate to draft your changes based on your specific modifications before you purchase the vellums, for a $50 fee. After you receive your estimate, if you decide to have us do the changes, the $50 estimate fee will be deducted from the cost of your modifications. If, however, you choose to use a different service, the $50 estimate fee is non-refundable. (Note: Personal checks cannot be accepted for the estimate.)

Within 5 days of receipt of your plans, you will be contacted by the Design Staff with an estimate for design services to draw those changes. A 50% deposit is required before we begin making the actual modifications to your plans.

Once the design changes have been completed to your vellum plan, a representative will call to inform you that your modified Vellum plan is complete and will be shipped as soon as the final payment has been made. For additional information call us at 1-860-343-5977. Please refer to the Modification Pricing Guide for estimated modification costs.

OPTION #2

Reproducible Vellums for Local Modification Ease

If you decide not to use Garlinghouse for your modifications, we recommend that you follow our same procedure of purchasing our Vellums. You then have the option of using the services of the original designer of the plan, a local professional designer, or architect to make the modifications to your plan.

With a Vellum copy of our plans, a design professional can alter the drawings just the way you want, then you can print as many copies of the modified plans as you need to build your house. And, since you have already started with our complete detailed plans, the cost of those expensive professional services will be significantly less than starting from scratch. Refer to the price schedule for Vellum costs.

IMPORTANT RETURN POLICY: Upon receipt of your Vellums, if for some reason you decide you do not want a modified plan, then simply return the Kit and the unopened Vellums. Reproducible Vellum copies of our home plans are copyright protected and only sold under the terms of a license agreement that you will receive with your order. Should you not agree to the terms, then the Vellums may be returned, **unopened,** for a full refund less the shipping and handling charges, plus a 20% restocking fee. For any additional information, please call us at 1-860-343-5977.

MODIFICATION PRICING GUIDE

CATEGORIES	ESTIMATED COST
KITCHEN LAYOUT — PLAN AND ELEVATION	$175.00
BATHROOM LAYOUT — PLAN AND ELEVATION	$175.00
FIREPLACE PLAN AND DETAILS	$200.00
INTERIOR ELEVATION	$125.00
EXTERIOR ELEVATION — MATERIAL CHANGE	$140.00
EXTERIOR ELEVATION — ADD BRICK OR STONE	$400.00
EXTERIOR ELEVATION — STYLE CHANGE	$450.00
NON BEARING WALLS (INTERIOR)	$200.00
BEARING AND/OR EXTERIOR WALLS	$325.00
WALL FRAMING CHANGE — 2X4 TO 2X6 OR 2X6 TO 2X4	$240.00
ADD/REDUCE LIVING SPACE — SQUARE FOOTAGE	QUOTE REQUIRED
NEW MATERIALS LIST	QUOTE REQUIRED
CHANGE TRUSSES TO RAFTERS OR CHANGE ROOF PITCH	$300.00
FRAMING PLAN CHANGES	$325.00
GARAGE CHANGES	$325.00
ADD A FOUNDATION OPTION	$300.00
FOUNDATION CHANGES	$250.00
RIGHT READING PLAN REVERSE	$575.00
ARCHITECTS SEAL (Available for most states.)	$300.00
ENERGY CERTIFICATE	$150.00
LIGHT AND VENTILATION SCHEDULE	$150.00

Questions?

"How to obtain a construction cost calculation based on labor rates and building material costs in <u>your</u> Zip Code area!"

ZIP-QUOTE!
HOME COST CALCULATOR

WHY?

Do you wish you could quickly find out the building cost for your new home without waiting for a contractor to compile hundreds of bids? Would you like to have a benchmark to compare your contractor(s) bids against? **Well, Now You Can!!,** with **Zip-Quote** Home Cost Calculator. Zip-Quote is only available for zip code areas within the United States.

HOW?

Our new **Zip-Quote** Home Cost Calculator will enable you to obtain the calculated building cost to construct your new home, based on labor rates and building material costs within your zip code area, without the normal delays or hassles usually associated with the bidding process. Zip-Quote can be purchased in two separate formats, an itemized or a bottom line format.

"How does **Zip-Quote** actually work?" When you call to order, you must choose from the options available, for your specific home, in order for us to process your order. Once we receive your **Zip-Quote** order, we process your specific home plan building materials list through our Home Cost Calculator which contains up-to-date rates for all residential labor trades and building material costs in your zip code area. "The result?" A calculated cost to build your dream home in your zip code area. This calculation will help you (as a consumer or a builder) evaluate your building budget. This is a valuable tool for anyone considering building a new home.

All database information for our calculations is furnished by Marshall & Swift, L.P. For over 60 years, Marshall & Swift L.P. has been a leading provider of cost data to professionals in all aspects of the construction and remodeling industries.

OPTION 1

The **Itemized Zip-Quote** is a detailed building material list. Each building material list line item will separately state the labor cost, material cost and equipment cost (if applicable) for the use of that building material in the construction process. Each category within the building material list will be subtotaled and the entire Itemized cost calculation totaled at the end. This building materials list will be summarized by the individual building categories and will have additional columns where you can enter data from your contractor's estimates for a cost comparison between the different suppliers and contractors who will actually quote you their products and services.

OPTION 2

The **Bottom Line Zip-Quote** is a one line summarized total cost for the home plan of your choice. This cost calculation is also based on the labor cost, material cost and equipment cost (if applicable) within your local zip code area.

COST

The price of your **Itemized Zip-Quote** is based upon the pricing schedule of the plan you have selected, in addition to the price of the materials list. Please refer to the pricing schedule on our order form. The price of your initial **Bottom Line Zip-Quote** is $29.95. Each additional **Bottom Line Zip-Quote** ordered in conjunction with the initial order is only $14.95. **Bottom Line Zip-Quote** may be purchased separately and does NOT have to be purchased in conjunction with a home plan order.

FYI

An **Itemized Zip-Quote** Home Cost Calculation can ONLY be purchased in conjunction with a Home Plan order. The **Itemized Zip-Quote** can not be purchased separately. The **Bottom Line Zip-Quote** can be purchased separately and doesn't have to be purchased in conjunction with a home plan order. Please consult with a sales representative for current availability. If you find within 60 days of your order date that you will be unable to build this home, then you may exchange the plans and the materials list towards the price of a new set of plans (see order info pages for plan exchange policy). The **Itemized Zip-Quote** and the **Bottom Line Zip-Quote** are NOT returnable. The price of the initial **Bottom Line Zip-Quote** order can be credited towards the purchase of an **Itemized Zip-Quote** order only. Additional **Bottom Line Zip-Quote** orders, within the same order can not be credited. Please call our Customer Service Department for more information.

Itemized Zip-Quote is available for plans where you see this symbol. 🖼

Bottom Line Zip-Quote is available for all plans under 4,000 square feet.

SOME MORE INFORMATION

Itemized and Bottom Line Zip-Quotes give you approximated costs for constructing the particular house in your area. These costs are not exact and are only intended to be used as a preliminary estimate to help determine the affordability of a new home and/or as a guide to evaluate the general competitiveness of actual price quotes obtained through local suppliers and contractors. However, Zip-Quote cost figures should never be relied upon as the only source of information in either case. Land, sewer systems, site work, landscaping and other expenses are not included in our building cost figures. Garlinghouse and Marshall & Swift L.P. can not guarantee any level of data accuracy or correctness in a Zip-Quote and disclaim all liability for loss with respect to the same, in excess of the original purchase price of the Zip-Quote product. All Zip-Quote calculations are based upon the actual blueprints and do not reflect any differences or options that may be shown on the published house renderings, floor plans, or photographs.

Ignoring Copyright Laws Can Be
A $1,000,000 Mistake

Recent changes in the US copyright laws allow for statutory penalties of up to **$100,000** per incident for copyright infringement involving any of the copyrighted plans found in this publication. The law can be confusing. So, for your own protection, take the time to understand what you can and cannot do when it comes to home plans.

···WHAT YOU CANNOT DO···

You Cannot Duplicate Home Plans

Purchasing a set of blueprints and making additional sets by reproducing the original is **illegal**. If you need multiple sets of a particular home plan, then you must purchase them.

You Cannot Copy Any Part of a Home Plan to Create Another

Creating your own plan by copying even part of a home design found in this publication is called "creating a derivative work" and is **illegal** unless you have permission to do so.

You Cannot Build a Home Without a License

You must have specific permission or license to build a home from a copyrighted design, even if the finished home has been changed from the original plan. It is **illegal** to build one of the homes found in this publication without a license.

What Garlinghouse Offers

Home Plan Blueprint Package

By purchasing a multiple set package of blueprints or a vellum from Garlinghouse, you not only receive the physical blueprint documents necessary for construction, but you are also granted a license to build one, and only one, home. You can also make simple modifications, including minor non-structural changes and material substitutions, to our design, as long as these changes are made directly on the blueprints purchased from Garlinghouse and no additional copies are made.

Home Plan Vellums

By purchasing vellums for one of our home plans, you receive the same construction drawings found in the blueprints, but printed on vellum paper. Vellums can be erased and are perfect for making design changes. They are also semi-transparent making them easy to duplicate. But most importantly, the purchase of home plan vellums comes with a broader license that allows you to make changes to the design (ie, create a hand drawn or CAD derivative work), to make an unlimited number of copies of the plan, and to build one home from the plan.

License To Build Additional Homes

With the purchase of a blueprint package or vellums you automatically receive a license to build one home and only one home, respectively. If you want to build more homes than you are licensed to build through your purchase of a plan, then additional licenses may be purchased at reasonable costs from Garlinghouse. Inquire for more information.

IMPORTANT INFORMATION TO READ BEFORE YOU PLACE YOUR ORDER

How Many Sets Of Plans Will You Need?

The Standard 8-Set Construction Package

Our experience shows that you'll speed every step of construction and avoid costly building errors by ordering enough sets to go around. Each tradesperson wants a set — the general contractor and all subcontractors; foundation, electrical, plumbing, heating/air conditioning and framers. Don't forget your lending institution, building department and, of course, a set for yourself. * Recommended For Construction *

The Minimum 4-Set Construction Package

If you're comfortable with arduous follow-up, this package can save you a few dollars by giving you the option of passing down plan sets as work progresses. You might have enough copies to go around if work goes exactly as scheduled and no plans are lost or damaged by subcontractors. But for only $50 more, the 8-set package eliminates these worries. * Recommended For Bidding *

The Single Study Set

We offer this set so you can study the blueprints to plan your dream home in detail. They are stamped "study set only-not for construction", and you cannot build a home from them. In pursuant to copyright laws, it is _illegal_ to reproduce any blueprint.

An Important Note About Building Code Requirements:

All plans are drawn to conform to one or more of the industry's major national building standards. However, due to the variety of local building regulations, your plan may need to be modified to comply with local requirements — snow loads, energy loads, seismic zones, etc. Do check them fully and consult your local building officials.

A few states require that all building plans used be drawn by an architect registered in that state. While having your plans reviewed and stamped by such an architect may be prudent, laws requiring non-conforming plans like ours to be completely redrawn forces you to unnecessarily pay very large fees. If your state has such a law, we strongly recommend you contact your state representative to protest.

The rendering, floor plans, and technical information contained within this publication are not guaranteed to be totally accurate. Consequently, no information from this publication should be used either as a guide to constructing a home or for estimating the cost of building a home. Complete blueprints must be purchased for such purposes.

Order Form

Plan prices guaranteed until 2/15/01— After this date call for updated pricing

Order Code No. **CHP13**

Foundation _____

_____ set(s) of blueprints for plan #_____ $_____

_____ Vellum & Modification kit for plan #_____ $_____

_____ Additional set(s) @ $30 each for plan #_____ $_____

_____ Mirror Image Reverse @ $50 each $_____

_____ Right Reading Reverse $_____

_____ Materials list for plan #_____ $_____

_____ Detail Plans @ $19.95 each $_____

_____ ❏ Construction ❏ Plumbing ❏ Electrical $_____

_____ Bottom line ZIP Quote @ $29.95 for plan #_____ $_____

Additional Bottom Line Zip Quote

@ $14.95 for plan(s) #_____ $_____

Zip Code where you are building _____

Itemized ZIP Quote for plan(s) #_____ $_____

Shipping (see charts on opposite page) $_____

Subtotal $_____

Sales Tax (CT residents add 6% sales tax, KS residents add 6.15% sales tax) (Not required for all states) $_____

TOTAL AMOUNT ENCLOSED $_____

Email address _____

Send your check, money order or credit card information to:
(No C.O.D.'s Please)

Please submit all United States & Other Nations orders to:

Garlinghouse Company
P.O. Box 1717
Middletown, CT. 06457

ADDRESS INFORMATION:

NAME: _____

STREET: _____

CITY: _____ STATE: _____ ZIP: _____

DAYTIME PHONE: _____

Credit Card Information

Charge To: ❏ Visa ❏ Mastercard

Card # | | | | | | | | | | | | | | | | |

Signature _____ Exp. ____/____

ORDER TOLL FREE — 1-800-235-5700
Monday-Friday 8:00 a.m. to 8:00 p.m. Eastern Time
or FAX your Credit Card order to 1-860-343-5984
All foreign residents call 1-800-343-5977

Please have ready: **1. Your credit card number** **2. The plan number** **3. The order code number** ⇨ **CHP13**

Garlinghouse 2000 Blueprint Price Code Schedule

Additional sets with original order $30

PRICE CODE	A	B	C	D	E	F	G	H
8 SETS OF SAME PLAN	$405	$445	$490	$530	$570	$615	$655	$695
4 SETS OF SAME PLAN	$355	$395	$440	$480	$520	$565	$605	$645
1 SINGLE SET OF PLANS	$305	$345	$390	$430	$470	$515	$555	$595
VELLUMS	$515	$560	$610	$655	$700	$750	$795	$840
MATERIALS LIST	$60	$60	$65	$65	$70	$70	$75	$75
ITEMIZED ZIP QUOTE	$75	$80	$85	$85	$90	$90	$95	$95

Shipping — (Plans 1-59999)

	1-3 Sets	4-6 Sets	7+ & Vellums
Standard Delivery (UPS 2-Day)	$25.00	$30.00	$35.00
Overnight Delivery	$35.00	$40.00	$45.00

Shipping — (Plans 60000-99999)

	1-3 Sets	4-6 Sets	7+ & Vellums
Ground Delivery (7-10 Days)	$15.00	$20.00	$25.00
Express Delivery (3-5 Days)	$20.00	$25.00	$30.00

International Shipping & Handling

	1-3 Sets	4-6 Sets	7+ & Vellums
Regular Delivery Canada (7-10 Days)	$25.00	$30.00	$35.00
Express Delivery Canada (5-6 Days)	$40.00	$45.00	$50.00
Overseas Delivery Airmail (2-3 Weeks)	$50.00	$60.00	$65.00

Our Reorder and Exchange Policies

If you find after your initial purchase that you require additional sets of plans you may purchase them from us at special reorder prices (please call for pricing details) provided that you reorder within 6 months of your original order date. There is a $28 reorder processing fee that is charged on all reorders. For more information on reordering plans please contact our Customer Service Department.

Your plans are custom printed especially for you once you place your order. For that reason we cannot accept any returns.

If for some reason you find that the plan you have purchased from us does not meet your needs, then you may exchange that plan for any other plan in our collection. We allow you sixty days from your original invoice date to make an exchange. At the time of the exchange you will be charged a processing fee of 20% of the total amount of your original order plus the difference in price between the plans (if applicable) plus the cost to ship the new plans to you. Call our Customer Service Department for more information. Please Note: Reproducible vellums can only be exchanged if they are unopened.

Important Shipping Information

Please refer to the shipping charts on the order form for service availability for your specific plan number. Our delivery service must have a street address or Rural Route Box number — never a post office box. (PLEASE NOTE: Supplying a P.O. Box number only will delay the shipping of your order.) Use a work address if no one is home during the day.

Orders being shipped to APO or FPO must go via First Class Mail.

For our International Customers, only Certified bank checks and money orders are accepted and must be payable in U.S. currency. For speed, we ship international orders Air Parcel Post. Please refer to the chart for the correct shipping cost.

Legend:
- **BL** — Bottom-line Zip Quote Available
- **ML** — Materials List Available
- **ZQ** — Zip Quote Available
- **RR** — Right Reading Reverse
- **DX** — Duplex Plan